Go Recipes

A Problem-Solution Approach

Shiju Varghese

Apress®

Go Recipes: A Problem-Solution Approach

Shiju Varghese
Chettiyadan House, Cheranalloor
India

ISBN-13 (pbk): 978-1-4842-1189-2   ISBN-13 (electronic): 978-1-4842-1188-5
DOI 10.1007/978-1-4842-1188-5

Library of Congress Control Number: 2016959568

Managing Director: Welmoed Spahr
Lead Editor: Steve Anglin
Technical Reviewer: Jan Newmarch
Editorial Board: Steve Anglin, Pramila Balan, Laura Berendson, Aaron Black, Louise Corrigan, Jonathan Gennick, Robert Hutchinson, Celestin Suresh John, Nikhil Karkal, James Markham, Susan McDermott, Matthew Moodie, Natalie Pao, Gwenan Spearing
Coordinating Editor: Mark Powers
Copy Editor: Teresa F. Horton
Compositor: SPi Global
Indexer: SPi Global
Artist: SPi Global

Distributed to the book trade worldwide by Springer Science+Business Media New York, 233 Spring Street, 6th Floor, New York, NY 10013. Phone 1-800-SPRINGER, fax (201) 348-4505, e-mail orders-ny@springer-sbm.com, or visit www.springeronline.com. Apress Media, LLC is a California LLC and the sole member (owner) is Springer Science + Business Media Finance Inc (SSBM Finance Inc). SSBM Finance Inc is a **Delaware** corporation.

For information on translations, please e-mail rights@apress.com, or visit www.apress.com.

Apress and friends of ED books may be purchased in bulk for academic, corporate, or promotional use. eBook versions and licenses are also available for most titles. For more information, reference our Special Bulk Sales–eBook Licensing web page at www.apress.com/bulk-sales.

Any source code or other supplementary materials referenced by the author in this text are available to readers at www.apress.com. For detailed information about how to locate your book's source code, go to www.apress.com/source-code/. Readers can also access source code at SpringerLink in the Supplementary Material section for each chapter.

Printed on acid-free paper

I would like to dedicate this book to my late father Varghese,
my wife Rosmi, and my daughter Irene Rose.

—*Shiju Varghese*

Contents at a Glance

Contents

About the Author

Shiju Varghese is a solutions architect focused on building highly scalable, cloud-native applications with a special interest in APIs, microservices, containerized architecture, and distributed systems. He currently specializes in Go, Google Cloud, and container technologies. He is an early adopter of the Go programming language, and provides consulting and training for building scalable back-end systems and microservices with the Go ecosystem. He has been a mentor to various organizations for the technology transformation to Go. He worked extensively in C# and Node.js before adopting Go as the primary technology stack.

About the Technical Reviewer

Jan Newmarch is Head of ICT (Higher Education) at Box Hill Institute, Adjunct Professor at Canberra University, and Adjunct Lecturer in the School of Information Technology, Computing, and Mathematics at Charles Sturt University. He is interested in more aspects of computing than he has time to pursue, but the major thrust over the last few years has developed from user interfaces under Unix into Java, the Web, and now general distributed systems. Jan has developed a number of publicly available software systems in these areas. Right now, he is looking at sound for Linux systems and programming the Raspberry Pi's GPU.

Introduction

Go, also commonly referred to as Golang, is a general-purpose programming language conceived at Google in 2007 by Robert Griesemer, Rob Pike, and Ken Thompson. The language first appeared in November 2009 as an open source project. The Go open source project is available at `https://github.com/golang/go`. Version 1.0 of Go was released in March 2012, providing a stable version that includes language specification, standard libraries, and custom tools. Go borrows the basic syntax of C and has the same philosophy as C: Enable maximum capability with a minimum set of features. You can say that Go is a modern C with the productivity of a dynamically typed language, although it is a statically typed language. The Go web site (`https://golang.org/`) defines Go this way: "Go is an open source programming language that makes it easy to build simple, reliable, and efficient software."

When Go was conceived at Google, there were numerous challenges in the software engineering of systems. Many of our software systems were not able to leverage the emergence of multicore computers. Our modern computers now have evolved to include many CPU cores and we are still using the languages and tools that were designed to write software for single-core machines. There was an emergence of the use of dynamically typed language for the sake of productivity, but it causes performance problems when applications are scaling, and debugging those applications is extremely difficult. C and C++ were widely used for writing systems software, but compiling larger applications with C and C++ was always painful due to the time-consuming compilation process. Another challenge is that we have many existing programming languages, but we use different languages for different purposes. For example, we might use C and C++ for writing high-performance systems software, but we use a different language for writing web applications. Using different programming languages for each techncial domain is really painful for many organizations, especially startup organizations.

First and foremost, Go is a great general-purpose programming language, designed to be simple, minimal, pragmatic. Go is a compiled, concurrent, garbage-collected, statically typed language that lets you write high-performance, scalable systems with high productivity. Go is efficient, scalable, and productive. Go compiles programs quickly into native machine code. It will surprise you with its simplicity and pragmatism. Go is designed for solving real-world problems rather than focusing too much on academic theories and programming language theory (PLT). Concurrency is a built-in feature of Go that enables you write efficient, high-performance software systems by leveraging the power of modern computers that have many CPU cores. Although Go is a statically typed language, it provides the productivity of a dynamically typed language thanks to its pragmatic design. As a general-purpose programming language, Go can be used for building a variety of software systems.

The book provides a problem-solution approach with various code recipes. Each recipe is a self-contained solution to a practical programming problem in Go. The first four chapters of the book are focused on the Go programming language and its various features. The remaining chapters help you to build real-world applications.

The source code for the book is available on GitHub at `https://github.com/shijuvar/go-recipes`. This will provide source code for each recipe discussed in the book. This GitHub repository will also provide additional example code that is not presented in the book.

CHAPTER 1

Beginning Go

Go, also commonly referred to as Golang, is a general-purpose programming language, developed by a team at Google and many contributors from the open source community (http://golang.org/contributors). The Go language was conceived in September 2007 by Robert Griesemer, Rob Pike, and Ken Thompson at Google. Go first appeared in November 2009, and the first version of the language was released in December 2012. Go is an open source project that is distributed under a BSD-style license. The official web site of the Go project is available at http://golang.org/. Go is a statically typed, natively compiled, garbage-collected, concurrent programming language that belongs primarily to the C family of languages in terms of basic syntax.

Introduction to Go

The Go programming language can be simply described in three words: simple, minimal, and pragmatic. The design goal of Go is to be a simple, minimal, and expressive programming language that provides all the essential features for building reliable and efficient software systems. Every language has its own design goal and a unique philosophy. Simplicity can't be added later in the language, so it must be built with simplicity in mind. Go is designed for simplicity. By combining Go's simplicity and pragmatism, you can build highly efficient software systems with a higher level of productivity.

Go is a statically typed programming language with its syntax loosely derived from C, sometimes referred to as a modern C for the 21st century. From C, Go borrows its basic syntax, control-flow statements, and basic data types. Like C and C++, Go programs compile into native machine code. Go code can be compiled into native machine code for a variety of processors (ARM, Intel) under a variety of operating systems (Linux, Windows, macOS). It is important to note that Go code can be compiled into Android and iOS platforms. Unlike Java and C#, Go doesn't need any virtual machine or language runtime to run compiled code because it compiles into native machine code. This will give you great opportunities when you build applications for modern systems. Go compiles programs faster than C and C++, hence compiling larger programs with Go solves the problem of delays in compiling larger programs with many of the existing programming languages. Although Go is a statically typed language, it provides the developer productivity similar to a dynamically type language because of its pragmatic design.

In the last decade, computer hardware has evolved to having many CPU cores and more power. Nowadays we heavily leverage cloud platforms for building and running applications where servers on the cloud have more power. Although modern computers and virtual machine instances on the cloud have more power and many CPU cores, we still can't leverage the power of modern computers using most of the existing programming languages and tools. Go is designed to effectively use the power of modern computers for running high-performance applications. Go provides concurrency as a built-in feature, and it is designed for writing high-performance concurrent applications that allow developers to build and run high-performance, massively scalable applications for modern computers. Go is a great choice of language in the era of cloud computing.

Electronic supplementary material The online version of this chapter (doi:10.1007/978-1-4842-1188-5_1) contains supplementary material, which is available to authorized users.

The Go Ecosystem

Go is an ecosystem that also provides essential tools and libraries for writing a variety of software systems. The Go ecosystem is consists of the following:

- Go language

- Go libraries

- Go tooling

The Go language provides essential syntax and features that allow you to write your programs. These programs leverage libraries as reusable pieces of functionality, and tooling for formatting code, compiling code, running tests, installing programs, and creating documentation. The Go installation comes with a lot of reusable libraries known as standard library packages. The Go developer community has been building a huge set of reusable libraries known as third-party packages. When you build Go applications, you can leverage packages (reusable libraries) provided by Go itself and the Go community. You use Go tooling to manage your Go code. Go tooling allows you to format, verify, test, and compile your code.

1-1. Installing Go Tools

Problem

You want to install Go tools in your development machine.

Solution

Go provides binary distributions for FreeBSD, Linux, macOS, and Windows. Go also provides installer packages for macOS and Windows.

How It Works

Go provides binary distributions for Go tools for the FreeBSD (release 8-STABLE and above), Linux, macOS (10.7 and above), and Windows operating systems and the 32-bit (386) and 64-bit (amd64) x86 processor architectures. If a binary distribution is not available for your combination of operating system and architecture, you can install it from source. The binary distributions for the Go tools are available at https://golang.org/dl/. You can also install the Go tools by building from the source. If you are building from source, follow the source installation instructions at https://golang.org/doc/install/source.

Figure 1-1 shows the installer packages and archived source for various platforms, including macOS, Windows, and Linux, which is listed on the download page of the Go web site (https://golang.org/dl/). Go provides installers for both macOS and Windows operating systems.

Stable versions

go1.6 ▾

File name	Kind	OS	Arch	Size	SHA256 Checksum
go1.6.src.tar.gz	**Source**			**12MB**	a96cce8ce43a9bf9b2a4c7d470bc7ee0cb00410da815980681c8353218dcf146
go1.6.darwin-amd64.tar.gz	Archive	OS X	64-bit	81MB	8b686ace24c0166738fd9f6003503+9d55ce03b7+24c963b043ba7b056f43000
go1.6.darwin-amd64.pkg	**Installer**	**OS X**	**64-bit**	**81MB**	cabae263fe1a8c3bb42539943348a69f94e3f96b5310a96e24df29ff745aaf5c
go1.6.freebsd-386.tar.gz	Archive	FreeBSD	32-bit	69MB	67+0278e0650b303156adbfe012317b9ce75396e3a28cbc0a8210284bb07ab85
go1.6.freebsd-amd64.tar.gz	Archive	FreeBSD	64-bit	81MB	3763815cdc7971e10f90fb5bec80d885e9956f836277dcb35a2166ffbd7af9b5
go1.6.linux-386.tar.gz	Archive	Linux	32-bit	69MB	7a240a0f45e559d47ea07319d9fa+838225eb9e18174+56a76ccaf9860dbb9b1
go1.6.linux-amd64.tar.gz	**Archive**	**Linux**	**64-bit**	**81MB**	5470eac05d273c74ff8bac7bef5bad0b5abbd1c4052efbdbc8db45332e836b0b
go1.6.linux-armv6l.tar.gz	Archive	Linux	ARMv6	67MB	c6c1859acd3727+23f900bde855b5+d0+74d3Gb1d10f6dd7beddeb+b57513d0b
go1.6.windows-386.zip	Archive	Windows	32-bit	74MB	ac41a46f44d0ea5b83ad7e6a55ee1d58c6a01b7ab7342e243f232510342f16f0
go1.6.windows-386.msi	Installer	Windows	32-bit	61MB	be2+9e1c85b+c55b3bea8+1e48ac+4a8117+bcd6c7f372aa9++9+74429+18a35
go1.6.windows-amd64.zip	Archive	Windows	64-bit	87MB	1be06afa469666d636a00928755c4bcd6403a01f5761946b2b13b8a664f86bac
go1.6.windows-amd64.msi	**Installer**	**Windows**	**64-bit**	**71MB**	9e185fe7985505e3a65633f5e4db76664607f67f8331f0ce4986ba69b51015b7

Figure 1-1. *Binary distributions and archived source for Go for various platforms*

A package installer is available for macOS that installs the Go distribution at /usr/local/go and configures the /usr/local/go/bin directory in your PATH environment variable.

In macOS, you can also install Go using Homebrew (http://brew.sh/). The following command will install Go on macOS:

```
brew install go
```

An MSI installer is available for Windows OS that installs the Go distribution at c:\Go. The installer also configures the c:\Go\bin directory in your PATH environment variable.

Figure 1-2 shows the package installer running on macOS.

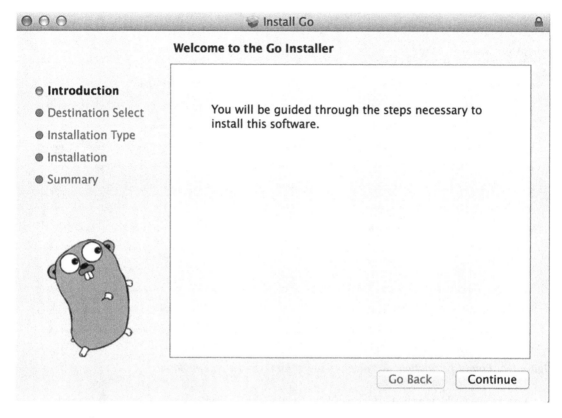

Figure 1-2. *Package installer for Go running on macOS*

A successful installation of Go automatically sets up the GOROOT environment variable in the location in which the Go tools are installed. By default, this will be /usr/local/go under macOS and c:\Go under Windows. To verify the installation of Go tools, type the go command with any of the subcommands in the command-line window as shown here:

```
go version
```

Here is the result that displays in macOS:

```
go version go1.6 darwin/amd64
```

Here is the result that displays on a Windows system:

```
go version go1.6 windows/amd64
```

The following go command provides the help for the Go tool:

```
go help
```

1-2. Setting Up Go Development Environment

Problem

You want to set up the development environment for Go on your development machine so that you can write programs in Go.

Solution

To write programs in Go, you must set up a *Go Workspace* on your development machine. To set up a directory as a Go Workspace, create a Go Workspace directory to contain all your Go programs, and configure the GOPATH environment variable with the directory that you have created for setting up the Go Workspace.

How It Works

Once you have installed the Go tools and set up the GOPATH environment variable to point to Go Workspace, you can start writing programs with Go. GOPATH is the directory in which you organize your Go programs as packages. We discuss packages in greater detail later. For now, think of packages as directories in which you organize your Go program that produces an executable program (often referred as *commands* on the Go web site) or a shared library after compilation. Once you set up a Workspace directory for your Go programs on a developer machine, you must configure the directory as GOPATH by setting the GOPATH environment variable.

Setting Up the Go Workspace

Go programs are organized in a specific way that helps you easily compile, install, and share Go code. Go programmers keep all their Go programs in a specific directory called *Go Workspace* or *GOPATH*. The Workspace directory contains the following subdirectories at its root:

- src: This directory contains the source files organized into packages.
- pkg: This directory contains the Go package objects.
- bin: This directory contains executable programs (commands).

Create a Go Workspace directory with the three subdirectories src, pkg, and bin. Put all Go source files into the src subdirectory under the Go Workspace. A Go programmer writes Go programs as packages into the src directory. Go source files are organized into directories called packages, in which a single directory will be used for a single package. You write Go source files with the .go extension. There are two types of packages in Go:

- Packages compiled into an executable program.
- Packages compiled into a shared library.

The Go tool compiles the Go source and installs the resulting binary into appropriate subdirectories under Workspace using the Go tool by running the go command. The go install command compiles the Go packages and moves the resulting binaries into the pkg directory if it is a shared library, and into the bin directory if it is an executable program. The pkg and bin directories are therefore used for the binary output of the packages based on the package type.

Configuring the GOPATH Environment Variable

You organize Go code in the Workspace directory, which you should manually specify so that Go runtime knows the Workspace location. You can configure the Go Workspace by setting up the GOPATH environment variable with value as the location of the Workspace.

Here we configure the GOPATH environment variable in macOS by specifying the location of the Workspace directory:

```
$ export GOPATH=$HOME/gocode
```

In the preceding command, you configure the Go Workspace at $HOME/gocode by specifying the GOPATH environment variable. For convenience, add the Workspace's bin subdirectory to your PATH so that you can run the executable commands from any location in the command-line window:

```
$ export PATH=$PATH:$GOPATH/bin
```

Note that you can have multiple Workspace directories on a single development machine, but Go programmers typically keep all their Go code in a single Workspace directory.

1-3. Declaring Variables

Problem

You want to declare variables in Go.

Solution

The keyword var is used for declaring variables. In addition to using the var keyword, Go provides various options to declare variables that provide expressiveness to language and productivity to programmers.

How It Works

Although Go borrows the basic syntax of the C family of languages, it uses different idioms for declaring variables. The keyword var is used for declaring variables of a particular data type. Here is the syntax for declaring variables:

```
var name type = expression
```

When you declare a variable you may omit either type or expression for the initialization, but you should specify at least one. If the type is omitted from the variable declaration, it is determined from the expression used for initialization. If the expression is omitted, the initial value is 0 for numeric types, false for boolean type, and "" for string type. Listing 1-1 shows a program that declares variables using the var keyword.

Listing 1-1. Declare Variables Using the var Keyword

```
package main

import "fmt"

func main() {
    var fname string
    var lname string
    var age int
    fmt.Println("First Name:", fname)
    fmt.Println("Last Name:", lname)
    fmt.Println("Age:", age)
}
```

Let's run the program using the go tool:

```
go run main.go
```

You should see the following output:

```
First Name:
Last Name:
Age: 0
```

In this program, we declare variables using the var keyword by explicitly specifying its data type. Because we didn't initialize and assign values to the variables, it takes the zero value of the corresponding type; "" for string type and 0 for int type. We can declare mutiple variables of the same type in a single statement as shown here:

```
var fname,lname string
```

You can declare and initialize the values for multiple variables in a single statement as shown here:

```
var fname, lname string = "Shiju", "Varghese"
```

If you are using an initializer expression for declaring variables, you can omit the type using **short variable declaration** as shown here:

```
fname, lname := "Shiju", "Varghese"
```

We use the operator : = for declaring and initializing variables with short variable declaration. When you declare variables with this method, you can't specify the type because the type is determined by the initializer expression. Go provides lot of productivity and expressiveness like a dynamically typed language with the features of a statically typed language. Note that short variable declaration is allowed only for declaring local variables, variables declared within the function. When you declare variables outside the function (package variables), you must do so using the var keyword. Listing 1-2 shows a program that demonstrates short variable declaration in functions and declaration of package variables.

Listing 1-2. Short Variable Declarations and Declaration of Package Variables

```go
package main

import "fmt"

// Declare constant
const Title = "Person Details"

// Declare package variable
var Country = "USA"

func main() {
    fname, lname := "Shiju", "Varghese"
    age := 35
    // Print constant variable
    fmt.Println(Title)
    // Print local variables
    fmt.Println("First Name:", fname)
    fmt.Println("Last Name:", lname)
    fmt.Println("Age:", age)
    // Print package variable
    fmt.Println("Country:", Country)
}
```

In this program, we declare variables using a short variable declaration statement in the main function. Because short variable declaration is not possible for declaring package variables, we use the var keyword for declaring package variables, omitting the type because we provide the initializer expression. We use the keyword const for declaring constants.

1-4. Building an Executable Program

Problem

You would like to build a Go executable program to get started with Go programming.

Solution

The Go installation comes with standard library packages that provide many shared libraries for writing Go programs. The standard library package fmt implements formatted I/O functions, which can be used to print formatted output messages. When you write your first program in Go, it is important to note that Go programs must be organized into packages.

How It Works

You must write Go source files into packages. In Go, there are two types of packages:

- Packages compiled into executable programs.
- Packages compiled into a shared library.

In this recipe you will write an executable program to print an output message into the console window. A special package main is used for compiling into executable programs. We write all Go programs in src subdirectory of Go Workspace ($GOPATH/src).

Create a subdirectory named hello under the $GOPATH/src directory. Listing 1-3 shows a "Hello, World" program that demonstrates the basic facets of writing Go programs.

Listing 1-3. An Executable Program in main.go Under $GOPATH/src/hello

```
package main

import "fmt"

func main() {
    fmt.Println("Hello, World")
}
```

Let's explore the program to understand the basic aspects for writing Go programs. Unlike the C family of languages, in Go you don't need to explicitly put a semicolon (;) at the end of statements. We write a Go source file named main.go and organize this into package main.

```
package main
```

The package declaration specifies what package the Go source file belongs to. Here we specify that the main.go file is part of the main package. Note that all source files in a single directory (package directory) should declare with the same package name. The compilation of the main package results in an executable program.

The import statement is used to import packages (shared libraries) so that you can reuse the functions of an imported package. Here we import the package fmt provided by the standard library. The standard library packages are found in the GOROOT location (Go installation directory).

```
import "fmt"
```

We use the func keyword to declare functions, followed by the function name. The function main is a special function that works as the entry point for an executable program. A main package must have a function main to work as the entry point for the executable programs. We use the Println function of the fmt package to print the output data.

```
func main() {
    fmt.Println("Hello, World")
}
```

It's time to build and run the program to see the output. You can build the program using the go tool. Navigate to the package directory in the command-line window, and run the following command to compile the program:

```
go build
```

The build command compiles the package source and generates an executable program with the name of the directory that contains Go source files for the package main. Because we are using the directory named hello, the executable command will be hello (or hello.exe under Windows). Run the command hello from the hello directory in a command-line window to view the output.

You should see the following output:

```
Hello, World
```

In addition to using the go build command, you can use go install to compile the source and put the resulting binary into the bin directory of GOPATH.

```
go install
```

You can now run the executable command by typing the command from the bin directory of GOPATH. If you have added $GOPATH/bin to your PATH environment variable, you can run the executable program from any location in a command-line window.

If you just want to compile and run your program, you can use the go run command followed by the file name to run the program.

```
go run main.go
```

1-5. Writing a Package as a Shared Library

Problem

You would like to write packages to be reused for other packages to share your Go code.

Solution

In Go, you can write a package as a shared library so that it can be reused in other packages.

How It Works

The design philosophy of Go programming is to develop small software components as packages and build larger applications by combining these small packages. In Go, code reusability is achieved through its package ecosystem. Let's build a small utility package to demonstrate how to develop a reusable piece of code in Go. We used package main in the previous code examples in this chapter, which is used to build executable programs. Here we want to write a shared library to share our code with other packages.

Listing 1-4 shows a program that provides a shared library with a package named strutils. Package strutils provides three string utility functions.

Listing 1-4. A Shared Library for String Utility Functions

```
package strutils

import (
    "strings"
    "unicode"
)

// Returns the string changed with uppercase.
func ToUpperCase(s string) string {
```

```
    return strings.ToUpper(s)
}

// Returns the string changed with lowercase.
func ToLowerCase(s string) string {
    return strings.ToLower(s)
}

// Returns the string changed to uppercase for its first letter.
func ToFirstUpper(s string) string {
    if len(s) < 1 { // if the empty string
        return s
    }
    // Trim the string
    t := strings.Trim(s, " ")
    // Convert all letters to lower case
    t = strings.ToLower(t)
    res := []rune(t)
    // Convert first letter to upper case
    res[0] = unicode.ToUpper(res[0])
    return string(res)
}
```

Note that the name of all functions starts with an uppercase letter. Unlike other programming languages, in Go, there are not any keywords like public and private. In Go, all package identifiers are exported to other packages if the first letter of the name is an uppercase letter. If the name of the package identifiers starts with a lowercase letter, it will not be exported to other packages, and the accessibility is limited to within the package. In our example program, we used two standard library packages, strings and unicode, in which identifiers of all reusable functions start with an uppercase letter. When you learn more about Go, it will surprise you with its simplicity and the way it solves problems.

In our package, we provide three string utility functions: ToUpperCase, ToLowerCase, and ToFirstUpper. The ToUpperCase function returns a copy of the string parameter with all Unicode letters mapped to their uppercase. We use the ToLower function of the strings package (standard library) to change the case.

```
func ToUpperCase(s string) string {
    return strings.ToUpper(s)
}
```

The ToLowerCase function returns a copy of the string parameter with all Unicode letters mapped to lowercase. We use the ToLower function of the strings package to change the letter case.

```
func ToLowerCase(s string) string {
    return strings.ToLower(s)
}
```

The ToFirstUpper function returns a copy of the string parameter with the first letter of its Unicode letter mapped to uppercase.

```
func ToFirstUpper(s string) string {
    if len(s) < 1 { // if the empty string
        return s
```

11

```
    }
    // Trim the string
    t := strings.Trim(s, " ")
    // Convert all letters to lowercase
    t = strings.ToLower(t)
    res := []rune(t)
    // Convert first letter to uppercase
    res[0] = unicode.ToUpper(res[0])
    return string(res)
}
```

In the ToFirstUpper function, we first convert all letters to lowercase, and then convert the first letter of the string to uppercase. In this function, we use a Slice (a data structure for storing collections of a particular type) of type rune. We discuss a lot more about various data structures for holding collections of values later in the book. The expression string (res) converts the value res to the type string.

▪ **Note**   Go language defines the type rune as an alias for the type int32 to represent a Unicode code point. A string in Go is a sequence of runes.

Organizing the Code Path

The Go package ecosystem is designed to be easily shared with other packages, and it considers that Go code might be shared through remote repositories. The third-party packages are shared through remote repositories hosted on code-sharing web sites such as GitHub. We organize the Go code in a special way to easily share code through remote repositories. For example, we put all example code for this book on GitHub at https://github.com/shijuvar/go-recipes. So when I wrote the code, I put the source code into the github.com/shijuvar/go-recipes directory structure under the $GOPATH/src directory. I wrote the source code of the strutils package into github.com/shijuvar/go-recipes/ch01/strutils under the $GOPATH/src directory. Once I committed the source into its remote repository location, GitHub.com in this example, users can access the package using go get by providing the location of the remote repository as shown here:

```
go get github.com/shijuvar/go-recipes/ch01/strutils
```

The go get command fetches the source from the remote repository and installs the package using the following procedure.

1. Fetch the source from the remote repository and put the source into the github.com/shijuvar/go-recipes/ch01/strutils directory under the $GOPATH/src directory.

2. Install the package that put the package object strutils into the github.com/shijuvar/go-recipes/ch01 directory under the platform-specific directory (darwin_amd64 directory in macOS) under the $GOPATH/pkg directory.

Compiling the Package

Let's build the strutils package so that we can make it a shared library to be used with other packages in our Go Workspace. Navigate to the package directory, then run the go install command:

```
go install
```

The install command compiles (similar to the action of the go build command) the package source, and then installs the resulting binary into the pkg directory of GOPATH. When we reuse this package from other packages, we can import it from the GOPATH location. All standard library packages reside in the GOROOT location and all custom packages are in the GOPATH location. We write the source of the strutils package in github.com/shijuvar/go-recipes/ch01/strutils directory structure under the $GOPATH/src directory. When you run the go install command it compiles the source and puts the resulting binary into the github.com/shijuvar/go-recipes/ch01/strutils directory under the platform-specific subdirectory in the $GOPATH/pkg directory. Figure 1-3 and Figure 1-4 show the directory structure of the package object strutils in the $GOPATH/pkg directory.

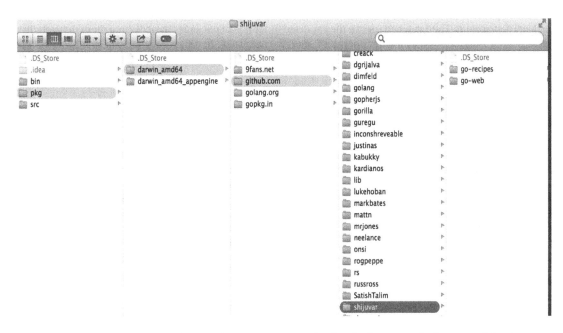

Figure 1-3. *Directory structure of go-recipes repository under the platform-specific directory of the pkg directory*

Figure 1-4. *Directory structure of package object strutils under the go-recipes repository*

We explore more about packages later in this chapter.

1-6. Reusing a Shared Library Package

Problem

You have developed a shared library package. Now, you would like to reuse the shared library package with other packages in your Go Workspace.

Solution

You can import the packages using the import statement specified at the top of your Go source files after the package declaration. Then you can invoke the exported functions of packages by accessing them through the package identifier, followed by the dot operator (.) and the exported identifier that you want to call.

How It Works

The Go installation installs the standard library packages that reside in the pkg directory of GOROOT. When you write custom packages, the resulting binary of these packages goes into the pkg directory of the GOPATH location. When you import the packages of the standard library you just need to specify the short path of the packages because most of these packages directly reside in the $GOROOT/pkg directory. When you import the fmt package, you just need to refer to fmt in the import block. Some standard library packages such as http reside under another root package directory (within $GOROOT/pkg); for http it is the net package directory, so when you import the http package you need to refer to net/http. When you import packages from GOPATH, you must specify the full path of the package location, for which it starts after the platform-specific directory of $GOPATH/pkg. Let's reuse the strutils package we developed in Listing 1-4, where the location of the package is github.com/shijuvar/go-recipes/ch01/strutils.

Listing 1-5 shows a program that reuses the exported functions of the strutils package.

Listing 1-5. Package main That Reuses the strutils Package

```go
package main

import (
    "fmt"

    "github.com/shijuvar/go-recipes/ch01/strutils"
)

func main() {
    str1, str2 := "Golang", "gopher"
    // Convert to uppercase
    fmt.Println("To Upper Case:", strutils.ToUpperCase(str1))

    // Convert to lowercase
    fmt.Println("To Lower Case:", strutils.ToUpperCase(str1))

    // Convert first letter to uppercase
    fmt.Println("To First Upper:", strutils.ToFirstUpper(str2))
}
```

We import the strutils package from the github.com/shijuvar/go-recipes/ch01/strutils path that resides in $GOPATH/pkg. In the import block, we differentiate the standard library packages and the custom packages by putting a blank line. It is not necessary to do so, but it is a recommended practice among Go programmers.

```
import (
    "fmt"

    "github.com/shijuvar/go-recipes/ch01/strutils"
)
```

We access the exported identifiers of the package using the package identifier strutils. You should see the following output when you run the program:

```
To Upper Case: GOLANG
To Lower Case: GOLANG
To First Upper: Gopher
```

1-7. Managing Source Code Using Go Tool

Problem

You would like to use Go tool for managing your Go source code.

Solution

The Go ecosystem provides tooling support through a command-line tool. You can run the Go tool by running the go command associated with a subcommand.

How It Works

The Go ecosystem consists of the Go language, the Go tool, and packages. The Go tool is a very important component for a Go programmer. It allows you to format, build, install, and test Go packages and commands. We used the Go tool in the previous sections of this chapter to compile, install, and run Go packages and commands. Run the go help command to obtain documentation on the go command.

Here is the documentation for the various subcommands provided by the go command:

```
Go is a tool for managing Go source code.

Usage:

        go command [arguments]

The commands are:

        build               compile packages and dependencies
        clean               remove object files
        doc                 show documentation for package or symbol
        env                 print Go environment information
```

15

```
fix                 run go tool fix on packages
fmt                 run gofmt on package sources
generate         generate Go files by processing source
get                 download and install packages and dependencies
install             compile and install packages and dependencies
list                     list packages
run                 compile and run Go program
test                test packages
tool                run specified go tool
version          print Go version
vet                 run go tool vet on packages
```

Use "go help [command]" for more information about a command.

Additional help topics:

```
c                         calling between Go and C
buildmode      description of build modes
filetype              file types
gopath               GOPATH environment variable
environment  environment variables
importpath       import path syntax
packages         description of package lists
testflag              description of testing flags
testfunc     description of testing functions
```

Use "go help [topic]" for more information about that topic.

If you want help on a specific command, run go help with the command for which you want help. Let's look for the help on the install subcommand:

```
go help install
```

Here is the documentation for the install command:

```
usage: go install [build flags] [packages]


Install compiles and installs the packages named by the import paths,
along with their dependencies.

For more about the build flags, see 'go help build'.
For more about specifying packages, see 'go help packages'.

See also: go build, go get, go clean.
```

Formatting Go Code

The go command provides a command fmt that automatically formats Go code. The go fmt command formats the source code by applying predefined styles to the source files, which formats the source with correct placement of curly brackets, tabs, and spaces, and alphabetically sorts the package imports. It uses tabs (width = 8) for indentation and blanks for alignment. Go programmers typically run the fmt command before committing their source code into version control systems. When you save the source files from Go integrated development environments (IDEs), most of them automatically call the fmt command to format the Go code. The fmt command can be used to format code at the directory level or for a specific Go source file.

The fmt command formats the package import block in alphabetical order. Listing 1-6 shows the package import block before applying go fmt, where we listed the packages without any order.

Listing 1-6. Package import Block Before Applying go fmt

```
import (
    "unicode"
    "log"
    "strings"
)
```

Listing 1-7 shows the package import block after applying the go fmt command to Listing 1-6. You can see that go fmt formats the import block in alphabetical order.

Listing 1-7. Package import Block After Applying go fmt on Listing 1-6

```
import (
    "log"
    "strings"
    "unicode"
)
```

Vetting Go Code for Common Errors

The go vet command lets you validate your Go code for common errors. The vet command verifies your Go code and reports suspicious constructs if it finds any. The compiler can't find some common errors, which might be able to be identified using go vet. This command examines the source code and reports errors such as Printf calls with arguments that do not align with the format string. Listing 1-8 shows a program on which an argument of a Printf call uses a wrong format specifier for printing a floating-point number.

Listing 1-8. Program That Uses the Wrong Format Specifier for Printing a Floating-Point Number

```
package main

import "fmt"

func main() {
    floatValue:=4.99
    fmt.Printf("The value is: %d",floatValue)
}
```

You need to use the format identifier %f for printing floating-point numbers, but provided %d, which is the wrong format identifier. When you compile this program, you will not get any error, but you will get an error when running the program. If you can verify your code with go vet, however, it shows the formatting error. Let's run the go vet command:

```
go vet main.go
```

The Go tool shows the following error:

```
main.go:7: arg floatValue for printf verb %d of wrong type: float64
exit status 1
```

It is recommended that you use the go vet command before committing your Go code into version control systems so that you can avoid some errors. You can run the go vet command at the directory level or on a specific Go source file.

Go Documentation with GoDoc

When you write code, providing proper documentation is an important practice so that programmers can easily understand the code later on, and it is easy to explore when looking at others' code and reusing third-party libraries. Go provides a tool named godoc that provides documentation infrastructure to Go programmers from their Go code itself, which simplifies the development process because you don't need to look for any other infrastructure for documentation.

The godoc tool generates the documentation from your Go code itself by leveraging the code and comments. Using the godoc tool, you can access the documentation from two places: a command-line window and a browser interface. Let's say that you want documentation for standard library package fmt. You would run the following command from the command-line window:

```
godoc fmt
```

Running this command provides the documentation directly in your command-line window. You can use the godoc tool to view the documentation of your own custom packages. Let's run the godoc tool to view the documentation for the strutils package we have developed in Listing 1-4:

```
godoc github.com/shijuvar/go-recipes/ch01/strutils
```

Running this command gives you the documentation for the strutils package in your command-line window, as shown here:

```
PACKAGE DOCUMENTATION

package strutils
    import "github.com/shijuvar/go-recipes/ch01/strutils"

    Package strutils provides string utility functions

FUNCTIONS

func ToFirstUpper(s string) string
    Returns the string changed to upper case for its first letter.

func ToLowerCase(s string) string
    Returns the string changed with lower case.

func ToUpperCase(s string) string
    Returns the string changed with upper case.
```

It would be difficult to look at and navigate the documentation from the command-line window. The godoc tool provides an elegant interface for documentation from a web browser window. To use the web browser interface, you need to run a web server locally using the godoc tool. The following command runs a documentation server locally by listening at the given port:

```
godoc -http=:3000
```

Running that command starts a web server. You can then navigate the documentation at http://localhost:3000. Figure 1-5 shows the index page of the documentation interface.

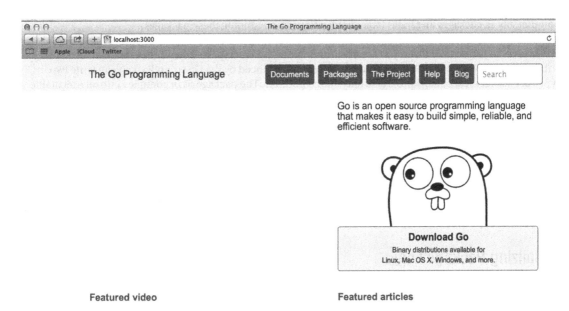

Figure 1-5. *Index page of the documentation user interface generated by the* godoc *tool*

This user interface provided by the godoc tool is exactly like the Go web site at https://golang.org/. By clicking the Packages link, you obtain the documentation for the packages from GOROOT and from GOPATH. When you run the godoc server locally, it simply looks in both GOROOT and GOPATH and generates the documentation for the packages resident in those locations. It is a good habit to write comments in your Go code so that you will produce better documentation for your Go code without leveraging any external infrastructure.

1-8. Writing and Reusing Packages

Problem

You want to write and reuse packages. You also want to provide initialization logic in packages and want to use a package alias for the package identifier.

Solution

You write `init` functions to write initialization logic for packages. When you reuse packages, you access their exported using a package identifier. You can also use a package alias for accessing the package's identifiers if you could provide the alias when you import the packages in the `import` block.

How It Works

Go provides the modularity and code reusability through its package ecosystem that lets you write highly maintainable and reusable code. The idiomatic way of writing Go applications is to write smaller software components as packages and build larger applications by combining these packages.

It is important to understand Go Workspace before writing packages. Recipe 1-1 covers the Go Workspace, so please read that if you are unsure about the Go Workspace. You write Go code in the `src` subdirectory of Workspace. Based on the binary output produced by the Go compiler, you can write two types of packages: executable programs and shared libraries. The package `main` compiles into an executable program. When you write package `main`, you must provide a function named `main` to make it the entry point of the executable program. When you write packages as shared libraries, you can choose a name as the package identifier. You organize Go source files into directories called packages. All source files that belong to a particular directory are part of that package. You must give the same package name to all source files under a single directory. Go programmers typically give a package name that is the same as the directory name in which they write Go source files for the package. When you write packages as shared libraries, you must give the package the same name as the directory name. When you run `go install` on the package directory, the resulting binary goes to the `bin` subdirectory of Workspace if it is a package `main`, and goes to the `pkg` subdirectory of Workspace if it is a shared library package.

Initializing Package Logic

When you write packages you might need to write some initialization logic. Let's say that you write a library package for persisting data into a database, and you want to establish a connection to the database automatically whenever this package is referenced from other packages. In this context, you can write a special function named `init` to write initialization logic for the package. Whenever packages reference from other packages, all `init` functions of the referenced packages will be automatically invoked. You don't need to explicitly call the `init` functions of the packages. When you refer a package from package `main`, the `init` functions of referenced packages will be invoked before executing the `main` function of the package `main`.

```
// Initialization logic for the package
func init() {
 // Initialization logic goes here
}
```

Writing an Example Package

Let's write an example package to be reused as a shared library. Write the source at `github.com/shijuvar/go-recipes/ch01/lib directory` under the `$GOPATH/src` directory. Because the directory name is `lib` the package name must be specified as `lib` in the package declaration statement.

```
package lib
```

In this example package, we persist a `string` of a collection of your favorite items into an in-memory collection. We want to provide some default favorite items for the in-memory collection so we write this logic in the `init` function. Listing 1-9 shows the core functionality of the `lib` package.

Listing 1-9. Favorites.go in the `lib` Package

```
package lib

// Stores favorites
var favorites []string

// Initialization logic for the package
func init() {
    favorites = make([]string, 3)
    favorites[0] = "github.com/gorilla/mux"
    favorites[1] = "github.com/codegangsta/negroni"
    favorites[2] = "gopkg.in/mgo.v2"
}

// Add a favorite into the in-memory collection
func Add(favorite string) {
    favorites = append(favorites, favorite)
}

// Returns all favorites
func GetAll() []string {
    return favorites
}
```

Favorites.go provides the core functionality for the `lib` package. It allows you to add favorite items to the collection using the Add function and returns the all the favorite items using the GetAll function. The Add and GetAll functions are to be exported to other packages, so the identifier names start with an uppercase letter. To store the data of favorite items, we used a data structure of a collection, named Slice, to store a collection of strings (Chapter 2 contains recipes that deal with slices). For now, think of it as a dynamic array to hold string values of favorite items. The identifier of the package variable favorites starts with a lowercase letter so that this will not be exported to other packages, but within the `lib` packages it can be accessed from all functions. The data for the favorite items is exposed to other packages using the GetAll function. In the init function, we add some default favorite items into the collection. The init function will be automatically invoked when we import this package into other packages.

Now write another source file into the `lib` package to provide utility functions on the favorite items. For the sake of this example, simply add a function in the new source file utils.go, to print the value of the favorite items in the console window. Listing 1-10 shows the source of utils.go.

Listing 1-10. utils.go in the `lib` Package

```
package lib

import (
    "fmt"
)

// Print all favorites
```

```
func PrintFavorites() {
    for _, v := range favorites {
        fmt.Println(v)
    }
}
```

In the PrintFavorites function, we iterate over the favorites data and print the value of each item. In this function, we use a special control statement provided by the Go language for iterating over the collection type. The range iterates over elements in a variety of data structures of collection types, and provides an index and value of each item in the iteration. Here is the basic syntax for iterating over the collection using range:

```
for index, value := range collection{
    // code statements
 }
```

In our range statement in the PrintFavorites function, we use each item value for printing into the console window, but we don't use the index value. If you declare a variable and never use it, Go compiler shows an error. We use a blank identifier (_) in place of an index variable to avoid a compiler error.

```
for _, v := range favorites {
    fmt.Println(v)
}
```

Build the package using the go install command:

```
go install
```

Running this command from the package directory compiles the source and puts the package object lib into the github.com/shijuvar/go-recipes/ch01 directory structure under the $GOPATH/pkg directory. Figure 1-6 shows the compiled package object of the lib package.

Figure 1-6. *Compiled package object of* lib

Reusing Packages

To reuse a package, you need to import that package. The import block is used to import packages. The following code block shows the import block that imports a standard library package and a custom package.

```
import (
    "fmt"

    "github.com/shijuvar/go-recipes/ch01/lib"
)
```

When you import the custom packages you should provide the full path to the packages under the $GOPATH/pkg directory. The lib package object is available at github.com/shijuvar/go-recipes/ch01 under the $GOPATH/pkg directory so we import the package with its full location.

Listing 1-11 shows a program that reuses the functions of the lib package.

Listing 1-11. Program Reuses the lib Package

```
package main

import (
    "fmt"

    "github.com/shijuvar/go-recipes/ch01/lib"
)

func main() {
    // Print default favorite packages
    fmt.Println("****** Default favorite packages ******\n")
    lib.PrintFavorites()
    // Add couple of favorites
    lib.Add("github.com/dgrijalva/jwt-go")
    lib.Add("github.com/onsi/ginkgo")
    fmt.Println("\n****** All favorite packages ******\n")
    lib.PrintFavorites()
    count := len(lib.GetAll())
    fmt.Printf("Total packages in the favorite list:%d", count)
}
```

■ **Note**   When you import packages in the import block, it is recommended that you first import the standard library packages in alphabetical order, then put a blank line, followed by third-party packages and your own packages (custom packages). If you import both third-party packages and your own packages, differentiate them by putting a blank line between both package lists.

You should see the following output when you run the program:

```
****** Default favorite packages ******

github.com/gorilla/mux
github.com/codegangsta/negroni
gopkg.in/mgo.v2

****** All favorite packages ******

github.com/gorilla/mux
github.com/codegangsta/negroni
gopkg.in/mgo.v2
github.com/dgrijalva/jwt-go
github.com/onsi/ginkgo
Total packages in the favorite list:5
```

Using a Package Alias

In Listing 1-11, we imported the package lib and accessed the exported identifiers of the package using the identifier lib. If you want to provide an alias for your packages, you can do this and access the exported identifiers of the packages using an alias instead of its original name. Here is the code block that shows the import statement using an alias.

```
import (
    fav "github.com/shijuvar/go-recipes/ch01/lib"
)
```

In this import statement we give the alias fav to the lib package. Here is the code block that accesses the exported identifiers of the lib package using an alias.

```
fav.PrintFavorites()
fav.Add("github.com/dgrijalva/jwt-go")
fav.Add("github.com/onsi/ginkgo")
```

You can also use alias names for packages to avoid package name ambiguity. Because packages are referenced from their full path, you can give the same name to multiple packages. When you use multiple packages with the same name inside a program, however, it creates name ambiguity. In this context, you can use a package alias to avoid name ambiguity. Listing 1-12 shows an example code block that imports two packages of the same name, but it uses a package alias to avoid name ambiguity.

Listing 1-12. Package Alias to Avoid Name Ambiguity

```
package main

import (
        mongo "app/libs/mongodb/db"
        redis "app/libs/redis/db"
)

func main() {
   mongo.Connect() //calling method of package "app/libs/mongodb/db"
   redis.Connect() //calling method of package "app/libs/redis/db"
}
```

Using a Blank Identifier as a Package Alias

We discussed that init functions of the referenced packages will be automatically invoked within the programs. Because init functions are primarily used for providing initialization logic on packages, you might need to reference packages just for invoking their init function. In some contexts, this might be needed when you don't need to call any functions other than init. The Go compiler shows an error when you import a package but never used it. In this context, to avoid a compilation error, you can use a blank identifier (_) as the package alias, so the compiler ignores the error of not using the package identifier, but the init functions will be automatically invoked.

Here is the code block that uses a blank identifier (_) as the package alias to avoid a compilation error.

```
import (
        _ "app/libs/mongodb/db"
)
```

Let's say that the package db has a function init that is used just for connecting to a database and initializing database objects. You don't want to invoke package identifiers from a specific source file, but you want to invoke the database initialization logic. Here you can call package identifiers from other source files of the same package.

Installing Third-Party Packages

The Go ecosystem is enriched with a vast number of third-party packages. The Go standard library provides the essential components for building a variety of applications. The Go developer community is very enthusiastic about building packages for numerous use cases. When you build real-world applications you might use several third party packages. To use a third-party package, you must download it into your GOPATH location. The go get command fetches the third-party packages from remote repositories and installs the packages into your GOPATH location. This puts the source code of packages into $GOPATH/src and package objects into $GOPATH/pkg.

The following command downloads and installs the thrid-party package gorethink (RethinkDB Driver for Go) into your GOPATH:

```
go get github.com/dancannon/gorethink
```

Once you have installed the third-party packages into your GOPATH location, you can reuse them in your programs by importing the package. Listing 1-13 shows an example program that uses the third-party package gorethink to connect with the RethinkDB database. We explore many third-party packages, including the gorethink package, later in this book.

Listing 1-13. Using a Third-Party Package

```
package main


import (
    r "github.com/dancannon/gorethink"
)

var session *r.Session

func main() {
session, err := r.Connect(r.ConnectOpts{
    Address: "localhost:28015",
})
}
```

CHAPTER 2

Go Fundamentals

Chapter 1 provided an overview of the Go programming language and the major components of the Go ecosystem. This chapter contains recipes dealing with the core fundamentals of Go language. Go is a simple programming language that provides the essential features for building scalable software systems. Unlike other programming languages such as C# and Java, Go provides minimal features in the language specification to keep to its design goal of being a simple, minimal language. Although it is a minimal language, Go provides the necessities in the language to build reliable and efficient software systems. The recipes in this chapter deal with writing functions, working with various collection types, error handling, and the unique features of Go implemented with the keywords defer, panic, and recover, among other things.

2-1. Writing Functions in Go

Problem

How do you manage Go code in functions?

Solution

The keyword func is used to declare functions. A function is declared with a name, a list of parameters, an optional list of return types, and a body to write the logic for the function.

How It Works

A function in Go is a reusable piece of code that organizes a sequence of code statements as a unit, which can be called from within the packages, and also from other packages if the functions are exported to other packages. Because functions are reusable piece of code, you can call this form multiple times. When you write shared library packages, the functions with names that start with an uppercase letter will be exported to other packages. If the function name starts with a lowercase letter, it won't be exported to other packages, but you can call this function within the same package.

Declaring Functions

Here is the syntax for writing functions in Go:

```
func name(list of parameters)  (list of return types)
{
    function body
}
```

© Shiju Varghese 2016
S. Varghese, *Go Recipes*, DOI 10.1007/978-1-4842-1188-5_2

The function parameters specify name and type. When a caller calls a function, it provides the arguments for the function parameters. In Go, a function can return multiple values. The list of return types specifies the types of values that the function returns. You write the code statements in the function body. Listing 2-1 shows an example function to add two integer values.

Listing 2-1. An Example Function That Adds Two Integer Values

```go
func Add(x, y int) int {
    return x + y
}
```

A function Add is declared, which has two parameters with the type integer, and the function returns an integer value. You provide the return values of functions using the return statement.

Listing 2-2 shows the code block that calls this Add function.

Listing 2-2. Code Block That Calls the Add Function

```go
x, y := 20, 10
result := Add(x, y)
```

Two integer variables x and y are initialized to provide arguments for calling the Add function. The local variable result initializes with the return value that the Add function returns.

Listing 2-3 shows an example program that declares two functions and calls it from a main function.

Listing 2-3. Example Program That Defines and Calls Functions

```go
package main

import (
    "fmt"
)

func Add(x, y int) int {
    return x + y
}

func Subtract(x, y int) int {
    return x - y
}

func main() {
    x, y := 20, 10

    result := Add(x, y)
    fmt.Println("[Add]:", result)

    result = Subtract(x, y)
    fmt.Println("[Subtract]:", result)
}
```

In this program, two functions are declared: Add and Subtract. These two functions are called from the main function.

You should see the following output when you run the program:

```
[Add]: 30
[Subtract]: 10
```

Naming Return Values

When you write functions, you can name the return values by defining variables at the top of the function. Listing 2-4 shows the Add function with named return values.

Listing 2-4. Add Function with Named Return Values

```
func Add(x, y int) (result int) {
    result = x + y
    return
}
```

A variable result of integer type is specified in the function declaration for the value that the function returns. When you specify the named return values, you can assign the return values to the named variables and can exit from functions by simply specifying the return keyword, without providing the return values along with the return statement.

```
    result = x + y
    return
```

This return statement returns the named return values specified in the function declaration. This is known as a *naked* return. I would not recommend this approach, as it could affect the readability of your programs.

Returning Multiple Values

Go is a language that provides lot of pragmatism in its language design. In Go, you can return multiple values from a function, which is a helpful feature in many practical scenarios.

Listing 2-5 shows an example program that declares a function with two return values and calls it from a main function.

Listing 2-5. An Example Program That Uses a Function with Multiple Return Values

```
package main

import (
    "fmt"
)

func Swap(x, y string) (string, string) {
    return y, x
}

func main() {
    x, y := "Shiju", "Varghese"
    fmt.Println("Before Swap:", x, y)
```

```
    x, y = Swap(x, y)
    fmt.Println("After Swap:", x, y)
}
```

A function named Swap is declared with two return values of string type. The Swap function swaps two string values. We call the Swap function from main function.

You should see the following output when you run the program:

```
Before Swap: Shiju Varghese
After Swap: Varghese Shiju
```

Variadic Functions

A *variadic function* is a function that accepts a variable number of arguments. This type of function is useful when you don't know the number of arguments you are passing to the function. The built-in Println function of the fmt package is an example of variadic function that can accept a variable number of arguments.

Listing 2-6 shows an example program that provides a variadic function Sum, which accepts a variable number of arguments of integer type.

Listing 2-6. Example Program with Variadic Function

```
package main

import (
    "fmt"
)

func Sum(nums ...int) int {
    total := 0
    for _, num := range nums {
        total += num
    }
    return total
}

func main() {
    // Providing four arguments
    total := Sum(1, 2, 3, 4)
    fmt.Println("The Sum is:", total)

    // Providing three arguments
    total = Sum(5, 7, 8)
    fmt.Println("The Sum is:", total)
}
```

The expression . . . is used to specify the variable length of a parameter list. When a caller provides the value to the nums parameter, it can provide a variable number of arguments with integer values. The Sum function provides the sum of the variable number of arguments provided by its caller. The function iterates over the values of the nums parameter using the range construct, to get the total value of the arguments provided by the caller. In the main function, Sum function is called twice. Each time you provide a variable number of arguments.

You should see the following output when you run the program:

```
The Sum is: 10
The Sum is: 20
```

When you call the variadic functions, you can provide slices (a dynamic array) as arguments. You will learn about slices later in this chapter. Listing 2-7 shows the code block that calls a variadic function by providing a slice as an argument.

Listing 2-7. Code Block That Calls a Variadic Function with a Slice

```go
// Providing a slice as an argument
nums := []int{1, 2, 3, 4, 5}
total = Sum(nums...)
fmt.Println("The Sum is:", total)
```

When you provide a slice as an argument, you must provide the expression ... after the Slice value.

Function Values, Anonymous Functions, and Closures

Go's pragmatism gives developers productivity like a dynamically typed language although Go is a statically typed language. Functions in Go provide a great deal of flexibility for Go programmers. Functions are like values, which means that you can pass function values as arguments to other functions that return values. Go also provides support for anonymous functions and closures. An *anonymous function* is a function definition without a function name. This is useful when you want to form a function inline without providing a function identifier.

Listing 2-8 shows an example program that demonstrates passing an anonymous function as an argument to another function, in which the anonymous function closes over the variables to form closure.

Listing 2-8. Example Program Demonstrating Passing Function as Value, Anonymous Function, and Closure

```go
package main

import (
    "fmt"
)

func SplitValues(f func(sum int) (int, int)) {
    x, y := f(35)
    fmt.Println(x, y)

    x, y = f(50)
    fmt.Println(x, y)
}

func main() {
    a, b := 5, 8
    fn := func(sum int) (int, int) {
        x := sum * a / b
        y := sum - x
```

```
        return x, y
    }

    // Passing function value as an argument to another function
    SplitValues(fn)

    // Calling the function value by providing argument
    x, y := fn(20)
    fmt.Println(x, y)
}
```

In the main function, an anonymous function is declared and assigned the value of anonymous function to a variable named fn.

```
    a, b := 5, 8
    fn := func(sum int) (int, int) {
        x := sum * a / b
        y := sum - x
        return x, y
    }
```

The anonymous function is declared within the main function. In Go, you can write functions within the function. The anonymous function split a value into two values using an arbitrary logic. To form the arbitrary logic, it accesses the values of a couple of variables declared in an outer function in the main function.

The anonymous function is assigned to variable fn and passes the function value to another function named SplitValues.

```
SplitValues(fn)
```

The SplitValues function receives a function as an argument.

```
func SplitValues(f func(sum int) (int, int)) {
    x, y := f(35)
    fmt.Println(x, y)

    x, y = f(50)
    fmt.Println(x, y)
}
```

Within the SplitValues function the parameter value that is a function that passes as an argument is called couple of times to split the values into two values. The returned values are printed to the console window.

Let's go back to the anonymous function. Within the main function, the value of the anonymous function is used for two things: calling the SplitValues function by passing the function value as an argument, and directly calling the function value by providing a value as an argument to split an integer value.

```
// Passing function value as an argument to another function
    SplitValues(fn)
```

```
// Calling the function value by providing argument
x, y := fn(20)
fmt.Println(x, y)
```

It is important to note that the anonymous function is accessing the two variables declared in the outer function:

```
a, b := 5, 8.
```

The variables a and b are declared in the main function, but the anonymous function (inner function) can access those variables. When you call the SplitValues function by passing the value of anonymous function as an argument, the anonymous function can also access the variables a and b. The anonymous function closes over the values of a and b, making it closure. Regardless of from where the value of the anonymous function is invoked, it can access the variables a and b declared in an outer function.

You should see the following output when you run the preceding program:

```
21 14
31 19
12 8
```

2-2. Working with Arrays

Problem

You would like to store a collection of elements into a fixed length of array types.

Solution

Go's array type allows you to store a fixed-size collection of elements of a single type.

How It Works

An *array* is a data structure that consists of a collection of elements of a single type. An array is a fixed-size data structure, which is declared by specifying a length and an element type.

Declaring and Initializing Arrays

Here is the code block that declares an array:

```
var x [5]int
```

A variable x is declared as an array of five elements of int type. Array x allows you to store five elements of integer values. You assign values to an array by specifying the index, which starts from 0. Here is the expression that assigns a value to the first element of array x:

```
x[0]=5
```

The expression x[4]=25 assigns a value to the last element (fifth element) of the array x.

You can also use an *array literal* to declare and initialize arrays as shown here:

```
y := [5]int {5,10,15,20,25}
```

When arrays are initialized using an array literal, you can provide values for specific elements as shown here:

```
langs := [4]string{0: "Go", 3: "Julia"}
```

An array of string type is declared with four as the size, but provides values only for the first element (index 0) and the last element (index 3). You will get default values for the elements that didn't get initialized. For string type it is empty string, for integer type it is 0, and for boolean type it is false. If you try to return the value of langs[1], you will get an empty string. You can provide values for the rest of elements at any time as usual:

```
langs[1] = "Rust"
langs[2] = "Scala"
```

When you declare and initialize arrays with the array literal you can provide the initialization expression in a multiline statement as shown here:

```
y := [5]int {
    5,
    10,
    15,
    20,
    25,
}
```

When you initialize array elements in a multiline statement, you must provide a comma after all elements, including the last element. This enables usability when you modify code. Because a comma is put after each element, you can easily remove or comment an element initialization or add a new element at any position, including the last position.

When you declare arrays, you always specify the length of the array, but when you declare and initialize arrays, you can use the expression ... instead of specifying the length, as shown here:

```
z := [...] { 5,10,15,20,25}
```

Here the length of the array is determined by the number of elements provided in the initialization expression.

Iterating over Arrays

Because an array is a collection type, you might want to iterate over the elements of arrays. Here is the code block that iterates over the elements of an array using the normal for loop:

```
langs := [4]string{"Go", "Rust", "Scala","Julia"}
for i := 0; i < len(langs); i++ {
        fmt.Printf("langs[%d]:%s \n", i, langs[i])
    }
```

Here we iterate over the elements of the langs array and simply print the value of each element by specifying the index value. The len function gets the length of the values of collection types.

■ **Note**   The Go language has only one looping construct, which is the for loop. Unlike many other languages, Go does not support the while looping construct. If you want a looping construct like while, you can use the for loop (e.g., for i< 1000{}).

Go has a range construct that lets you iterate over elements in various collection types. Go programmers typically use the range construct for iterating over the elements of data structures such as arrays, slices, and maps. Here is the code block that iterates over the elements of an array:

```
for k, v := range langs {
      fmt.Printf("langs[%d]:%s \n", k, v)
 }
```

The range construct on arrays provides both the index and value for each element in the collection. In our example code block, variable k gets the index and variable v gets the value of the element. If you don't want to use the value of any variable you declare on the left side, you can ignore it by using a blank identifier (_) as shown here:

```
for _, v := range langs {
      fmt.Printf(v)
   }
```

Inside this range block, the value of the element is used but the index is not, so a blank identifier (_) is used in place of the index variable to avoid a compilation error. The Go compiler shows an error if a variable is declared and never used.

Example Program

Listing 2-9 shows an example program that explores the array type.

Listing 2-9. Example Program on Arrays

```
package main

import (
    "fmt"
)

func main() {
    // Declare arrays
    var x [5]int
    // Assign values at specific index
    x[0] = 5
    x[4] = 25
    fmt.Println("Value of x:", x)

    x[1] = 10
```

```go
    x[2] = 15
    x[3] = 20
    fmt.Println("Value of x:", x)

    // Declare and initialize array with array literal
    y := [5]int{10, 20, 30, 40, 50}
    fmt.Println("Value of y:", y)

    // Array literal with ...
    z := [...]int{10, 20, 30, 40, 50}
    fmt.Println("Value of z:", z)
    fmt.Println("Length of z:", len(z))

    // Initialize values at specific index with array literal
    langs := [4]string{0: "Go", 3: "Julia"}
    fmt.Println("Value of langs:", langs)
    // Assign values to remaining positions
    langs[1] = "Rust"
    langs[2] = "Scala"

    // Iterate over the elements of array
    fmt.Println("Value of langs:", langs)
    fmt.Println("\nIterate over arrays\n")
    for i := 0; i < len(langs); i++ {
        fmt.Printf("langs[%d]:%s \n", i, langs[i])
    }
    fmt.Println("\n")

    // Iterate over the elements of array using range
    for k, v := range langs {
        fmt.Printf("langs[%d]:%s \n", k, v)
    }
}
```

You should see the following output when you run the program:

```
Value of x: [5 0 0 0 25]
Value of x: [5 10 15 20 25]
Value of y: [10 20 30 40 50]
Value of z: [10 20 30 40 50]
Length of z: 5
Value of langs: [Go   Julia]
Value of langs: [Go Rust Scala Julia]

Iterate over arrays

langs[0]:Go
langs[1]:Rust
langs[2]:Scala
langs[3]:Julia
```

```
langs[0]:Go
langs[1]:Rust
langs[2]:Scala
langs[3]:Julia
```

2-3. Working with Dynamic Arrays Using Slices

Problem

You would like to store collections of data into dynamic arrays because you don't know the size of the array when you declare it.

Solution

Go's slice type allows you to store a dynamic length of elements of a single type.

How It Works

When you declare data structures for storing a collection of elements, you might not know its size. For example, let's say that you want to query data from a database table or from a NoSQL collection and put the data into a variable. In this context, you can't declare an array by providing the size, because the size of the array could vary at any time based on the data contained in the database table. A slice is a data structure that is built on top of Go's array type, which allows you to store a dynamic length of elements of a single type. In your Go applications, the use of arrays might be limited, and you might often use slices because they provide a flexible and extensible data structure.

The slice data structure has length and capacity. The *length* is the number of elements referred to by the slice. The *capacity* is the number of elements for which there is space allocated in the slice. The length of the slice cannot go beyond the value of capacity because it is the highest value length that can be reached. The length and capacity of slices can be determined by using the len and cap functions, respectively. Due to the dynamic nature of slices, length and capacity of a slice can be varied at any time when slices are growing.

Declaring nil Slice

Declaring a slice is similar to declaring an array, but when you declare slices, you don't need to specify the size because it is a dynamic array. Here is the code block that declares a nil slice:

```
var x []int
```

A slice x is declared as a nil slice of integers. At this moment, the length and capacity of the slice is zero. Although the length of x is now zero, you can modify the length and initialize values later because slices are dynamic arrays. Go provides a function append that can be used to enlarge any slice (nil or nonnil) later on.

Initializing Slices Using make Function

A slice must be initialized before assigning values. In the preceding declaration, the slice x was declared, but it was not initialized, so if you try to assign values to it this will cause a runtime error. Go's built-in make function is used to initialize slices. When slices are declared using the make function, length and capacity are provided as arguments.

Here is the code block that creates a slice using the make function specifying the length and capacity:

```
y:= make ([]int, 3,5)
```

A slice y is declared and initialized with a length of 3 and capacity of 5 using the make function. When the capacity argument is omitted from the arguments of the make function, the value of capacity defaults to the specified value of length.

```
y:= make ([]int, 3)
```

A slice y is declared and initialized with length of 3 and capacity of 3. Because the value of capacity is not provided, it defaults to the value of length.

You can assign values to slice y similar to an array:

```
y[0] = 10
y[1] = 20
y[2] = 30
```

Creating Slices Using a Slice Literal

In addition to creating slices using the make function, you can also create slices using a *slice literal,* which is similar to an array literal. Here is the code block that creates a slice using a slice literal:

```
z:= []int {10,20,30}
```

A slice z is declared and initialized with length of 3 and capacity of 3. When you initialize the values, you can provide values to specific indexes as shown here:

```
z:= []int {0:10, 2:30}
```

A slice z is created and initialized with length of 3 and capacity of 3. When you create slices using this approach, the length is determined by the highest index value you have specified, so you can also create a slice by simply providing the highest index, as shown here:

```
z:= []int {2:0}
```

A slice z is created by initializing a zero value for index 2, so the capacity and length of the slice will be 3. By using a slice literal, you can also create an empty slice:

```
z:= []int{}
```

A slice z is created with zero elements of value. An empty slice is useful when you want to return empty collections from functions. Let's say that you provide a function that queries data from a database table and returns a slice by filling in the data of the table. Here you can return an empty slice if the table doesn't contain any data. Note that nil slices and empty slices are different. If z is an empty slice, a code expression z == nil returns false, but if it is a nil slice, the expression z == nil returns true.

Enlarging Slices with copy and append Functions

Because slices are dynamic arrays, you can enlarge them whenever you want. When you want to increase the capacity of a slice, one approach is to create a new, bigger slice and copy the elements of the original slice into newly created one. Go's built-in copy function is used to copy data from one slice to another. Listing 2-10 shows an example program that uses the copy function to increase the size of a slice.

Listing 2-10. Program to Enlarge a Slice Using the copy Function

```
package main

import (
    "fmt"
)

func main() {
    x := []int{10, 20, 30}
    fmt.Printf("[Slice:x] Length is %d Capacity is %d\n", len(x), cap(x))
    // Create a bigger slice
    y := make([]int, 5, 10)
    copy(y, x)
    fmt.Printf("[Slice:y] Length is %d Capacity is %d\n", len(y), cap(y))
    fmt.Println("Slice y after copying:", y)
    y[3] = 40
    y[4] = 50
    fmt.Println("Slice y after adding elements:", y)
}
```

You should see the following output when you run the program:

```
 [Slice:x] Length is 3 Capacity is 3
[Slice:y] Length is 5 Capacity is 10
Slice y after copying: [10 20 30 0 0]
Slice y after adding elements: [10 20 30 40 50]
```

A slice x is created with a length of 3 and capacity of 3. To increase the capacity and add more elements to the slice, a new slice y is created with a length of 5 and capacity of 10. The copy function then copies data from slice x to the destination slice y.

You can also enlarge slices by appending data to the end of a existing slice using Go's built-in append function. The append function automatically increases the size of the slice if it is necessary, and returns the updated slice with newly added data. Listing 2-11 shows an example program that uses the append function to increase a slice.

Listing 2-11. Program That Enlarges a Slice Using the append Function

```
package main

import (
    "fmt"
)

func main() {
```

```
x := make([]int, 2, 5)
x[0] = 10
x[1] = 20recipes for arrays
fmt.Println("Slice x:", x)
fmt.Printf("Length is %d Capacity is %d\n", len(x), cap(x))
// Create a bigger slice
x = append(x, 30, 40, 50)
fmt.Println("Slice x after appending data:", x)

fmt.Printf("Length is %d Capacity is %d\n", len(x), cap(x))

x = append(x, 60, 70, 80)
fmt.Println("Slice x after appending data for the second time:", x)
fmt.Printf("Length is %d Capacity is %d\n", len(x), cap(x))

}
```

You should see the following output when you run the program:

```
Slice x: [10 20]
Length is 2 Capacity is 5
Slice x after appending data: [10 20 30 40 50]
Length is 5 Capacity is 5
Slice x after appending data for the second time: [10 20 30 40 50 60 70 80]
Length is 8 Capacity is 10
```

A slice x is created with length of 2 and capacity of 5. Then three more data elements are appended to the slice. This time the length and capacity are both 5. Three more data elements are then appended to the slice. This time you are trying to increase the length of the slice to 8, but the capacity of the slice is 5. The append function can automatically grow the capacity if it is necessary. Here it increases to 10.

You can append data to a nil slice where it allocates a new underlying array as shown in Listing 2-12.

Listing 2-12. Appending Data to a Nil Slice

```
package main

import "fmt"

func main() {
    // Declare a nil slice
    var x []int
    fmt.Println(x, len(x), cap(x))
    x = append(x, 10, 20, 30)
    fmt.Println("Slice x after appending data:", x)
}
```

You should see the following output when you run the program:

```
[] 0 0
Slice x after appending data: [10 20 30]
```

Iterating Over Slices

An idiomatic approach for iterating over the elements of a slice is to use a `range` construct. Listing 2-13 shows an example program that iterates over the elements of a slice.

Listing 2-13. Program to Iterate Over the Elements of a Slice

```
package main

import (
    "fmt"
)

func main() {
    x := []int{10, 20, 30, 40, 50}
    for k, v := range x {
        fmt.Printf("x[%d]: %d\n", k, v)
    }
}
```

You should see the following output when you run the program:

```
x[0]: 10
x[1]: 20
x[2]: 30
x[3]: 40
x[4]: 50
```

The `range` construct on a slice provides both an index and value for each element in the collection. In our example program, variable k gets the index and variable v gets the value of the data element.

2-4. Persisting Key/Value Pairs Using Map

Problem

You would like to persist the collection of key/value pairs into a collection type similar to a hash table.

Solution

Go's map type allows you to store a collection of key/value pairs into a structure similar to a hash table.

How It Works

Go's *map* type is a data structure that provides an implementation of a hash table (known as HashMap in Java). A hash table implementation allows you to persist data elements as keys and values. A hash table provides fast lookups on the data element, as you can easily retrieve a value by providing the key.

Declaring and Initializing Maps

Here is a definition of a map type:

```
map[KeyType]ValueType
```

Here KeyType is the type of key and ValueType is the type of value. Here is the code block that declares a map:

```
var chapts  map[int]string
```

A map chapts is declared with int as the type for key and string as the type for value. At this moment, the value of map chapts is nil because the map doesn't get initialized. An attempt to write values to a nil map will cause a runtime error. You need to initialize maps before writing values to them. The built-in make function is used to initialize maps, as shown here:

```
chapts = make(map[int] string)
```

The map chapts is initialized using the make function. Let's add a few data values to the map:

```
chapts[1]="Beginning Go"
chapts[2]="Go Fundamentals"
chapts[3]="Structs and Interfaces"
```

It is important to note that you cannot add duplicate keys to the map.
You can also declare and initialize a map using a *map literal,* as shown here:

```
langs := map[string]string{
            "EL": "Greek",
            "EN": "English",
            "ES": "Spanish",
            "FR": "French",
            "HI": "Hindi",
     }
```

A map langs is declared with string as the type for both key and value, and values are initialized using the map literal.

Working with Maps

Maps provide fast lookups on the data elements in the data structure. You can easily retrieve the value of an element by providing the key shown here:

```
lan, ok := langs["EN"]
```

A lookup performed on the map by providing a key returns two values: the value of the element and a boolean value that indicates whether or not the lookup was successful. The variable lan gets the value of the element for the key "EN", and the variable ok gets a boolean value: true if a value exists for the key "EN" and false if the key doesn't exist. Go provides a convenient syntax for writing an if statement that can be used for writing a lookup statement:

```
if lan, ok := langs["EN"]; ok {
      fmt.Println(lan)
}
```

When writing an `if` statement as multiple statements on a single line, the statements are separated by semicolon (;) and the last expression should have a boolean value.

To remove items from a map, use the built-in function `delete` by providing the key. The `delete` function removes an element for the given key from the map and doesn't return anything. Here is the code block that deletes an element from `langs` map for the key `"EL"`.

```
delete(langs,"EL")
```

This deletes an element of the key `"EL"`. If the specified key doesn't exist, it won't do anything.

The range construct is typically used for iterating over the elements of map like other collection types. Listing 2-14 shows an example program that demonstrates various operations on maps.

Listing 2-14. Various operations on maps

```go
package main

import (
    "fmt"
)

func main() {
    // Declares a nil map
    var chapts map[int]string

    // Initialize map with make function
    chapts = make(map[int]string)

    // Add data as key/value pairs
    chapts[1] = "Beginning Go"
    chapts[2] = "Go Fundamentals"
    chapts[3] = "Structs and Interfaces"

    // Iterate over the elements of map using range
    for k, v := range chapts {
        fmt.Printf("Key: %d Value: %s\n", k, v)
    }

    // Declare and initialize map using map literal
    langs := map[string]string{
        "EL": "Greek",
        "EN": "English",
        "ES": "Spanish",
        "FR": "French",
        "HI": "Hindi",
    }

    // Delete an element
    delete(langs, "EL")

    // Lookout an element with key
    if lan, ok := langs["EL"]; ok {
        fmt.Println(lan)
```

```
    } else {
        fmt.Println("\nKey doesn't exist")
    }
}
```

You should see output similar to this:

```
Key: 3 Value: Structs and Interfaces
Key: 1 Value: Beginning Go
Key: 2 Value: Go Fundamentals

Key doesn't exist
```

Iteration Order of Maps

When you iterate over a map with a range construct, the iteration order is not specified and hence the same result is not guaranteed from one iteration, as Go randomizes map iteration order. If you want to iterate a map with a specific order, you must maintain a data structure to specify that order. Listing 2-15 shows an example program that iterates over a map with an order. To specify the order, this example maintains a slice to store sorted keys of a map.

Listing 2-15. Iterate over a Map With an Order

```go
package main

import (
        "fmt"
        "sort"
)

func main() {
        // Initialize map with make function
        chapts := make(map[int]string)

        // Add data as key/value pairs
        chapts[1] = "Beginning Go"
        chapts[2] = "Go Fundamentals"
        chapts[3] = "Structs and Interfaces"

        // Slice for specifying the order of the map
        var keys []int
        // Appending keys of the map
        for k := range chapts {
                keys = append(keys, k)
        }
        // Ints sorts a slice of ints in increasing order.
        sort.Ints(keys)
        // Iterate over the map with an order
        for _, k := range keys {
                fmt.Println("Key:", k, "Value:", chapts[k])
        }
}
```

You should see the following output:

```
Key: 1 Value: Structs and Interfaces
Key: 2 Value: Go Fundamentals
Key: 3 Value: Beginning Go
```

The order of the output will be same for all iterations because you specified an order.

2-5. Writing Clean-Up Code in Functions

Problem

You would like to write clean-up logic in functions to execute clean-up actions after the surrounding function returns.

Solution

Go provides a `defer` statement that allows you to write clean-up logic in functions.

How It Works

A `defer` statement in a function pushes a function call or a code statement onto a list of saved calls. You can add multiple `defer` statements inside a function. These deferred function calls from the saved list are executed after the surrounding function returns. A `defer` statement is commonly used to write clean-up logic inside functions to release resources that you have created in them. For example, let's say that you have opened a database connection object inside a function, where you can schedule the connection object to close to clean up the resources of the connection object after the function returns. The `defer` statement is often used for `close`, `disconnect`, and `unlock` statements against `open`, `connect`, or `lock` statements. The `defer` statement ensures that the deferred list of function calls is invoked in all cases, even when an exception occurs.

Listing 2-16 shows a code block that uses a `defer` statement to close a file object that is opened for reading.

Listing 2-16. Defer Statement Used to Close a File Object

```
import (
    "io/ioutil"
    "os"
)

func ReadFile(filename string) ([]byte, error) {
    f, err := os.Open(filename)
    if err != nil {
        return nil, err
    }
    defer f.Close()
    return ioutil.ReadAll(f)
}
```

We open a file object f to read its contents. To ensure object f is releasing its resources, we add the code statement f.Close() to the deferred list of function calls. A defer statement to release a resource is often written after the resource has been created without any error. We write defer f.Close() immediately after the object f has been successfully created.

```
f, err := os.Open(filename)
if err != nil {
    return nil, err
}
defer f.Close()
```

Using defer for writing clean-up logic is similar to using finally blocks in other programming languages like C# and Java. In the try/catch/finally block, you write clean-up logic in the finally block for the resources that have been created in the try block. Go's defer is more powerful than the finally block of a conventional programming language. For example, combining defer and recover statements, you can regain control from a panicking function. We cover panic and recover in the next sections of this chapter.

2-6. Stopping the Execution Flow of Control Using Panic

Problem

You would like to stop the execution flow of control in functions and begin panicking when your program is having critical errors.

Solution

Go provides a built-in panic function that stops the normal execution of a program and begins panicking.

How It Works

When the Go runtime detects any unhandled error during execution, it panics and stop the execution. Therefore, all runtime errors cause panic in your program. By explicitly calling the built-in panic function, you can create the same situation; it stops the normal execution and begins panicking. The panic function is often called in situations in which continuing the execution is almost impossible. For example, if you are trying to connect to a database and are unable to, then continuing the execution of the program doesn't make any sense because your application depends on the database. Here you can call the panic function to stop the normal execution and panic your program. The panic function accepts a value of any type as an argument. When a panic is happening inside a function, it stops normal execution of the function, all deferred function calls in that function are executed, and then the caller function gets a panicking function. It is important that all deferred functions are executed before stopping the execution. The Go runtime ensures that defer statements are executed in all cases, including a panic situation.

Listing 2-17 shows a code block that calls panic when attempting to open a file results in an error; it calls panic by providing an error object as an argument.

Listing 2-17. Using panic to Panic a Function

```
import (
    "io/ioutil"
```

```
    "os"
)

func ReadFile(filename string) ([]byte, error) {
    f, err := os.Open(filename)
    if err != nil {
        panic (err)  // calls panic
    }
    defer f.Close()
    return ioutil.ReadAll(f)
}
```

The function ReadFile tries to open a file to read its contents. If the Open function gets an error, the panic function is called to start a panicking function. When you write real-world applications you will rarely call the panic function; your objective should be to handle all errors to avoid a panic situation, log error messages, and show the proper error messages to the end user.

2-7. Recovering a Panicking Function Using Recover

Problem

You would like to regain control of a panicking function.

Solution

Go provides a built-in recover function that lets you regain control of a panicking function; hence, it is used only with deferred functions. The recover function is used inside the deferred functions to resume normal execution of a panicking function.

How It Works

When a function is panicking, all deferred function calls in that function are executed before normal execution stops. Here a call to recover inside the deferred function gets the value given to panic and regains control of normal execution. In short, you can resume normal execution using recover even after a panick situation.

Listing 2-18 shows an example of panic recovery using recover.

Listing 2-18. Example that demonstrates recover

```
package main

import (
    "fmt"
)

func panicRecover() {
```

```
    defer fmt.Println("Deferred call - 1")
    defer func() {
        fmt.Println("Deferred call - 2")
        if e := recover(); e != nil {
            // e is the value passed to panic()
            fmt.Println("Recover with: ", e)
        }
    }()
    panic("Just panicking for the sake of example")
    fmt.Println("This will never be called")
}

func main() {
    fmt.Println("Starting to panic")
    panicRecover()
    fmt.Println("Program regains control after the panic recovery")
}
```

This example program demonstrates how to resume the normal execution of a panicking function using the recover function. Inside the function panicRecover, two deferred functions have been added. Of the two deferred function calls, the second one is an anonymous function in which recover is called to resume execution even after a panic situation. It is important to understand that you can add any number of deferred function calls inside a function. The order of the execution of deferred functions is last added, first in order. For example, panic is explicitly called by providing a string value as an argument. This value can be retrieved by calling the recover function. When the panic function is called, the flow of control goes to deferred functions, where the recover function is called from the second deferred function (this will be invoked first when deferred function calls are executing). When the recover is called it receives the value given to panic and resumes normal execution and the program runs as normal.

You should see the following output when you run the program:

```
Starting to panic
Deferred call - 2
Recover with:  Just panicking for the sake of example
Deferred call - 1
Program regains control after the panic recovery
```

The result also illustrates the order in which the deferred functions are executed. The deferred function added last is executed before the first deferred function call.

2-8. Performing Error Handling

Problem

You would like to perform error handling in Go applications.

Solution

Go provides a built-in error type that is used to signal errors in functions. Go functions can return multiple values. This can be used to implement exception handling in functions by returning an error value along with other return values, and hence caller functions can check whether the functions provide an error value.

How It Works

Unlike many other programming languages, Go does not provide a try/catch block to handle exceptions. Instead of it, you can use the built-in error type to signal exceptions to caller functions. If you can look into the function of standard library packages you will get a better understanding about how to handle exceptions in Go. Most of the functions of standard library packages return multiple values, including an error value. An idiomatic way of returning an error value in functions is to provide the error value after other values provided in the return statement. In the return statement, therefore, the error value would be the last argument. In Listing 2-14, you called the Open function of the standard library package os to open a file object.

```
f, err := os.Open(filename)
    if err != nil {
        return nil, err
    }
```

The Open function returns two values: a file object and an error value. Check the returned error value to identify whether any exception has occurred while opening the file. If the error value returns a nonnil value, it means that an error has occurred.

Here is the source of the Open function in the os package:

```
// Open opens the named file for reading.  If successful, methods on
// the returned file can be used for reading; the associated file
// descriptor has mode O_RDONLY.
// If there is an error, it will be of type *PathError.
func Open(name string) (*File, error) {
        return OpenFile(name, O_RDONLY, 0)
}
```

Just as the standard library packages use exception handling by returning an error value, you can take the same approach in your Go code. Listing 2-19 shows an example function that returns an error value.

Listing 2-19. Example Function That Provides error Value

```
func Login(user User) (User, error) {
            var u User
        err = C.Find(bson.M{"email": user.Email}).One(u)
        if err != nil {
                return nil, err
        }
        err = bcrypt.CompareHashAndPassword(u.HashPassword, []byte(user.Password))
        if err != nil {
                return nil, err
        }
        return u, nil
}
```

The Login function returns two values, including an error value. Here is the code block that calls the Login function and verifies if the function returns any nonnil error value:

```
if user, err := repo.Login(loginUser); err != nil {
    fmt.Println(err)
}
// Implementation here if error is nil
```

In this code block, the caller function checks the returned error value; if the error value returns a non-nil. value, it indicates that the function returns an error. If the returned error value is nil, it indicates that the function call was successful without any error. When the fmt.Println function gets an error value as an argument, it formats the error value by calling its Error() string method. Ther Error method of error value returns the error message as string. The caller functions can be used with the Error method to get error messages as strings.

```
Message := err.Error()
```

When you return error values, you can provide descriptive error values to the caller functions. By using the New function of the errors package, you can provide descriptive error values as shown here:

```
func Login(user User) (User, error) {
        var u User
        err = C.Find(bson.M{"email": user.Email}).One(u)
        if err != nil {
                return nil, errors.New("Email doesn't exists")
        }
        // Validate password
        err = bcrypt.CompareHashAndPassword(u.HashPassword, []byte(user.Password))
        if err != nil {
                return nil, errors.New("Invalid password")
        }
        return u, nil
}
```

The errors.New function returns an error value that is used to provide descriptive error values to the caller functions. The Errorf function of the fmt package lets you use the formatting capabilities of the fmt package to create descriptive error values, as shown here:

```
func Login(user User) (User, error) {
        var u User
        err = C.Find(bson.M{"email": user.Email}).One(u)
        if err != nil {
                errObj:= fmt.Errorf("User %s doesn't exists. Error:%s, user.Email, err.
                Error())
                return nil, errObj
        }
        // Validate password
        err = bcrypt.CompareHashAndPassword(u.HashPassword, []byte(user.Password))
        if err != nil {
                errObj:= fmt.Errorf("Invalid password for the user:%s. Error:%s, user.Email,
                err.Error())
                return nil, errObj
        }
        return u, nil
}
```

The preceding code block uses the fmt.Errorf function to use the fmt package's formatting features to create descriptive error values.

A function in Go is a reusable piece of code that organizes a sequence of code statements as a unit. The keyword `func` is used to declare functions. Functions are exported to other packages if their names start with an uppercase letter. One unique feature of Go functions is that they can return multiple values.

Go provides three types of data structures to work with collections of data: arrays, slices, and maps. An array is a fixed-length type that contains sequence of elements of a single type. An array is declared by specifying a length and type. A slice is similar to an array, but its size can be varied at any time, so you don't have to specify the length of the slice. Slices are initialized using the built-in `make` function or the slice literal. Slices can be modified using two built-in functions: `append` and `copy`. A map is an implementation of a hash table that provides an unordered collection of key/value pairs. Maps are initialized using the built-in `make` function or using a map literal.

Go provides `defer`, which can be used to write clean-up logic in functions. A `defer` statement pushes a function call onto a saved list which is executed after the surrounding function returns. `Panic` is a built-in function that lets you stop normal execution and begins the panic of a function. `Recover` is a built-in function that regains control of a panicking function. `Recover` is used only inside the deferred functions.

Go uses a different and unique approach for implementing exception handling in Go code. Because Go functions can return multiple values, an `error` value is provided with the `return` statement, along with other return values. In this way, the caller functions can check the returned `error` value to identify whether there is any error or not.

CHAPTER 3

Structs and Interfaces

When you write programs, the type system of your choice of language is very important. Types allow you to organize your application data in a structured way that can be persisted into various data stores. When you write applications, especially business applications, you organize your application data using various types and persist the values of those types into persistence storage. When you write applications with Go, it is important to understand its type system and its design philosophy. Go provides various built-in types such as int, uint, float64, string, and bool. Data structures for storing collections of values such as arrays, slices, and maps are known as composite types because they are made up of other types—built-in types and user-defined types. In addition to the built-in types provided by Go, you can create your own types by combining with other types. This chapter contains recipes for user-defined types in Go.

Go provides simplicity and pragmatism for its type system, as the language does so much for various language specifications. Go's type system was designed for solving real-world problems instead of relying too much on academic theories, and it avoids a lot of complexity when you design data models for your applications. The object-oriented approach of Go is different from that of other languages, such as C++, Java, and C#. Go does not support inheritance in its type system, and it does not even have a class keyword. Go has a struct type, which is analogous to classes if you want to compare Go's type system with the type system of other object-oriented languages. The struct type in Go is a lightweight version of classes, following a unique design that favors *composition* over *inheritance*.

3-1. Creating User-Defined Types

Problem

You would like to create user-defined types to organize your application data.

Solution

Go has a struct type that allows you to create user-defined types by combining with other types.

How It Works

Go struct lets you create your own types by combining one or more types, including both built-in and user-defined types. Structs are the only way to create concrete user-defined types in Go. When you create your own types using struct, it is important to understand that Go does not provide support for inheritance in its type system, but it favors *composition* of types that lets you create larger types by combining smaller types. The design philosophy of Go is to create larger components by combining smaller and modular components. If you are a pragmatic programmer, you will appreciate the design philosophy of Go that favors composition over inheritance because of its practical benefits. The inheritance of types sometimes introduces practical challenges with regard to maintainability.

© Shiju Varghese 2016

S. Varghese, *Go Recipes*, DOI 10.1007/978-1-4842-1188-5_3

Declaring Struct Types

The keyword struct is used to declare a type as struct. Listing 3-1 shows an example struct that represents a customer's information.

Listing 3-1. Declare Struct Type

```
type Customer struct {
      FirstName string
      LastName  string
      Email     string
      Phone     string
}
```

A struct type Customer is declared that has four fields of string type. Note that the Customer struct and its fields are exported to other packages because identifiers are started with an uppercase letter. In Go, identifiers are exported to other packages if the name starts with an uppercase letter; otherwise accessibility will be limited within the packages. If a group of struct fields have a common type, you can organize the fields of the same type in a single-line statement as shown in Listing 3-2.

Listing 3-2. Declare Struct Type

```
type Customer struct {
    FirstName, LastName, Email, Phone string
}
```

Because all the fields of the Customer struct have string type, fields can be specified in a single statement.

Creating Instances of Struct Types

You can create instances of struct types by declaring a struct variable or using a *struct literal*. Listing 3-3 shows the code block that creates an instance of Customer struct by declaring a struct variable and assigning values to the fields of struct.

Listing 3-3. Creating a Struct Instance and Assigning Values

```
var c Customer
c.FirstName = "Alex"
c.LastName = "John"
c.Email = "alex@email.com"
c.Phone = "732-757-2923"
```

An instance of Customer type is created and values are assigned to the struct fields one by one. A struct literal can also be used for creating instances of struct types. Listing 3-4 shows the code block that creates an instance of Customer struct by using a struct literal and assigning values to the fields of the struct.

Listing 3-4. Creating a Struct Instance Using a Struct Literal

```
c := Customer{
        FirstName: "Alex",
        LastName:  "John",
        Email:     "alex@email.com",
        Phone:     "732-757-2923",
}
```

An instance of Customer type is created using the struct literal and values are assigned to the struct fields. Note that a comma is added even after the initialization to the last field of struct. When you create instances of a struct using the struct literal, you can initialize values as a multiline statement but you must put a comma even after end of the assignment to the struct fields. In Listing 3-4, you initialized values by specifying the struct fields. If you clearly know the order of the fields, you can omit the field identifiers while initializing the values as shown in the Listing 3-5.

Listing 3-5. Creating a Struct Instance Using a Struct Literal

```
c := Customer{
        "Alex",
        "John",
        "alex@email.com",
        "732-757-2923",
}
```

When you create struct instances using a struct literal, you can provide the values to specific fields of the struct as shown in Listing 3-6.

Listing 3-6. Creating a Struct Instance Using a Struct Literal by Specifying Values to a Few Fields

```
c := Customer{
        FirstName: "Alex",
        Email:     "alex@email.com",
}
```

Using User-Defined Types as the Type for Fields

The Customer struct was created using fields of built-in types. You can use other struct types as the type for the fields of structs. Let's expand the Customer struct by adding a new field to hold address information with a struct as the type for the new field. Listing 3-7 shows the Customer struct expanded by adding a new field with its type as a slice of Address type.

Listing 3-7. Customer Struct with a Slice of a User-Defined Type as the Type for Field

```
type Address struct {
    Street, City, State, Zip string
    IsShippingAddress        bool
}

type Customer struct {
    FirstName, LastName, Email, Phone string
    Addresses                         []Address
}
```

The Customer struct has been expanded by adding a new field, Addresses, for which the type is specified as a slice of a struct named Address. Using the Addresses field, you can specify multiple addresses for a customer. The IsShippingAddress field is used to specify a default shipping address. Listing 3-8 shows the code block that creates an instance of this modified Customer struct.

Listing 3-8. Creating an Instance of Customer Struct

```
c := Customer{
    FirstName: "Alex",
    LastName:  "John",
    Email:     "alex@email.com",
    Phone:     "732-757-2923",
    Addresses: []Address{
        Address{
            Street:             "1 Mission Street",
            City:               "San Francisco",
            State:              "CA",
            Zip:                "94105",
            IsShippingAddress: true,
        },
        Address{
            Street: "49 Stevenson Street",
            City:   "San Francisco",
            State:  "CA",
            Zip:    "94105",
        },
    },
}
```

The Addresses field is initialized by creating a slice of Address type with a length of two values.

3-2. Adding Methods to Struct Types

Problem

You would like to add behaviors to struct types to provide operations on the struct to be called as methods.

Solution

Go's type system allows you to add methods to struct types using a *method receiver*. The method receiver specifies which type has to associate a function as a method to that type.

How It Works

In Go, a method is a function that is specified with a receiver. Let's add a method to the Customer struct.

```
func (c Customer) ToString() string {
    return fmt.Sprintf("Customer: %s %s, Email:%s", c.FirstName, c.LastName, c.Email)
}
```

A method `ToString` is added to the `Customer` struct. The receiver is specified using an extra parameter section preceding the method name. Inside the methods, you can access the fields of receiver type using the identifier of receiver. The `ToString` method returns the customer name and email as a string by accessing the struct fields.

```
return fmt.Sprintf("Customer: %s %s, Email:%s", c.FirstName, c.LastName, c.Email)
```

Listing 3-9 shows an example program that declares the `Customer` struct and adds a couple of methods to it.

Listing 3-9. Struct with Methods

```go
package main

import (
        "fmt"
)

type Address struct {
        Street, City, State, Zip string
        IsShippingAddress        bool
}

type Customer struct {
        FirstName, LastName, Email, Phone string
        Addresses                         []Address
}

func (c Customer) ToString() string {
        return fmt.Sprintf("Customer: %s %s, Email:%s", c.FirstName, c.LastName, c.Email)
}
func (c Customer) ShippingAddress() string {
        for _, v := range c.Addresses {
                if v.IsShippingAddress == true {
                        return fmt.Sprintf("%s, %s, %s, Zip - %s", v.Street, v.City, v.State, v.Zip)
                }
        }
        return ""
}

func main() {
        c := Customer{
                FirstName: "Alex",
                LastName:  "John",
                Email:     "alex@email.com",
                Phone:     "732-757-2923",
                Addresses: []Address{
                        Address{
                                Street:          "1 Mission Street",
                                City:            "San Francisco",
                                State:           "CA",
```

```
                        Zip:                  "94105",
                        IsShippingAddress: true,
                },
                Address{
                        Street: "49 Stevenson Street",
                        City:   "San Francisco",
                        State:  "CA",
                        Zip:    "94105",
                },
            },
        }
        fmt.Println(c.ToString())
        fmt.Println(c.ShippingAddress())

}
```

The Customer struct is attached to a couple of methods by specifying the method receiver. The ToString returns the customer name and email and ShippingAddress returns the default shipping address from the list of addresses stored in the Addresses field. Inside the main function, an instance of the Customer struct is created and its methods are invoked.

You should see the following output when you run the program:

```
Customer: Alex John, Email:alex@email.com
1 Mission Street, San Francisco, CA, Zip - 94105
```

A method is a function with a receiver. There are two types of method receivers: the *pointer receiver* and the *value receiver*. The program in Listing 3-9 uses a value receiver to add methods to the Customer struct. When a method is specified with a pointer receiver, the method is invoked with a pointer to the receiver value, and a copy of the receiver value is used when the method is specified with a value receiver. Hence you must use a pointer receiver if you want to mutate the state (value of fields) of the receiver.

Let's add a new method to the Customer struct (see Listing 3-9) to explore the pointer receiver. First, let's add the method by specifying the receiver without a pointer.

```
func (c Customer) ChangeEmail(newEmail string) {
        c.Email = newEmail
}
```

The newly added ChangeEmail method assigns a new email address to the Email field. Let's create an instance of Customer struct and invoke the ChangeEmail method by passing a new email address.

```
c := Customer{
            FirstName: "Alex",
            LastName:  "John",
            Email:     "alex@gmail.com",
            Phone:     "732-757-2923",
            Addresses: []Address{
                    Address{
                            Street:          "1 Mission Street",
                            City:            "San Francisco",
                            State:           "CA",
                            Zip:             "94105",
```

```
                        IsShippingAddress: true,
                },
                Address{
                        Street: "49 Stevenson Street",
                        City:   "San Francisco",
                        State:  "CA",
                        Zip:    "94105",
                },
        },
    }

    // Call ChangeEmail
            c.ChangeEmail("alex.john@gmail.com")
    fmt.Println(c.ToString())
```

You should see the following output when you run the program:

```
Customer: Alex John, Email:alex@gmail.com
```

You have provided a new email to the ChangeEmail method to change the email address, but it is not reflected when you call the ToString method. You are still getting the old email from the Email field. To modify the state of the struct values inside the methods, you must declare methods with a pointer receiver so that a change to the field values will be reflected outside the methods. Listing 3-10 modifies the ChangeEmail method by specifying with a pointer receiver so that the change to the Email field will be reflected outside the ChangeEmail method.

Listing 3-10. A Method to Customer Struct with a Pointer Receiver

```
func (c *Customer) ChangeEmail(newEmail string) {
        c.Email = newEmail
}
```

Let's create an instance of Customer struct and invoke the ChangeEmail method by passing a new email address.

```
c := Customer{
            FirstName: "Alex",
            LastName:  "John",
            Email:     "alex@gmail.com",
            Phone:     "732-757-2923",
}

// Call ChangeEmail
 c.ChangeEmail(alex.john@gmail.com)
 fmt.Println(c.ToString())
```

You should see the following output when you run the program:

```
Customer: Alex John, Email:alex.john@gmail.com
1 Mission Street, San Francisco, CA, Zip - 94105
```

The output shows that the value of the Email field has been changed. Here a value of type Customer is used to call the ChangeEmail method that was specified with a pointer receiver.

Here is the code block that uses a pointer of type Customer to call the ChangeEmail method that is specified with a pointer receiver:

```
c := $Customer{
                FirstName: "Alex",
                LastName:  "John",
                Email:     "alex@gmail.com",
                Phone:     "732-757-2923",
        }

// Call ChangeEmail
 c.ChangeEmail(alex.john@gmail.com)
```

It is important to note that you can add methods to any type, including built-in types. You can add methods to primitive types, composite types, and user-defined types. You can define methods for either pointer or value receiver types, so it is important to understand when to use a value or a pointer for the receiver on methods. In a nutshell, if the method needs to change the state of the receiver, the receiver must be a pointer. If the receiver is a large struct, array, or slice, a pointer receiver is more efficient because it avoids copying the value of the large data structure on method calls. If a method is specified with a pointer receiver that might be intended for changing the receiver, then it is better to use a pointer receiver on all methods of the same receiver type, which provides better usability and readability for the user.

The ChangeEmail method of the Customer struct needs to change its receiver. Hence, let's modify the other methods as well for better usability and clarity. Listing 3-11 modifies the program of Listing 3-9, with all methods specified with a pointer receiver.

Listing 3-11. Struct with Pointer Receiver on Methods

```
package main

import (
        "fmt"
)

type Address struct {
        Street, City, State, Zip string
        IsShippingAddress         bool
}

type Customer struct {
        FirstName, LastName, Email, Phone string
        Addresses                         []Address
}

func (c *Customer) ToString() string {
        return fmt.Sprintf("Customer: %s %s, Email:%s", c.FirstName, c.LastName, c.Email)
}
func (c *Customer) ChangeEmail(newEmail string) {
        c.Email = newEmail
}
func (c *Customer) ShippingAddress() string {
```

```go
        for _, v := range c.Addresses {
                if v.IsShippingAddress == true {
                        return fmt.Sprintf("%s, %s, %s, Zip - %s", v.Street, v.City,
v.State, v.Zip)
                }
        }
        return ""
}

func main() {

        c := &Customer{
                FirstName: "Alex",
                LastName:  "John",
                Email:     "alex@email.com",
                Phone:     "732-757-2923",
                Addresses: []Address{
                        Address{
                                Street:            "1 Mission Street",
                                City:              "San Francisco",
                                State:             "CA",
                                Zip:               "94105",
                                IsShippingAddress: true,
                        },
                        Address{
                                Street: "49 Stevenson Street",
                                City:   "San Francisco",
                                State:  "CA",
                                Zip:    "94105",
                        },
                },
        }

        fmt.Println(c.ToString())
        c.ChangeEmail("alex.john@gmail.com")
        fmt.Println("Customer after changing the Email:")
        fmt.Println(c.ToString())
        fmt.Println(c.ShippingAddress())

}
```

Because the ChangeEmail method needs to alter the receiver, all methods are defined with a pointer receiver. It is important to note that you can mix up methods with value and pointer receivers. In the preceding program, a pointer of Customer is created by using the address-of operator (&):

```go
c := &Customer{}
```

The Customer pointer c is used for invoking methods of the Customer struct:

```go
fmt.Println(c.ToString())
c.ChangeEmail("alex.john@gmail.com")
```

```
fmt.Println(c.ToString())
fmt.Println(c.ShippingAddress())
```

You should see the following output when you run the program:

```
Customer: Alex John, Email:alex@email.com
Customer after changing the Email:
Customer: Alex John, Email:alex.john@gmail.com
1 Mission Street, San Francisco, CA, Zip - 94105
```

3-3. Composing Types Using Type Embedding

Problem

You would like create types by composing from other types.

Solution

Go provides support for embedding types into other types that allows you to create types by combining other types.

How It Works

Go's type system enforces the design philosophy of *composition* over *inheritance* that allows you to create types by embedding other types into them. By using the composition design philosophy implemented via type embedding, you can create larger types by combining smaller types.

Let's create types by embedding other types into them. Listing 3-12 shows the data model that can be used to represent an order in an e-commerce system.

Listing 3-12. Data Model for Order Entity

```
type Address struct {
        Street, City, State, Zip string
        IsShippingAddress        bool
}

type Customer struct {
        FirstName, LastName, Email, Phone string
        Addresses                         []Address
}

type Order struct {
        Id int
        Customer
        PlacedOn   time.Time
        Status     string
        OrderItems []OrderItem
}
```

```go
type OrderItem struct {
        Product
        Quantity int
}

type Product struct {
        Code, Name, Description string
        UnitPrice                      float64
}
```

In Listing 3-12, the Order struct is declared with embedding another type, the Customer struct. The Order struct is used to place an order for a customer so that the Customer struct is embedded into the Order struct. To embed a type, just specify the name of the type that you would like to embed into another type.

```go
type Order struct {
        Customer
}
```

The fields and behaviors of the Customer struct are available in the Order struct because of the type embedding. The Customer struct uses the slice of Address struct to the Addresses field. The Order struct uses the slice of OrderItem struct to the OrderItems field. The Product struct is embedded into the OrderItem struct. Here you create a bigger type Order struct by combining several other struct types.

Let's add operations to the struct types that are declared for representing order information. Listing 3-13 shows the completed version of the data model for Order with various behaviors.

Listing 3-13. Data Model for Order Entity with Operations in models.go

```go
package main

import (
    "fmt"
    "time"
)

type Address struct {
    Street, City, State, Zip string
    IsShippingAddress        bool
}

type Customer struct {
    FirstName, LastName, Email, Phone string
    Addresses                         []Address
}

func (c Customer) ToString() string {
    return fmt.Sprintf("Customer: %s %s, Email:%s", c.FirstName, c.LastName, c.Email)
}
func (c Customer) ShippingAddress() string {
    for _, v := range c.Addresses {
        if v.IsShippingAddress == true {
            return fmt.Sprintf("%s, %s, %s, Zip - %s", v.Street, v.City, v.State, v.Zip)
        }
```

```go
    }
    return ""
}

type Order struct {
    Id int
    Customer
    PlacedOn   time.Time
    Status     string
    OrderItems []OrderItem
}

func (o *Order) GrandTotal() float64 {
    var total float64
    for _, v := range o.OrderItems {
        total += v.Total()
    }
    return total
}
func (o *Order) ToString() string {
    var orderStr string
    orderStr = fmt.Sprintf("Order#:%d, OrderDate:%s, Status:%s, Grand Total:%f\n", o.Id,
o.PlacedOn, o.Status, o.GrandTotal())
    orderStr += o.Customer.ToString()
    orderStr += fmt.Sprintf("\nOrder Items:")
    for _, v := range o.OrderItems {
        orderStr += fmt.Sprintf("\n")
        orderStr += v.ToString()
    }
    orderStr += fmt.Sprintf("\nShipping Address:")
    orderStr += o.Customer.ShippingAddress()
    return orderStr
}
func (o *Order) ChangeStatus(newStatus string) {
    o.Status = newStatus
}

type OrderItem struct {
    Product
    Quantity int
}

func (item OrderItem) Total() float64 {
    return float64(item.Quantity) * item.Product.UnitPrice
}
func (item OrderItem) ToString() string {
    itemStr := fmt.Sprintf("Code:%s, Product:%s -- %s, UnitPrice:%f, Quantity:%d, Total:%f",
        item.Product.Code, item.Product.Name, item.Product.Description, item.Product.
        UnitPrice, item.Quantity, item.Total())
    return itemStr

}
```

```
type Product struct {
    Code, Name, Description string
    UnitPrice               float64
}
```

The ToString method of the Order struct returns a string value that provides all information about an order. The ToString invokes the ToString and ShippingAddress methods of its embedded type Customer. The ToString method also invokes the ToString method of the OrderItem struct by iterating over the OrderItems field, which is a slice of OrderItem.

```
orderStr += o.Customer.ToString()
    orderStr += fmt.Sprintf("\nOrder Items:")
    for _, v := range o.OrderItems {
        orderStr += fmt.Sprintf("\n")
        orderStr += v.ToString()
    }
    orderStr += fmt.Sprintf("\nShipping Address:")
    orderStr += o.Customer.ShippingAddress()
```

The GrandTotal method of the Order struct returns the grand total value of an order, which invokes the Total method of the OrderItem struct to determine the total value for each order item.

```
func (o *Order) GrandTotal() float64 {
    var total float64
    for _, v := range o.OrderItems {
        total += v.Total()
    }
    return total
}
```

Note that the ChangeStatus method of the Order struct changes the state of the Status field and hence a pointer receiver is used for the method.

```
func (o *Order) ChangeStatus(newStatus string) {
    o.Status = newStatus
}
```

Because the ChangeStatus method requires a pointer receiver, all other methods of the Order struct are defined with a pointer receiver.

Listing 3-14 shows the main function, which is used to create an instance of the Order struct and call its ToString method to get the information about an order.

Listing 3-14. Entry Point of the Program That Creates an Instance of the Order struct in main.go

```
package main

import (
    "fmt"
    "time"
)
```

```go
func main() {
    order := &Order{
        Id: 1001,
        Customer: Customer{
            FirstName: "Alex",
            LastName:  "John",
            Email:     "alex@email.com",
            Phone:     "732-757-2923",
            Addresses: []Address{
                Address{
                    Street:            "1 Mission Street",
                    City:              "San Francisco",
                    State:             "CA",
                    Zip:               "94105",
                    IsShippingAddress: true,
                },
                Address{
                    Street: "49 Stevenson Street",
                    City:   "San Francisco",
                    State:  "CA",
                    Zip:    "94105",
                },
            },
        },
        Status:   "Placed",
        PlacedOn: time.Date(2016, time.April, 10, 0, 0, 0, 0, time.UTC),
        OrderItems: []OrderItem{
            OrderItem{
                Product: Product{
                    Code:        "knd100",
                    Name:        "Kindle Voyage",
                    Description: "Kindle Voyage Wifi, 6 High-Resolution Display",
                    UnitPrice:   220,
                },
                Quantity: 1,
            },
            OrderItem{
                Product: Product{
                    Code:        "fint101",
                    Name:        "Kindle Case",
                    Description: "Fintie Kindle Voyage SmartShell Case",
                    UnitPrice:   10,
                },
                Quantity: 2,
            },
        },
    }

    fmt.Println(order.ToString())
    // Change Order status
    order.ChangeStatus("Processing")
```

```
    fmt.Println("\n")
    fmt.Println(order.ToString())
}
```

An instance of the Order struct is created by providing the values for its fields, including the embedded types. A pointer variable is used here to call the methods of the Order struct. The ToString method provides all of the information about an order placed by a customer. The ChangeStatus method is used to change the status of an order that changes the value of the Status field. When you embed a type, you can provide values similar to the normal fields of a struct.

You should see the following output when you run the program:

```
Order#:1001, OrderDate:2016-04-10 00:00:00 +0000 UTC, Status:Placed, Grand Total:240.000000
Customer: Alex John, Email:alex@email.com
Order Items:
Code:knd100, Product:Kindle Voyage -- Kindle Voyage Wifi, 6 High-Resolution Display,
UnitPrice:220.000000, Quantity:1, Total:220.000000
Code:fint101, Product:Kindle Case -- Fintie Kindle Voyage SmartShell Case,
UnitPrice:10.000000, Quantity:2, Total:20.000000
Shipping Address:1 Mission Street, San Francisco, CA, Zip - 94105


Order#:1001, OrderDate:2016-04-10 00:00:00 +0000 UTC, Status:Processing, Grand
Total:240.000000
Customer: Alex John, Email:alex@email.com
Order Items:
Code:knd100, Product:Kindle Voyage -- Kindle Voyage Wifi, 6 High-Resolution Display,
UnitPrice:220.000000, Quantity:1, Total:220.000000
Code:fint101, Product:Kindle Case -- Fintie Kindle Voyage SmartShell Case,
UnitPrice:10.000000, Quantity:2, Total:20.000000
Shipping Address:1 Mission Street, San Francisco, CA, Zip - 94105
```

That output shows the order information, including the grand total, which is calculated by calling corresponding methods of the types.

3-4. Working with Interfaces

Problem

You would like to create an interface type to provide it as a contract for other types.

Solution

Go has a user-defined interface type that can be used as a contract for concrete types. Go's interface type provides lot of extensibility and composability for your Go applications. An interface type is defined with the keyword interface.

How It Works

Go's interface type provides lot of extensibility and composability for your Go applications. Programming languages like C# and Java support interface type, but Go's interface type is unique in design philosophy.

Declaring Interface Types

Unlike C# and Java, in Go, you don't need to explicitly implement an interface into a concrete type by specifying any keyword. To implement an interface into a concrete type, just provide the methods with the same signature that is defined in the interface type. Listing 3-15 shows an interface type.

Listing 3-15. Interface Type TeamMember

```
type TeamMember interface {
    PrintName()
    PrintDetails()
}
```

The interface type TeamMember is a contract for creating various employee types in a team. The TeamMember interface provides two behaviors in its contract: PrintName and PrintDetails.

Implementing an Interface into Concrete Types

Let's create a concrete type of TeamMember interface by implementing its two behaviors, PrintName and PrintDetails. Listing 3-16 shows a concrete type of TeamMember that implements the methods defined in the interface type.

Listing 3-16. Concrete Type of TeamMember

```
type Employee struct {
    FirstName, LastName string
    Dob                 time.Time
    JobTitle, Location  string
}

func (e Employee) PrintName() {
    fmt.Printf("\n%s %s\n", e.FirstName, e.LastName)
}

func (e Employee) PrintDetails() {
    fmt.Printf("Date of Birth: %s, Job: %s, Location: %s\n", e.Dob.String(), e.JobTitle,
e.Location)
}
```

A struct Employee is declared with fields for holding its state and methods implemented based on the behaviors defined in the TeamMember interface. You don't need to use any syntax for implementing an interface into a type. Instead, just provide the methods with the same signature defined in the interface, just as you did for the Employee type for implementing the TeamMember interface.

The greatest benefit of an interface type is that it allows you to create different implementations for the same interface type, which enables a greater level of extensibility.

Listing 3-17 shows an implementation of the TeamMember interface created by embedding the Employee type, which is an implementation of the TeamMember interface.

Listing 3-17. Type Developer Implements TeamMember Interface

```
type Developer struct {
    Employee //type embedding for composition
    Skills   []string
}
```

A struct Developer is declared in which the type Employee is embedded. Here you create more concrete types of the TeamMember interface. Because type Employee is an implementation of the TeamMember interface, the type Developer is also an implementation of the TeamMember interface. All fields and methods defined in the Type Employee types are also available in the Developer type. In addition to the embedded type of Employee, the Developer struct provides a Skill field to represent the skill for Developer type.

Listing 3-18 shows the code block that creates an instance of Developer and calls the methods that are available through the embedded type Employee.

Listing 3-18. Create an Instance of Developer Type and Call Methods

```
d := Developer{
            Employee{
                    "Steve",
                    "John",
                    time.Date(1990, time.February, 17, 0, 0, 0, 0, time.UTC),
                    "Software Engineer",
                    "San Francisco",
            },
            []string{"Go", "Docker", "Kubernetes"},
    }
    d.PrintName()
    d.PrintDetails()
```

You should see the following output when you run the program:

```
Steve John
Date of Birth: 1990-02-17 00:00:00 +0000 UTC, Job: Software Engineer, Location: San
Francisco
```

The output shows that the methods defined in the Employee struct are accessible through the instance of the Developer struct.

The Developer struct is more of a concrete implementation of the TeamMember interface than an Employee type. The Employee type is defined for type embedding for making a more concrete implementation of the TeamMember interface, like the Developer struct. At this moment, the Developer struct uses the methods that were defined in the Employee struct. Because the Developer struct is more of a concrete implementation, it might have its own implementations for its methods. Here the Developer struct might need to override the methods defined in the Employee struct to provide extra functionalities. Listing 3-19 shows the code block that overrides the method PrintDetails for the Developer struct.

Listing 3-19. Overrides for the PrintDetails Method for the Developer struct

```
// Overrides the PrintDetails
func (d Developer) PrintDetails() {
    // Call Employee PrintDetails
    d.Employee.PrintDetails()
    fmt.Println("Technical Skills:")
    for _, v := range d.Skills {
        fmt.Println(v)
    }
}
```

Here you call the PrintDetails method of Employee and provide an extra functionality for the Developer struct.

Let's create another struct type to provide a different implementation of the TeamMember interface. Listing 3-20 shows a struct named Manager that implements the TeamMember interface by embedding the Employee type and overriding the PrintDetails method.

Listing 3-20. Type Manager Implements the TeamMember Interface

```
type Manager struct {
    Employee  //type embedding for composition
    Projects  []string
    Locations []string
}

// Overrides the PrintDetails
func (m Manager) PrintDetails() {
    // Call Employee PrintDetails
    m.Employee.PrintDetails()
    fmt.Println("Projects:")
    for _, v := range m.Projects {
        fmt.Println(v)
    }
    fmt.Println("Managing teams for the locations:")
    for _, v := range m.Locations {
        fmt.Println(v)
    }
}
```

In addition to the embedded type of Employee, the Manager struct provides Projects and Locations fields to represent the projects and locations managed by a manager.

Until now, you have created an interface type named TeamMember, and three concrete types that implement the TeamMember interface: Employee, Developer, and Manager. Let's create an example program to explore these types and demonstrate interface type. Listing 3-21 shows an example program that demonstrates interface by using the types that we have discussed in this section.

Listing 3-21. Example Program Demonstrates Interface with Type Embedding and Method Overriding

```
package main

import (
    "fmt"
    "time"
)

type TeamMember interface {
    PrintName()
    PrintDetails()
}

type Employee struct {
    FirstName, LastName string
    Dob                 time.Time
```

```go
    JobTitle, Location  string
}

func (e Employee) PrintName() {
    fmt.Printf("\n%s %s\n", e.FirstName, e.LastName)
}

func (e Employee) PrintDetails() {
    fmt.Printf("Date of Birth: %s, Job: %s, Location: %s\n", e.Dob.String(), e.JobTitle,
e.Location)
}

type Developer struct {
    Employee //type embedding for composition
    Skills   []string
}

// Overrides the PrintDetails
func (d Developer) PrintDetails() {
    // Call Employee PrintDetails
    d.Employee.PrintDetails()
    fmt.Println("Technical Skills:")
    for _, v := range d.Skills {
        fmt.Println(v)
    }
}

type Manager struct {
    Employee  //type embedding for composition
    Projects  []string
    Locations []string
}

// Overrides the PrintDetails
func (m Manager) PrintDetails() {
    // Call Employee PrintDetails
    m.Employee.PrintDetails()
    fmt.Println("Projects:")
    for _, v := range m.Projects {
        fmt.Println(v)
    }
    fmt.Println("Managing teams for the locations:")
    for _, v := range m.Locations {
        fmt.Println(v)
    }
}

type Team struct {
    Name, Description string
    TeamMembers       []TeamMember
}
```

```go
func (t Team) PrintTeamDetails() {
    fmt.Printf("Team: %s  - %s\n", t.Name, t.Description)
    fmt.Println("Details of the team members:")
    for _, v := range t.TeamMembers {
        v.PrintName()
        v.PrintDetails()
    }
}

func main() {
    steve := Developer{
        Employee{
            "Steve",
            "John",
            time.Date(1990, time.February, 17, 0, 0, 0, 0, time.UTC),
            "Software Engineer",
            "San Francisco",
        },
        []string{"Go", "Docker", "Kubernetes"},
    }
    irene := Developer{
        Employee{
            "Irene",
            "Rose",
            time.Date(1991, time.January, 13, 0, 0, 0, 0, time.UTC),
            "Software Engineer",
            "Santa Clara",
        },
        []string{"Go", "MongoDB"},
    }
    alex := Manager{
        Employee{
            "Alex",
            "Williams",
            time.Date(1979, time.February, 17, 0, 0, 0, 0, time.UTC),
            "Program Manger",
            "Santa Clara",
        },
        []string{"CRM", "e-Commerce"},
        []string{"San Francisco", "Santa Clara"},
    }

    // Create team
    team := Team{
        "Go",
        "Golang Engineering Team",
        []TeamMember{steve, irene, alex},
    }
    // Get details of Team
    team.PrintTeamDetails()
}
```

A struct named Team is declared to represent a team of employees, and employees of the team members are organized with the field TeamMembers with type of slice of the TeamMember interface. Because the type of TeamMembers field uses a slice of the TeamMember interface, you can provide any implementation of the TeamMember interface as the value. The type Employee is used just for embedding into Developer and Manager structs that are more of a concrete and specific implementation of an employee as a team member.

```
type Team struct {
    Name, Description string
    TeamMembers        []TeamMember
}
```

The PrintTeamDetails method of Team prints the information of a Team object. Inside the PrintTeamDetails method, it iterates over the elements of the TeamMembers collection and calls PrintName and PrintDetails methods to get information on each team member.

```
func (t Team) PrintTeamDetails() {
    fmt.Printf("Team: %s  - %s\n", t.Name, t.Description)
    fmt.Println("Details of the team members:")
    for _, v := range t.TeamMembers {
        v.PrintName()
        v.PrintDetails()
    }
}
```

Inside main function, an instance of team struct is created by providing values of the three objects that implemented the TeamMember interface. Among the three objects of TeamMember type, two are created with the Developer type and another is created with the Manager type. The value of the TeamMembers field contains the value of different types; the connecting factor of all objects is the TeamMember interface. You just provide the different implementation of the TeamMember interface. The PrintTeamDetails method of the Team struct is finally called to get information about the value of the Team type.

```
func main() {
    steve := Developer{
        Employee{
            "Steve",
            "John",
            time.Date(1990, time.February, 17, 0, 0, 0, 0, time.UTC),
            "Software Engineer",
            "San Francisco",
        },
        []string{"Go", "Docker", "Kubernetes"},
    }
    irene := Developer{
        Employee{
            "Irene",
            "Rose",
            time.Date(1991, time.January, 13, 0, 0, 0, 0, time.UTC),
            "Software Engineer",
            "Santa Clara",
        },
        []string{"Go", "MongoDB"},
    }
```

```go
    alex := Manager{
        Employee{
            "Alex",
            "Williams",
            time.Date(1979, time.February, 17, 0, 0, 0, 0, time.UTC),
            "Program Manger",
            "Santa Clara",
        },
        []string{"CRM", "e-Commerce"},
        []string{"San Francisco", "Santa Clara"},
    }

    // Create team
    team := Team{
        "Go",
        "Golang Engineering Team",
        []TeamMember{steve, irene, alex},
    }
    // Get details of Team
    team.PrintTeamDetails()
}
```

You should see the following output when you run the program:

```
Team: Go  - Golang Engineering Team
Details of the team members:

Steve John
Date of Birth: 1990-02-17 00:00:00 +0000 UTC, Job: Software Engineer, Location: San
Francisco
Technical Skills:
Go
Docker
Kubernetes

Irene Rose
Date of Birth: 1991-01-13 00:00:00 +0000 UTC, Job: Software Engineer, Location: Santa Clara
Technical Skills:
Go
MongoDB

Alex Williams
Date of Birth: 1979-02-17 00:00:00 +0000 UTC, Job: Program Manger, Location: Santa Clara
Projects:
CRM
e-Commerce
Managing teams for the locations:
San Francisco
Santa Clara
```

CHAPTER 4

Concurrency

We are living in the era of cloud computing in which you can quickly provision virtual machines in high-powered servers. Although our modern computers evolved now have more CPU cores, we still cannot leverage the full power of modern servers when we run our applications. Sometimes our applications are running slow, but when we look at the CPU utilization, it might be underutilized. The problem is that we are still using some tools that were designed for the era of single-core machines. We can improve the performance of many of our applications by writing concurrent programs that let you write programs as a composition of several autonomous activities. Some of our existing programming languages provide support for concurrency by using a framework or a library, but not a built-in feature of the core language.

Go's support for concurrency is one of its major selling points. Concurrency is a built-in feature of Go, and the Go runtime has great control over the programs that run with its concurrency features. Go provides concurrency via two paradigms: *goroutine* and *channel*. Goroutines let you run functions independent of each other. A concurrently executing function in Go is called a goroutine, and each one is treated as a unit of work that performs a specific task. You write concurrent programs by combining these autonomous tasks. In addition to the capability of running functions independent of each other, Go has the capability of synchronizing of goroutines by sending and receiving data between goroutines using channels. A channel is a communication mechanism to send and receive data between goroutines.

4-1. Writing Concurrent Programs

Problem

You would like to write concurrent programs by running functions as autonomous activity.

Solution

Go has the ability to run functions concurrently by running it as a goroutine. Goroutines are created by calling the go statement followed by the function or method that you want to run as an autonomous activity.

How It Works

In the examples in previous chapters, all programs were sequential programs. That means that within the program, you call functions sequentially: Each function call blocks the program to complete the execution of that function and then calls the next function. For example, let's say that you write a program that needs to call two functions from the main function. Here you might need to call the first function and then call the next function. The execution of the second function will happen after the execution of first function. Using the concurrency capability provided by Go, through goroutines, you can execute both functions at the same time, independent of each other

© Shiju Varghese 2016
S. Varghese, *Go Recipes*, DOI 10.1007/978-1-4842-1188-5_4

To run a function as a goroutine, call that function prefixed with the go statement. Here is the example code block:

```
f() // A normal function call that executes f synchronously and waits for completing it
go f() // A goroutine that executes f asynchronously and doesn't wait for completing it
```

The only difference between a normal function call and a goroutine is that a goroutine is created with the go statement. An executable Go program does have at least one goroutine; the goroutine that calls the main function is known as the main goroutine. Listing 4-1 shows an example program that creates two goroutines to print an addition table and a multiplication table. This program also synchronizes the execution using sync.WaitGroup while executing the goroutines; here function main is waiting for completion of the execution of goroutines using sync.WaitGroup.

Listing 4-1. Example Program Demonstrates how to Create Goroutines

```go
package main

import (
    "fmt"
    "math/rand"
    "sync"
    "time"
)

// WaitGroup is used to wait for the program to finish goroutines.
var wg sync.WaitGroup

func main() {

    // Add a count of two, one for each goroutine.
    wg.Add(2)

    fmt.Println("Start Goroutines")
    // Launch functions as goroutines
    go addTable()
    go multiTable()
    // Wait for the goroutines to finish.
    fmt.Println("Waiting To Finish")
    wg.Wait()
    fmt.Println("\nTerminating Program")
}

func addTable() {
    // Schedule the call to WaitGroup's Done to tell goroutine is completed.
    defer wg.Done()
    for i := 1; i <= 10; i++ {
        sleep := rand.Int63n(1000)
        time.Sleep(time.Duration(sleep) * time.Millisecond)
        fmt.Println("Addition Table for:", i)
        for j := 1; j <= 10; j++ {
            fmt.Printf("%d+%d=%d\t", i, j, i+j)
        }
```

```
        fmt.Println("\n")
    }
}
func multiTable() {
    // Schedule the call to WaitGroup's Done to tell goroutine is completed.
    defer wg.Done()
    for i := 1; i <= 10; i++ {
        sleep := rand.Int63n(1000)
        time.Sleep(time.Duration(sleep) * time.Millisecond)
        fmt.Println("Multiplication Table for:", i)
        for j := 1; j <= 10; j++ {
            //res = i + j
            fmt.Printf("%d*%d=%d\t", i, j, i*j)
        }
        fmt.Println("\n")
    }
}
```

The program creates two goroutines: One function is for printing an addition table and another function is for printing a multiplication table. Because both functions are running concurrently, both are printing output into the console window. The go statement is used to launch functions as goroutines.

```
go addTable()
go multiTable()
```

The program uses the WaitGroup type of sync package, which is used to wait for the program to finish all goroutines launched from the main function. Otherwise the goroutines would be launched from main function and then terminate the program before completing the execution of goroutines. The Wait method of the WaitGroup type waits for the program to finish all goroutines. The WaitGroup type uses a counter that specifies the number of goroutines, and Wait blocks the execution of the program until the WaitGroup counter is zero.

```
var wg sync.WaitGroup
wg.Add(2)
```

The Add method is used to add a counter to the WaitGroup so that a call to the Wait method blocks execution until the WaitGroup counter is zero. Here a counter of two is added into the WaitGroup, one for each goroutine. Inside the addTable and multiTable functions that are launched as goroutines, the Done method of WaitGroup is scheduled using a defer statement to decrement the WaitGroup counter. The WaitGroup counter therefore decrements by one after executing each goroutine.

```
func addTable() {
    // Schedule the call to WaitGroup's Done to tell goroutine is completed.
    defer wg.Done()
    for i := 1; i <= 10; i++ {
        sleep := rand.Int63n(1000)
        time.Sleep(time.Duration(sleep) * time.Millisecond)
        fmt.Println("Addition Table for:", i)
        for j := 1; j <= 10; j++ {
            //res = i + j
            fmt.Printf("%d+%d=%d\t", i, j, i+j)
```

```
        }
        fmt.Println("\n")
    }
}
```

When the `Wait` method is called inside the `main` function, it blocks execution until the `WaitGroup` counter reaches the value of zero and ensures that all goroutines are executed.

```
func main() {


    // Add a count of two, one for each goroutine.
    wg.Add(2)

    fmt.Println("Start Goroutines")
    // Launch functions as goroutines
    go addTable()
    go multiTable()
    // Wait for the goroutines to finish.
    fmt.Println("Waiting To Finish")
    wg.Wait()
    fmt.Println("\nTerminating Program")
}
```

You should see output similar to the following:

```
Start Goroutines
Waiting To Finish
Addition Table for: 1
1+1=2    1+2=3    1+3=4    1+4=5    1+5=6    1+6=7    1+7=8    1+8=9    1+9=10   1+10=11

Multiplication Table for: 1
1*1=1    1*2=2    1*3=3    1*4=4    1*5=5    1*6=6    1*7=7    1*8=8    1*9=9    1*10=10

Multiplication Table for: 2
2*1=2    2*2=4    2*3=6    2*4=8    2*5=10  2*6=12  2*7=14  2*8=16  2*9=18  2*10=20

Addition Table for: 2
2+1=3    2+2=4    2+3=5    2+4=6    2+5=7    2+6=8    2+7=9    2+8=10  2+9=11  2+10=12

Multiplication Table for: 3
3*1=3    3*2=6    3*3=9    3*4=12  3*5=15  3*6=18  3*7=21  3*8=24  3*9=27  3*10=30

Addition Table for: 3
3+1=4    3+2=5    3+3=6    3+4=7    3+5=8    3+6=9    3+7=10  3+8=11  3+9=12  3+10=13

Addition Table for: 4
4+1=5    4+2=6    4+3=7    4+4=8    4+5=9    4+6=10  4+7=11  4+8=12  4+9=13  4+10=14

Addition Table for: 5
5+1=6    5+2=7    5+3=8    5+4=9    5+5=10  5+6=11  5+7=12  5+8=13  5+9=14  5+10=15
```

```
Multiplication Table for: 4
4*1=4    4*2=8    4*3=12   4*4=16   4*5=20   4*6=24   4*7=28   4*8=32   4*9=36   4*10=40

Addition Table for: 6
6+1=7    6+2=8    6+3=9    6+4=10   6+5=11   6+6=12   6+7=13   6+8=14   6+9=15   6+10=16

Multiplication Table for: 5
5*1=5    5*2=10   5*3=15   5*4=20   5*5=25   5*6=30   5*7=35   5*8=40   5*9=45   5*10=50

Addition Table for: 7
7+1=8    7+2=9    7+3=10   7+4=11   7+5=12   7+6=13   7+7=14   7+8=15   7+9=16   7+10=17

Multiplication Table for: 6
6*1=6    6*2=12   6*3=18   6*4=24   6*5=30   6*6=36   6*7=42   6*8=48   6*9=54   6*10=60

Multiplication Table for: 7
7*1=7    7*2=14   7*3=21   7*4=28   7*5=35   7*6=42   7*7=49   7*8=56   7*9=63   7*10=70

Addition Table for: 8
8+1=9    8+2=10   8+3=11   8+4=12   8+5=13   8+6=14   8+7=15   8+8=16   8+9=17   8+10=18

Multiplication Table for: 8
8*1=8    8*2=16   8*3=24   8*4=32   8*5=40   8*6=48   8*7=56   8*8=64   8*9=72   8*10=80

Multiplication Table for: 9
9*1=9    9*2=18   9*3=27   9*4=36   9*5=45   9*6=54   9*7=63   9*8=72   9*9=81   9*10=90

Addition Table for: 9
9+1=10   9+2=11   9+3=12   9+4=13   9+5=14   9+6=15   9+7=16   9+8=17   9+9=18   9+10=19

Addition Table for: 10
10+1=11 10+2=12 10+3=13 10+4=14 10+5=15 10+6=16 10+7=17 10+8=18 10+9=19 10+10=20

Multiplication Table for: 10
10*1=10 10*2=20 10*3=30 10*4=40 10*5=50 10*6=60 10*7=70 10*8=80 10*9=90 10*10=100

Terminating Program
```

You can see that both addTable and multiTable functions are generating output simultaneously into the console window because both are executing concurrently. Inside the addTable and multiTable functions, the execution is delaying for a randomly generated time period just for the sake of demonstration. When you run the program, the order of the output would vary each time because the execution is randomly delaying inside the functions.

4-2. Managing the Number of CPUs in Concurrency

Problem

You would like to manage the number of CPUs to be used for executing goroutines in the Go runtime so that you manage the behavior of concurrent programming.

Solution

The GOMAXPROCS function of the runtime package is used to change the number of CPUs to be used for running concurrent programs.

How It Works

The Go runtime provides a *scheduler* that manages the goroutines during execution. The scheduler works closely with the operating system and controls everything during the execution of a goroutine. It schedules all goroutines to run against logical processors in which each logical processor is bound with a single operating system thread that runs against a physical processor. In short, the Go runtime scheduler runs goroutines against a logical processor that is bound with an operating system thread within an available physical processor. Keep in mind that a single logical processor with an operating system thread can execute tens of thousands of goroutines simultaneously.

While executing the programs, the Go runtime scheduler takes the value of the GOMAXPROCS setting to find out how many operating system threads will attempt to execute code simultaneously. For example, if the value of GOMAXPROCS is 8, then the program will only execute goroutines on 8 operating system threads at once. As of Go 1.5, the default value for GOMAXPROCS is the number of CPUs available, as determined by the NumCPU function of the runtime package. The NumCPU function returns the number of logical CPUs usable by the current process. Prior to Go 1.5, the default value of GOMAXPROCS was 1. The value of GOMAXPROCS can be modified using the GOMAXPROCS environment variable or calling the GOMAXPROCS function of the runtime package from within a program. The following code block sets the value of GOMAXPROCS to 1 so that the program will execute goroutines on one operating system thread at once:

```
import "runtime"
// Sets the value of GOMAXPROCS
runtime.GOMAXPROCS(1)
```

4-3. Creating Channels

Problem

You would like to send and receive data between goroutines so that one goroutine can communicate with others.

Solution

Go provides a mechanism called a *channel* that is used to share data between goroutines. There are two types of channels based on their behavior: unbuffered channels and buffered channels. An *unbuffered channel* is used to perform synchronous communication between goroutines; a *buffered channel* is used for perform asynchronous communication.

How It Works

Goroutines are a great mechanism to use to execute concurrent activities in concurrent programming. When you execute a concurrent activity as a goroutine you might need to send data from one goroutine to another. A channel handles this communication by acting as a conduit between goroutines. Based on the behavior of data exchange, channels are differentiated into unbuffered channels and buffered channels. An unbuffered channel is used to perform synchronous exchange of data. On other hand a buffered channel is used to perform the data exchange asynchronously.

Creating Channels

A channel is created by the make function, which specifies the chan keyword and a channel's element type. Here is the code block that creates an unbuffered channel:

```
// Unbuffered channel of integer type
counter := make(chan int)
```

An unbuffered channel of integer type is created using the built-in function make. The channel counter can act as a conduit for values of integer type. You can use both built-in types and user-defined types as the type of channel element.

A buffered channel is created by specifying its capacity. Here is the code block that declares a buffered channel:

```
// Buffered channel of integer type buffering up to 3 values
nums := make(chan int,3)
```

A buffered channel of integer type is created with capacity of 3. The channel nums is capable of buffering up to three elements of integer values.

Communication with Channels

A channel has three operations: send, receive, and close. A send operation sends a value or a pointer into a channel, and the value or pointer reads from the channel when a corresponding receive operation is executed. The communication operator <- is used for both send and receive operations:

```
counter <- 10
```

The preceding statement shows a send operation that sends a value to the channel named counter. When you write a value or pointer into a channel, the operator <- is put on the right side of the channel variable.

```
num = <- counter
```

The preceding statement shows a receive operation that receives a value from a channel named counter. When you receive a value or pointer from a channel, the operator <- is put on the left side of the channel variable.

A channel has a close operation that closes the channel so that a send operation on the channel cannot take place. A send operation on a closed channel will result in a panic. A receive operation on a closed channel returns the values that have already been sent into the channel before it closed; after that, a receive statement returns the zero value of the channel's element type.

Listing 4-2 shows an example program that sends and receives with both unbuffered and buffered channels.

Listing 4-2. Send and Receive Values with Unbuffered and Buffered Channels

```
package main

import (
    "fmt"
)
```

```go
func main() {
    // Declare a unbuffered channel
    counter := make(chan int)
    // Declare a buffered channel with capacity of 3
    nums := make(chan int, 3)
    go func() {
        // Send value to the unbuffered channel
        counter <- 1
        close(counter) // Closes the channel
    }()

    go func() {
        // Send values to the buffered channel
        nums <- 10
        nums <- 30
        nums <- 50
    }()
    // Read the value from unbuffered channel
    fmt.Println(<-counter)
    val, ok := <-counter // Trying to read from closed channel
    if ok {
        fmt.Println(val) // This won't execute
    }
    // Read the 3 buffered values from the buffered channel
    fmt.Println(<-nums)
    fmt.Println(<-nums)
    fmt.Println(<-nums)
    close(nums) // Closes the channel
}
```

An unbuffered channel named counter is created with an element type of integer. A buffered channel named nums is also created with an element type of integer and capacity of 3, which means it can buffer up to three values. An anonymous function is launched as a goroutine from the main function and writes a value to it. The channel counter closes after writing a value to it. Note that a send operation on the unbuffered channel blocks the execution on that channel until a corresponding receive operation is executed, so the channel will wait for a receive operation from another goroutine. Here the receive operation is executing from the main goroutine.

```go
go func() {
        // Send value to the unbuffered channel
        counter <- 1
        close(counter) // Closes the channel
    }()
```

Another anonymous function is launched as a goroutine to write values into the buffered channel. Unlike the unbuffered channel, a send operation on the buffered channel won't block the execution and you can buffer values up to its capacity, which here is 3.

```go
go func() {
        // Send values to the buffered channel
        nums <- 10
```

```
        nums <- 30
        nums <- 50
    }()
```

The program yields the value from the unbuffered channel. Before closing the channel counter, one value was sent into it so the program can perform one receive operation. Thereafter the channel would be empty.

```
// Read the value from unbuffered channel
    fmt.Println(<-counter)
```

A receive operation on the channel can identify whether the channel is empty. The following code block checks whether the channel is empty or not.

```
    val, ok := <-counter // Trying to read from closed channel
    if ok {
        fmt.Println(val) // This won't execute
    }
```

The receive operation can return two values. It returns an additional boolean value that indicates whether the communication succeeded or not. In the preceding code block, the value of ok would return true if the receive operation was delivered by a successful send operation to the channel, or false if a zero value is generated because the channel is closed and empty. In this program, the value of ok would be false because the channel is closed and empty.

The buffered channel buffers three values so the program can perform three receive operations to yield the value from the channel. Finally the buffered channel is closed so that no more send operations can be performed on it.

```
// Read the 3 values from the buffered channel
    fmt.Println(<-nums)
    fmt.Println(<-nums)
    fmt.Println(<-nums)
    close(nums) // Closes the channel
```

In this simple example, we haven't used the WaitGroup type to synchronize the execution becausse we focused on the behavior of channels. Use the WaitGroup type to synchronize execution if your programs want to wait for the execution to complete goroutines. You should see the following output when you run the program:

```
1
10
30
50
```

The send and receive operations of both buffered and unbuffered channels have different behaviors. We examine in detail both buffered and unbuffered channels in the next sections.

4-4. Using Channels for Synchronous Communication

Problem

You would like to exchange data between goroutines through channels in a synchronous manner so that you can ensure that a send operation would successfully deliver data with a corresponding receive operation.

Solution

An unbuffered channel provides for the exchange of data in a synchronous manner that ensures that a send operation on the channel from one goroutine would be successfully delivered to another goroutine with a corresponding receive operation on the same channel.

How It Works

An unbuffered channel ensures the exchange of data between a sending and a receiving goroutine. When a send operation performs on an unbuffered channel from one goroutine, a corresponding receive operation must be executed on the same channel from another goroutine to complete the send operation. A send operation therefore blocks the sending goroutine until a corresponding receive operation executes from another goroutine. The receive operation might be attempted before the send operation is performed. If the receive operation executes first, the receiving goroutine is blocked until a corresponding send operation executes from another goroutine. In short, completion of a send or receive operation from one goroutine requires execution of a corresponding send or receive operation from another goroutine. This kind of communication mechanism ensures the delivery of data from one goroutine to another.

Deadlock

To understand the blocking behavior of communication operations on the unbuffered channel, let's write a program. Listing 4-3 shows an example program that will create a deadlock; hence it will fail when running the program.

Listing 4-3. Example Program That Creates a Deadlock so That the Program Will Fail

```
package main

import (
    "fmt"
)

func main() {
    // Declare an unbuffered channel
    counter := make(chan int)
    // This will create a deadlock
    counter <- 10          // Send operation to a channel from main goroutine
    fmt.Println(<-counter) // Receive operation from the channel
}
```

You should see the following error when you run the program:

```
fatal error: all goroutines are asleep - deadlock!

goroutine 1 [chan send]:
```

This program will fail due to a deadlock because of the blocking behavior of the unbuffered channel when communication operations are executed. Here a `send` operation is performed from the main goroutine while the channel is trying to perform the `receive` operation from the same main goroutine. The `receive` operation is defined just after executing the `send` operation. When the `send` operation executes, it blocks the main goroutine, which means that it blocks the execution of the entire program because the `send` operation is waiting for a corresponding `receive` operation on the same channel. Because the `send` operation blocks execution, the `receive` operation cannot be executed, which causes a deadlock. In Listing 4-4, we fix the deadlock issue by writing the `send` operation in a goroutine.

Listing 4-4. Example Program That Fixes the Deadlock Caused in Listing 4-3

```
package main

import (
    "fmt"
)

func main() {
    // Declare an unbuffered channel
    counter := make(chan int)
    // Perform send operation by launching new goroutine
    go func() {
        counter <- 10
    }()
    fmt.Println(<-counter) // Receive operation from the channel
}
```

This program will run successfully without any issue because it executes the `send` operation by launching a new goroutine and the `receive` operation is executed in the main goroutine.

Example Program

Let's write an example program to understand the communication mechanism of unbuffered channels, as shown in Listing 4-5.

Listing 4-5. Example Program Demonstrating Unbuffered Channels

```
package main

import (
    "fmt"
    "sync"
)

// wg is used to wait for the program to finish.
var wg sync.WaitGroup

func main() {

    count := make(chan int)
    // Add a count of two, one for each goroutine.
    wg.Add(2)
```

```go
    fmt.Println("Start Goroutines")
    // Launch a goroutine with label "Goroutine-1"
    go printCounts("Goroutine-1", count)
    // Launch a goroutine with label "Goroutine-2"
    go printCounts("Goroutine-2", count)
    fmt.Println("Communication of channel begins")Sticky

    count <- 1
    // Wait for the goroutines to finish.
    fmt.Println("Waiting To Finish")
    wg.Wait()
    fmt.Println("\nTerminating the Program")
}

func printCounts(label string, count chan int) {
    // Schedule the call to WaitGroup's Done to tell goroutine is completed.
    defer wg.Done()
    for {
        // Receives message from Channel
        val, ok := <-count
        if !ok {
            fmt.Println("Channel was closed")
            return
        }
        fmt.Printf("Count: %d received from %s \n", val, label)
        if val == 10 {
            fmt.Printf("Channel Closed from %s \n", label)
            // Close the channel
            close(count)
            return
        }
        val++
        // Send count back to the other goroutine.
        count <- val
    }
}
```

An unbuffered channel of integer type named count is created and launches two goroutines. Both goroutines are executing the printCounts function by providing the channel count and a string label. After the two goroutines are launched, a send operation is performed on the channel count. This waits to get a corresponding receive operation on the same channel.

```go
// Launch a goroutine with label "Goroutine-1"
    go printCounts("Goroutine-1", count)
    // Launch a goroutine with label "Goroutine-2"
    go printCounts("Goroutine-2", count)
    fmt.Println("Communication of channel begins")
    count <- 1
```

The printCounts function prints the value received from the channel count and performs a send operation on the same channel by providing a new value to the count to share the data with other goroutines. After two goroutines are launched, an initial value of 1 is sent to the channel, so one goroutine can receive the initial value and the send operation can be completed. After receiving a value from the channel, the receiving goroutine sends an incremented value to the channel, so it blocks the goroutine until the other goroutine receives the value from the channel. The operation of both send and receive continue until the value of count reaches 10. When the value of the channel count gets to 10, the channel is closed so that no more send operations can be performed.

```go
func printCounts(label string, count chan int) {
    // Schedule the call to WaitGroup's Done to tell goroutine is completed.
    defer wg.Done()
    for {
        // Receives message from Channel
        val, ok := <-count
        if !ok {
            fmt.Println("Channel was closed")
            return
        }
        fmt.Printf("Count: %d received from %s \n", val, label)
        if val == 10 {
            fmt.Printf("Channel Closed from %s \n", label)
            // Close the channel
            close(count)
            return
        }
        val++
        // Send count back to the other goroutine.
        count <- val
    }
}
```

When a receive operation is performed on the channel, we check if the channel is closed or not, and exit from the goroutine if the channel is closed.

```go
val, ok := <-count
    if !ok {
        fmt.Println("Channel was closed")
        return
    }
```

You should see output similar to the following:

```
Start Goroutines
Communication of channel begins
Waiting To Finish
Count: 1 received from Goroutine-1
Count: 2 received from Goroutine-2
Count: 3 received from Goroutine-1
Count: 4 received from Goroutine-2
Count: 5 received from Goroutine-1
Count: 6 received from Goroutine-2
Count: 7 received from Goroutine-1
Count: 8 received from Goroutine-2
```

```
Count: 9 received from Goroutine-1
Count: 10 received from Goroutine-2
Channel Closed from Goroutine-2
Channel was closed

Terminating the Program
```

Note that order of the goroutines might change when you run the program each time.

Receive Values Using Range Expression

In Listing 4-5, you read the value from the channel using the communication operator <- and checking whether the channel was closed or not. You have used the range expression to iterate over the elements of various data structures such as arrays, slices, and maps. The range expression can also be used to yield the values from channels, which would be more convenient for most use cases. The range expression on the channel yields the values until the channel is closed. Listing 4-6 rewrites the code of Listing 4-5 with the range expression.

Listing 4-6. Example Program Demonstrates Unbuffered Channel and range Expression on Channel

```go
package main

import (
    "fmt"
    "sync"
)

// wg is used to wait for the program to finish.
var wg sync.WaitGroup

func main() {

    count := make(chan int)
    // Add a count of two, one for each goroutine.
    wg.Add(2)

    fmt.Println("Start Goroutines")
    // Launch a goroutine with label "Goroutine-1"
    go printCounts("Goroutine-1", count)
    // Launch a goroutine with label "Goroutine-2"
    go printCounts("Goroutine-2", count)
    fmt.Println("Communication of channel begins")
    count <- 1
    // Wait for the goroutines to finish.
    fmt.Println("Waiting To Finish")
    wg.Wait()
    fmt.Println("\nTerminating the Program")
}

func printCounts(label string, count chan int) {
    // Schedule the call to WaitGroup's Done to tell goroutine is completed.
```

```
    defer wg.Done()
    for val := range count {
        fmt.Printf("Count: %d received from %s \n", val, label)
        if val == 10 {
            fmt.Printf("Channel Closed from %s \n", label)
            // Close the channel
            close(count)
            return
        }
        val++
        // Send count back to the other goroutine.
        count <- val
    }
}
```

The range expression yields the value from channel count until the channel is closed.

```
for val := range count {
    fmt.Printf("Count: %d received from %s \n", val, label)
}
```

You should see output similar to the following:

```
Start Goroutines
Communication of channel begins
Waiting To Finish
Count: 1 received from Goroutine-1
Count: 2 received from Goroutine-2
Count: 3 received from Goroutine-1
Count: 4 received from Goroutine-2
Count: 5 received from Goroutine-1
Count: 6 received from Goroutine-2
Count: 7 received from Goroutine-1
Count: 8 received from Goroutine-2
Count: 9 received from Goroutine-1
Count: 10 received from Goroutine-2
Channel Closed from Goroutine-2

Terminating the Program
```

4-5. Using the Output of One Goroutine as the Input of Another

Problem

You would like to use the output of one goroutine as the input of another goroutine, and so on.

Solution

Pipeline is a concurrency pattern, which refers to a series of stages of goroutines connected by channels in which the output of one goroutine is the input of another goroutine, and so on.

How It Works

Let's write an example program to explore a pipeline. Listing 4-7 shows an example program that demonstrates a pipeline with goroutines and channels. The example program has a three-stage pipeline with three goroutines that are connected by two channels. In this pipeline, the goroutine of the first stage is used to randomly generate values with an upper limit of 50. The pipeline has an outbound channel to give inbound values to the goroutine of the second stage. The goroutine of the second stage has an inbound channel and an outbound channel. The inbound channel receives values from the first goroutine when it randomly generates each value and finds out the Fibonacci value. It then provides the resulting Fibonacci values to the goroutine of third stage, which just prints the outbound values from the goroutine of second stage. Here is the example program.

Listing 4-7. A Three-Stage Pipeline with Three Goroutines Connected by Two Channels

```go
package main

import (
    "fmt"
    "math"
    "math/rand"
    "sync"
)

type fibvalue struct {
    input, value int
}

var wg sync.WaitGroup
// Generates random values
func randomCounter(out chan int) {
    defer wg.Done()
    var random int
    for x := 0; x < 10; x++ {
        random = rand.Intn(50)
        out <- random
    }
    close(out)
}

// Produces Fibonacci values of inputs provided by randomCounter
func generateFibonacci(out chan fibvalue, in chan int) {
    defer wg.Done()
    var input float64
    for v := range in {
        input = float64(v)
        // Fibonacci using Binet's formula
        Phi := (1 + math.Sqrt(5)) / 2
        phi := (1 - math.Sqrt(5)) / 2
        result := (math.Pow(Phi, input) - math.Pow(phi, input)) / math.Sqrt(5)
        out <- fibvalue{
            input: v,
            value: int(result),
```

```
        }
    }
    close(out)
}

// Print Fibonacci values generated by generateFibonacci
func printFibonacci(in chan fibvalue) {
    defer wg.Done()
    for v := range in {
        fmt.Printf("Fibonacci value of %d is %d\n", v.input, v.value)
    }
}

func main() {
    // Add 3 into WaitGroup Counter
    wg.Add(3)
    // Declare Channels
    randoms := make(chan int)
    fibs := make(chan fibvalue)
    // Launching 3 goroutines
    go randomCounter(randoms)              // First stage of pipeline
    go generateFibonacci(fibs, randoms)    // Second stage of pipeline
    go printFibonacci(fibs)                // Third stage of pipeline
  // Wait for completing all goroutines
    wg.Wait()
}
```

The program prints Fibonacci values of 10 randomly generated values. Two unbuffered channels are used as inbound and outbound channels for the three-stage pipeline. The element type of channel randoms is integer and the element type of channel fibs is a struct type named fibvalue that consists of two fields for holding a random number and its Fibonacci value. Three goroutines are used for completing this pipeline.

```
go randomCounter(randoms)              // First stage of pipeline
go generateFibonacci(fibs, randoms)    // Second stage of pipeline
go printFibonacci(fibs)                // Third stage of pipeline
```

The goroutine of the first stage randomly generates values with an upper limit of 50.

```
func randomCounter(out chan int) {
    defer wg.Done()
    var random int
    for x := 0; x < 10; x++ {
        random = rand.Intn(50)
        out <- random
    }
    close(out)
}
```

In the first stage of three-stage pipeline, the randomCounter function provides inputs to the second stage, which is implemented in the generateFibonacci function. The randomCounter function uses a channel of integer that is being used to send 10 randomly generated values, and thereafter the channel is closed.

```go
func generateFibonacci(out chan fibvalue, in chan int) {
    defer wg.Done()
    var input float64
    for v := range in {
        input = float64(v)
        // Fibonacci using Binet's formula
        Phi := (1 + math.Sqrt(5)) / 2
        phi := (1 - math.Sqrt(5)) / 2
        result := (math.Pow(Phi, input) - math.Pow(phi, input)) / math.Sqrt(5)
        out <- fibvalue{
            input: v,
            value: int(result),
        }
    }
    close(out)
}
```

The generateFibonacci function uses two channels: one for receiving inputs from the goroutine of the first stage the other for providing inputs to the goroutine of the third stage. Inside the generateFibonacci function, the receive operation is performed on the inbound channel, which is getting values from the randomCounter function. The incoming values to generateFibonacci can be sent until the channel is closed from the randomCounter function. The generateFibonacci function generates the Fibonacci values for each incoming value. Those values are being sent to the outbound channel to provide inputs to the goroutine of the third stage.

```go
func printFibonacci(in chan fibvalue) {
    defer wg.Done()
    for v := range in {
        fmt.Printf("Fibonacci value of %d is %d\n", v.input, v.value)
    }
}
```

The final stage of the pipeline is implemented in the printFibonacci function, which prints the Fibonacci values received from the outbound channel of the generateFibonacci function. The incoming values to the printFibonacci function can be yielded until the channel is closed from the generateFibonacci function.

In this example program, the output of the first stage is used as the input for the second stage, then the output of second stage is used as the input for third stage. You should see output similar to the following:

```
Fibonacci value of 31 is 1346268
Fibonacci value of 37 is 24157816
Fibonacci value of 47 is 2971215072
Fibonacci value of 9 is 34
Fibonacci value of 31 is 1346268
Fibonacci value of 18 is 2584
Fibonacci value of 25 is 75025
Fibonacci value of 40 is 102334154
Fibonacci value of 6 is 8
Fibonacci value of 0 is 0
```

Channel Direction

In Listing 4-7, you used three goroutines connected by two channels. In these goroutines, one goroutine performs the send operation to a channel and from another goroutine values are received from the same channel. Here a channel within in a goroutine is used for either a send operation or a receive operation so that you can specify the channel direction (send or receive) when you specify channels as parameters.

```
func generateFibonacci(out chan<- fibvalue, in <-chan int) {
}
```

Here the declaration out chan<- fibvalue specifies that the channel out is used for the send operation and the in <-chan int specifies that the channel in is used for the receive operation. The communication operator <- put on the right side of the chan keyword specifies a channel to be used only for send operations; put on the left side of the chan keyword, the same operator specifies that a channel is to be used only for receive operations.

Example with Channel Direction

Listing 4-8 rewrites the example code of Listing 4-7 by clearly specifying the channel direction.

Listing 4-8. A Three-Stage Pipeline with Three Goroutines Connected by Two Channels

```
package main

import (
    "fmt"
    "math"
    "math/rand"
    "sync"
)

type fibvalue struct {
    input, value int
}

var wg sync.WaitGroup

func randomCounter(out chan<- int) {
    defer wg.Done()
    var random int
    for x := 0; x < 10; x++ {
        random = rand.Intn(50)
        out <- random
    }
    close(out)
}

func generateFibonacci(out chan<- fibvalue, in <-chan int) {
    defer wg.Done()
    var input float64
    for v := range in {
```

```
        input = float64(v)
        // Fibonacci using Binet's formula
        Phi := (1 + math.Sqrt(5)) / 2
        phi := (1 - math.Sqrt(5)) / 2
        result := (math.Pow(Phi, input) - math.Pow(phi, input)) / math.Sqrt(5)
        out <- fibvalue{
            input: v,
            value: int(result),
        }
    }
    close(out)
}

func printFibonacci(in <-chan fibvalue) {
    defer wg.Done()
    for v := range in {
        fmt.Printf("Fibonacci value of %d is %d\n", v.input, v.value)
    }
}

func main() {
    // Add 3 into WaitGroup Counter
    wg.Add(3)
    // Declare Channels
    randoms := make(chan int)
    fibs := make(chan fibvalue)
    // Launching 3 goroutines
    go randomCounter(randoms)
    go generateFibonacci(fibs, randoms)
    go printFibonacci(fibs)
    // Wait for completing all goroutines
    wg.Wait()
}
```

In the randomCounter function, the channel out is used only for the send operation. The generateFibonacci function uses two channels: The channel in is used for the receive operation and the channel out is used for send operations. The channel in the printFibonacci function is used only for the receive operation.

4-6. Using Channels for Asynchronous Communication

Problem

You would like to exchange data between goroutines through channels in an asynchronous manner, and the channel should be capable of buffering values.

Solution

The buffered channel is capable of buffering values up to its capacity and it provides asynchronous communication for data exchange.

How It Works

Unlike unbuffered channels, buffered channels can hold values up to their capacity. A buffered channel is like a queue on which a send operation doesn't block any goroutine because of its capability for holding elements. A send operation on the buffered channel is blocked only when the channel is full, which means that the channel has reached its buffering capacity. The capacity of a buffered channel is determined when it is created using the make function. The following statement creates a buffered channel that is capable of holding elements of three integer values.

```
nums := make(chan int, 3)
```

Here is the code block that makes three send operations into the channel nums:

```
nums <- 10
nums <- 30
nums <- 50
```

A send operation on a buffered channel doesn't block the sending goroutine. Here the channel nums is capable of holding elements of three integer values. A send operation inserts an element on the back of the channel and a receive operation removes an element from the front of the channel. This pattern ensures that the send and receive operations on a buffered channel are working on a first-in, first-out (FIFO) basis. The first inserted element through a send operation will be yielded for the first receive operation on the channel.

The following code block receives three values from the channel nums:

```
fmt.Println(<-nums) // Print 10 (first inserted item)
fmt.Println(<-nums) // Print 30 (second inserted item)
fmt.Println(<-nums) // Print 50 (third inserted item)
```

A buffered channel can hold elements up to its capacity. If one goroutine makes a send operation on a buffered channel that exceeds its capacity, which means that the channel is full and trying to perform another send operation on the same channel, it blocks the sending goroutine until a space is available to insert a new element on the channel by a receive operation of another goroutine. In the same way, a receive operation on an empty buffered channel blocks the receiving goroutine until an element is inserted into the channel by a send operation of another goroutine.

Let's explore buffered channels by writing an example program, shown in Listing 4-9. In this example, a buffered channel is used to hold information on tasks to be executed from a number of goroutines. The buffered channel is capable of holding elements of 10 pointers that contain information on jobs to be completed. These jobs are being executed using a predefined number of goroutines; here it is three. These three goroutines are simultaneously receiving values from a buffered channel and then executing the jobs.

Listing 4-9. Example Demonstrating Buffered Channels

```
package main

import (
    "fmt"
    "math/rand"
    "sync"
    "time"
)
```

```go
type Task struct {
    Id        int
    JobId     int
    Status    string
    CreatedOn time.Time
}

func (t *Task) Run() {

    sleep := rand.Int63n(1000)
    // Delaying the execution for the sake of example
    time.Sleep(time.Duration(sleep) * time.Millisecond)
    t.Status = "Completed"

}

// wg is used to wait for the program to finish.
var wg sync.WaitGroup

const noOfWorkers = 3

// main is the entry point for all Go programs.
func main() {
    // Create a buffered channel to manage the task queue.
    taskQueue := make(chan *Task, 10)

    // Launch goroutines to handle the work.
    // The worker process is distributing with the value of noOfWorkers.
    wg.Add(noOfWorkers)
    for gr := 1; gr <= noOfWorkers; gr++ {
        go worker(taskQueue, gr)
    }

    // Add Tasks into Buffered channel.
    for i := 1; i <= 10; i++ {
        taskQueue <- &Task{
            Id:        i,
            JobId:     100 + i,
            CreatedOn: time.Now(),
        }
    }

    // Close the channel
    close(taskQueue)

    // Wait for all the work to get done.
    wg.Wait()
}

// worker is launched as a goroutine to process Tasks from
// the buffered channel.
```

```
func worker(taskQueue <-chan *Task, workerId int) {
    // Schedule the call to Done method of WaitGroup.
    defer wg.Done()
    for v := range taskQueue {
        fmt.Printf("Worker%d: received request for Task:%d - Job:%d\n", workerId, v.Id,
v.JobId)
        v.Run()
        // Display we finished the work.
        fmt.Printf("Worker%d: Status:%s for Task:%d - Job:%d\n", workerId, v.Status, v.Id,
v.JobId)
    }
}
```

A struct type named Task is defined for representing a task to be executed. A method named Run is added to the Task type to replicate running a task, which will be executed from goroutines.

```
type Task struct {
    Id        int
    JobId     int
    Status    string
    CreatedOn time.Time
}

func (t *Task) Run() {

    sleep := rand.Int63n(1000)
    // Delaying the execution for the sake of example
    time.Sleep(time.Duration(sleep) * time.Millisecond)
    t.Status = "Completed"
}
```

A buffered channel is created by specifying a pointer to Task type as the element type and capacity of 10.

```
taskQueue := make(chan *Task, 10)
```

The buffered channel taskQueue holds the tasks to be executed from a predefined number of goroutines. From the main function, the program launches a predefined number of goroutines to distribute the work for which the information for completing the tasks is available from channel taskQueue. After launching three goroutines, the buffered channel is filled with 10 elements of pointers to Task values.

```
// wg is used to wait for the program to finish.
var wg sync.WaitGroup

const noOfWorkers = 3  // number of goroutines to be used for executing the worker

// main is the entry point for all Go programs.
func main() {
    // Create a buffered channel to manage the task queue.
    taskQueue := make(chan *Task, 10)
```

```go
    // Launch goroutines to handle the work.
    // The worker process is distributing with the value of noOfWorkers.
    wg.Add(noOfWorkers)
    for gr := 1; gr <= noOfWorkers; gr++ {
        go worker(taskQueue, gr)
    }

    // Add Tasks into Buffered channel.
    for i := 1; i <= 10; i++ {
        taskQueue <- &Task{
            Id:        i,
            JobId:     100 + i,
            CreatedOn: time.Now(),
        }
    }

    // Close the channel
    close(taskQueue)

    // Wait for all the work to get done.
    wg.Wait()
}
```

The function worker is used for launching goroutines to execute tasks by receiving values from the buffered channel. The channel contains the information for 10 tasks, and these tasks are distributed and executed from three goroutines by launching the worker function as goroutines. The worker function receives elements (pointer to Task) from a channel and then executes the Run method of Task type to completing the task.

```go
func worker(taskQueue <-chan *Task, workerId int) {
    // Schedule the call to Done method of WaitGroup.
    defer wg.Done()
    for v := range taskQueue {
        fmt.Printf("Worker%d: received request for Task:%d - Job:%d\n", workerId, v.Id,
v.JobId)
        v.Run()
        // Display we finished the work.
        fmt.Printf("Worker%d: Status:%s for Task:%d - Job:%d\n", workerId, v.Status, v.Id,
v.JobId)
    }
}
```

In short, in this example, a buffered channel is used to send 10 tasks to be executed for completing some work. Because buffered channels work like a queue, the channel can hold values up to its capacity, and a send operation on the channel doesn't block the goroutine. Here the work of 10 tasks is executed by three goroutines after launching a function so that the work for completing 10 tasks can be concurrently performed from a number of goroutines.

You should see output similar to the following:

```
Worker1: received request for Task:2 - Job:102
Worker3: received request for Task:1 - Job:101
Worker2: received request for Task:3 - Job:103
```

```
Worker1: Status:Completed for Task:2 - Job:102
Worker1: received request for Task:4 - Job:104
Worker1: Status:Completed for Task:4 - Job:104
Worker1: received request for Task:5 - Job:105
Worker3: Status:Completed for Task:1 - Job:101
Worker3: received request for Task:6 - Job:106
Worker2: Status:Completed for Task:3 - Job:103
Worker2: received request for Task:7 - Job:107
Worker3: Status:Completed for Task:6 - Job:106
Worker3: received request for Task:8 - Job:108
Worker3: Status:Completed for Task:8 - Job:108
Worker3: received request for Task:9 - Job:109
Worker3: Status:Completed for Task:9 - Job:109
Worker3: received request for Task:10 - Job:110
Worker1: Status:Completed for Task:5 - Job:105
Worker2: Status:Completed for Task:7 - Job:107
Worker3: Status:Completed for Task:10 - Job:110
```

The output shows that the work for executing 10 tasks is being distributed from three workers launched as goroutines.

4-7. Communicating on Multiple Channels

Problem

You would like to perform communication operations on multiple channels.

Solution

Go provides a select statement that lets a goroutine perform communication operations on multiple channels.

How It Works

When you build real-world concurrent programs with Go, you might need to deal with multiple channels in a single goroutine, which could require you to perform communication operations on multiple channels. The select statement is a powerful communication mechanism when it is used in conjunction with multiple channels. A select block is written with multiple case statements that lets a goroutine wait until one of the cases can run; it then executes the code block of that case. If multiple case blocks are ready for execution, it randomly picks one of them and executes the code block of that case.

Listing 4-10 shows an example program that performs a select block for reading values from multiple channels in a goroutine.

Listing 4-10. A select Block for Reading Values from Multiple Channels

```
package main

import (
    "fmt"
```

```go
    "math"
    "math/rand"
    "sync"
)

type (
    fibvalue struct {
        input, value int
    }
    squarevalue struct {
        input, value int
    }
)

func generateSquare(sqrs chan<- squarevalue) {
    defer wg.Done()
    for i := 1; i <= 10; i++ {
        num := rand.Intn(50)
        sqrs <- squarevalue{
            input: num,
            value: num * num,
        }
    }
}
func generateFibonacci(fibs chan<- fibvalue) {
    defer wg.Done()
    for i := 1; i <= 10; i++ {
        num := float64(rand.Intn(50))
        // Fibonacci using Binet's formula
        Phi := (1 + math.Sqrt(5)) / 2
        phi := (1 - math.Sqrt(5)) / 2
        result := (math.Pow(Phi, num) - math.Pow(phi, num)) / math.Sqrt(5)
        fibs <- fibvalue{
            input: int(num),
            value: int(result),
        }
    }
}
func printValues(fibs <-chan fibvalue, sqrs <-chan squarevalue) {
    defer wg.Done()
    for i := 1; i <= 20; i++ {
        select {
        case fib := <-fibs:
            fmt.Printf("Fibonacci value of %d is %d\n", fib.input, fib.value)
        case sqr := <-sqrs:
            fmt.Printf("Square value of %d is %d\n", sqr.input, sqr.value)
        }
    }
}

// wg is used to wait for the program to finish.
var wg sync.WaitGroup
```

```
func main() {
    wg.Add(3)
    // Create Channels
    fibs := make(chan fibvalue)
    sqrs := make(chan squarevalue)
    // Launching 3 goroutines
    go generateFibonacci(fibs)
    go generateSquare(sqrs)
    go printValues(fibs, sqrs)
    // Wait for completing all goroutines
    wg.Wait()
}
```

The program launches three goroutines: One is for generating Fibonacci values of 10 randomly generated numbers; another one is for generating square values of 10 randomly generated numbers; and the last one is for printing the resulting values generated by the first and second goroutines. From the main function, two channels are created for the communication of Fibonacci values and square values generated by corresponding goroutines. The function generateFibonacci is launched as a goroutine that performs a send operation into channel fibs to provide values of Fibonacci. The function generateSquare is launched as a goroutine that performs a send operation into channel sqrs to provide values of a square. The function printValues is launched as a goroutine that polls on both fibs and sqrs channels to print the resulting values whenever the values can receive from both channels.

Inside the printValues function, a select expression is used with two case blocks. The select block is 20 times using a for loop expression. We use the 20 times for printing 10 Fibonacci values and 10 square values. In a real-world scenario, you might be running this in an endless loop in which you might be continually communicating with channels.

```
func printValues(fibs <-chan fibvalue, sqrs <-chan squarevalue) {
    defer wg.Done()
    for i := 1; i <= 20; i++ {
        select {
        case fib := <-fibs:
            fmt.Printf("Fibonacci value of %d is %d\n", fib.input, fib.value)
        case sqr := <-sqrs:
            fmt.Printf("Square value of %d is %d\n", sqr.input, sqr.value)
        }
    }
}
```

Here the select expression is written with two case blocks: One is for the receive operation on the fibs channel and the other is for the receive operation on the sqrs channel. The select statement blocks the goroutine until any of these blocks can run, and then it executes that case block. If all case blocks are not ready for execution, it blocks until a value is sent into either of the two channels used in this program. If multiple case blocks are ready for execution, it randomly picks a case block, then executes it.

You can also add a default block inside a select expression, and this does execute if all other case blocks are not ready for an execution. It also possible to implement a timeout expression in the select block as shown here:

```
select {
  case fib := <-fibs:
      fmt.Printf("Fibonacci value of %d is %d\n", fib.input, fib.value)
```

```
  case sqr := <-sqrs:
    fmt.Printf("Square value of %d is %d\n", sqr.input, sqr.value)
  case <-time.After(time.Second * 3):
    fmt.Println("timed out")
}
```

In the preceding code block, a timeout expression is added into the select block. If the select statement is unable to run any of the case blocks within the specified timeout period, which is 3 seconds in this case, then the timeout block would be executed. The time.After function returns a channel (<-chan time.Time) that waits for the given duration to elapse and then sends the current time on the returned channel.

You should see output similar to the following:

```
Fibonacci value of 31 is 1346268
Square value of 47 is 2209
Fibonacci value of 37 is 24157816
Square value of 9 is 81
Square value of 31 is 961
Square value of 18 is 324
Fibonacci value of 25 is 75025
Fibonacci value of 40 is 102334154
Square value of 0 is 0
Fibonacci value of 6 is 8
Fibonacci value of 44 is 701408732
Square value of 12 is 144
Fibonacci value of 11 is 89
Square value of 39 is 1521
Square value of 28 is 784
Fibonacci value of 11 is 89
Square value of 24 is 576
Square value of 45 is 2025
Fibonacci value of 37 is 24157816
Fibonacci value of 6 is 8
```

CHAPTER 5

Using Standard Library Packages

Packages are a very important component in the Go ecosystem. Go code is organized as packages that enable reusability and composability to your Go programs. The Go installation comes with a lot of reusable packages called standard library packages. These packages extend the Go language and provide reusable libraries for building a variety of applications. They can help you quickly build applications because you don't need to write your own packages for many common functionalities. If you want to extend the standard library packages, you can either create your own or obtain third-party packages provided by the Go developer community. The standard library packages are very rich in functionality. You can build full-fledged web applications using only standard library packages, without using any third-party packages. This chapter's recipes cover how to use standard library packages for some common functionalities such as encoding and decoding JavaScript Object Notation (JSON) objects, parsing command-line flags, logging Go programs, and archiving files. The documentation of standard library packages is available from https://golang.org/pkg/.

5-1. Encoding and Decoding JSON

Problem

You would like to encode values of Go types into JSON objects and decode JSON objects into values of Go types.

Solution

The standard library package encoding/json is used for encoding and decoding JSON objects.

How It Works

JSON is a data interchange format that is widely used for communication between web back-end servers and front ends of web and mobile applications. When you build RESTful application programming interfaces (APIs) with Go, you might need to decode JSON values from the HTTP request body and parse those data into Go values, and encode Go values into JSON values for sending to the HTTP response.

Encoding JSON

The Marshal function of the json package is used to encode Go values into JSON values. To working with the json package, you must add the package encoding/json to the list of imports.

```
import (
        "encoding/json"
)
```

Here is the signature of function `Marshal`:

```
func Marshal(v interface{}) ([]byte, error)
```

The function `Marshal` returns two values: the encoded JSON data as `slice byte` and an `error` value. Let's declare a struct type to demonstrate parsing a value of struct type into JSON:

```
type Employee struct {
        ID                          int
        FirstName, LastName, JobTitle string
}
```

The following code block creates an instance of `Employee` struct and parses the value into JSON.

```
emp := Employee{
                ID:         100,
                FirstName: "Shiju",
                LastName:  "Varghese",
                JobTitle:  "Architect",
        }
    // Encoding to JSON
    data, err := json.Marshal(emp)
```

The function `Marshal` returns the JSON encoding of the value of the `Employee` struct. When you build JSON-based RESTful APIs, you mostly parse values of struct type into JSON objects. Using `Marshal`, you can easily encode values of struct type as JSON values that will help you to quickly build JSON-based APIs.

Decoding JSON

The function `Unmarshal` of the `json` package is used to decode JSON values into Go values. Here is the signature of function `Unmarshal`:

```
func Unmarshal(data []byte, v interface{}) error
```

The function `Unmarshal` parses the JSON-encoded data and stores the result into the second argument (`v interface{}`). The following code block decodes JSON data and stores the result into the value of the `Employee` struct:

```
b := []byte(`{"ID":101,"FirstName":"Irene","LastName":"Rose","JobTitle":"Developer"}`)
var emp1 Employee
// Decoding JSON data into the value of Employee struct
err = json.Unmarshal(b, &emp1)
```

The preceding statements parse the JSON data of variable `b` and store the result into the variable `emp1`. The JSON data is provided as a raw string literal using the back quotes. Within the back quotes, any character is valid except for the back quote. Now you can read the fields of the `Employee` struct like a normal struct value as shown here:

```
fmt.Printf("ID:%d, Name:%s %s, JobTitle:%s", emp1.ID, emp1.FirstName, emp1.LastName, emp1.JobTitle)
```

Example: Encoding and Decoding

Listing 5-1 shows an example program that demonstrates encoding a value of struct type into a JSON object and decoding a JSON object into a value of struct type.

Listing 5-1. Encoding and Decoding of JSON with a Struct Type

```go
package main

import (
        "encoding/json"
        "fmt"
)

// Employee struct
type Employee struct {
        ID                        int
        FirstName, LastName, JobTitle string
}

func main() {
        emp := Employee{
                ID:        100,
                FirstName: "Shiju",
                LastName:  "Varghese",
                JobTitle:  "Architect",
        }
    // Encoding to JSON
        data, err := json.Marshal(emp)
        if err != nil {
                fmt.Println(err.Error())
                return
        }
        jsonStr := string(data)
                fmt.Println("The JSON data is:")
        fmt.Println(jsonStr)

        b := []byte(`{"ID":101,"FirstName":"Irene","LastName":"Rose","JobTitle":"Developer"}`)
        var emp1 Employee
    // Decoding JSON data to a value of struct type
        err = json.Unmarshal(b, &emp1)
        if err != nil {
                fmt.Println(err.Error())
                return
        }
                fmt.Println("The Employee value is:")
        fmt.Printf("ID:%d, Name:%s %s, JobTitle:%s", emp1.ID, emp1.FirstName, emp1.LastName,
emp1.JobTitle)
}
```

You should see the following output when you run the program:

```
The JSON data is:
{"ID":100,"FirstName":"Shiju","LastName":"Varghese","JobTitle":"Architect"}
The Employee value is:
ID:101, Name:Irene Rose, JobTitle:Developer
```

■ **Note**   When you encode and decode JSON data with values of struct type, you must specify the all fields of the struct type as exported fields (identifier names start with uppercase letters) because the values of the struct fields are being used by the `json` package while calling the `Marshal` and `Unmarshal` functions.

Struct Tags

When you encode values of struct type into JSON you might need to use different fields in the JSON encoding than struct type's fields. For example, you would start with an uppercase letter to specify the name of struct fields to mark them as exported fields, but it's common use for the elements to start with lowercase letters in JSON. Here we can use struct tags to map the names of struct fields with the names of fields in JSON to be used when encoding and decoding JSON objects.

Here is the `Employee` struct specified with tags to be used and different names in JSON encoding:

```
type Employee struct {
        ID        int    `json:"id,omitempty"`
        FirstName string `json:"firstname"`
        LastName  string `json:"lastname"`
        JobTitle  string `json:"job"`
}
```

Note that back quotes (` `` `) are used to specify tags. Within the quotes, you put the metadata known as tags, for package `json`. Within the quotes, any character is valid except another back quote. The struct field ID is tagged with `id` for JSON representation. The `omitempty` flag specifies that the field is not being included in the JSON representation if that field has a default value. If you are not providing a value for the ID field of the `Employee` struct, the output of the JSON object doesn't include the `id` field when you parse the `Employee` values to JSON. All fields of the `Employee` struct are tagged with different names for JSON data.

If you want to skip fields from the struct, you can give the tag name as `"-"`. The `User` struct shown here specifies that the field `Password` must be skipped when encoding and decoding JSON objects:

```
type User struct {
    UserName string `json:"user"`
    Password string `json:"-"`
}
```

Example: Encoding and Decoding with Struct Tags

Listing 5-2 shows an example program that demonstrates encoding and decoding of JSON objects with struct tags.

Listing 5-2. Encoding and Decoding of JSON with Struct Tags

```go
package main

import (
        "encoding/json"
        "fmt"
)

// Employee struct with struct tags
type Employee struct {
        ID        int    `json:"id,omitempty"`
        FirstName string `json:"firstname"`
        LastName  string `json:"lastname"`
        JobTitle  string `json:"job"`
}

func main() {
        emp := Employee{
                FirstName: "Shiju",
                LastName:  "Varghese",
                JobTitle:  "Architect",
        }
        // Encoding to JSON
        data, err := json.Marshal(emp)
        if err != nil {
                fmt.Println(err.Error())
                return
        }
        jsonStr := string(data)
        fmt.Println("The JSON data is:")
        fmt.Println(jsonStr)

        b := []byte(`{"id":101,"firstname":"Irene","lastname":"Rose","job":"Developer"}`)
        var emp1 Employee
        // Decoding JSON to a struct type
        err = json.Unmarshal(b, &emp1)
        if err != nil {
                fmt.Println(err.Error())
                return
        }
        fmt.Println("The Employee value is:")
        fmt.Printf("ID:%d, Name:%s %s, JobTitle:%s", emp1.ID, emp1.FirstName, emp1.LastName,
emp1.JobTitle)
}
```

You should see the following output when you run the program:

```
The JSON data is:
{"firstname":"Shiju","lastname":"Varghese","job":"Architect"}
The Employee value is:
ID:101, Name:Irene Rose, JobTitle:Developer
```

The Employee struct is tagged with field names to be used with JSON objects. The value of the Employee struct is created without specifying the ID field so that the JSON object excludes the id field when encoding the value of Employee struct into JSON. The JSON output also shows the corresponding JSON field names that are tagged in the struct declaration. When we decode the JSON object, the id field is not empty so it is parsed into the ID field of the Employee struct.

5-2. Using Command-Line Flags

Problem

You would like to parse command-line flags to provide some values to the Go programs.

Solution

The standard library package flag is used to parse command-line flags.

How It Works

Sometimes you might need to receive values from an end user via command line when you run programs. This is an essential feature when you build command-line applications. A command-line option, also known as a flag, can be used to provide values to the program when you run the programs. The standard library package flag provides the functions for parsing command-line flags. The package flag provides the functions for parsing string, integer, and boolean values using flag.String(), flag.Bool(), and flag.Int().

To work with the flag package, you must it to the list of imports:

```
import (
        "flag"
)
```

Listing 5-3 shows an example program that demonstrates how to define flags in Go programs.

Listing 5-3. Defining Flags Using Package flag

```
package main

import (
        "flag"
        "fmt"
)

func main() {

        fileName := flag.String("filename", "logfile", "File name for the log file")
        logLevel := flag.Int("loglevel", 0, "An integer value for Level (0-4)")
        isEnable := flag.Bool("enable", false, "A boolean value for enabling log options")
        var num int
        // Bind the flag to a variable.
        flag.IntVar(&num, "num", 25, "An integer value")
```

```
        // Parse parses flag definitions from the argument list.
        flag.Parse()
        // Get the values from pointers
        fmt.Println("filename:", *fileName)
        fmt.Println("loglevel:", *logLevel)
        fmt.Println("enable:", *isEnable)
        // Get the value from a variable
        fmt.Println("num:", num)
        // Args returns the non-flag command-line arguments.
        args := flag.Args()
        if len(args) > 0 {
                fmt.Println("The non-flag command-line arguments are:")
                // Print the arguments
                for _, v := range args {
                        fmt.Println(v)
                }
        }

}
```

The function flag.String is used to define the flag for getting the string value via the command line.

```
fileName := flag.String("filename", "logfile", "File name for the log file")
```

The preceding statement declares a string flag, with flag name as filename and provides a default value as "logfile ". The user input for the filename flag (-filename) is stored in the pointer fileName, with type *string. The third argument provides a description for the usage of the flag. The functions flag.Bool() and flag.Int() are used for declaring flags for boolean and integer values.

```
logLevel := flag.Int("loglevel", 0, "An integer value for Level (0-4)")
isEnable := flag.Bool("enable", false, "A boolean value for enabling log options")
```

If you want to bind the flag to an existing variable, you can use the functions flag.IntVar, flag.BoolVar, and flag.StringVar. The following code block binds the flag num (-num) to the integer variable num.

```
var num int
// Bind the flag to a variable.
flag.IntVar(&num, "num", 25, "An integer value")
```

The function flag.Parse() parses flag definitions from the command line. Because the functions flag.String(), flag.Bool(), and flag.Int() are return pointers, we dereference the pointers to get the values.

```
fmt.Println("name:", *fileName)
fmt.Println("num:", *logLevel)
fmt.Println("enable:", *isEnable)
```

The function flag.IntVar returns an integer value, not a pointer, so that the value can be read without a dereference of the pointer.

```
fmt.Println("num:", num)
```

The package flag provides a function called Args that can be used to read nonflag command-line arguments. This function call returns a slice of string if you provide nonflag command-line arguments. Command-line arguments are positioned after the command-line flags. Here the command-line arguments are printing into the console if the user provides it.

```
args := flag.Args()
        if len(args) > 0 {
                fmt.Println("The non-flag command-line arguments are:")
                // Print the arguments
                for _, v := range args {
                        fmt.Println(v)
                }
        }
```

Let's build the program and run it with different command-line options:

```
$ go build
```

First, let's run the program by providing all flags and arguments.

```
$ ./ cmdflags -filename=applog -loglevel=2 -enable -num=50 10 20 30 test
filename: applog
loglevel: 2
enable: true
num: 50
The non-flag command-line arguments are:
10
20
30
test
```

The nonflag command-line arguments must be provided after giving the flags. The flag -h or --help provides help for the use of the command-line program. This help text will be generated from the flag definitions defined in the program. Let's run the program by providing the -h flag.

```
$ ./ cmdflags -h
Usage of cmdflags:
  -enable
        A boolean value for enabling log options
  -filename string
        File name for the log file (default "logfile")
  -loglevel int
        An integer value for Level (0-4)
  -num int
        An integer value (default 25)
```

Let's now run the program by providing few flags without nonflag arguments:

```
$ ./ cmdflags -filename=applog -loglevel=1
filename: applog
loglevel: 1
enable: false
num: 25
```

110

If the user does not provide values for flags, the default values will be taken for the same.

5-3. Logging Go Programs

Problem

You would like to implement logging for your Go programs.

Solution

The standard library package log provides a basic infrastructure for logging that can be used for logging your Go programs.

How It Works

Although there are many third-party packages available for logging, the standard library package log should be your choice of package if you want to stay with the standard library or use a simple package. The package log allows you to write log messages into all the standard output devices that support the io.Writer interface. The struct type log.Logger is the major component in the package log, which provides several methods for logging that also support formatting log data.

To work with package log, you must add it to the list of imports:

```
import (
        "log"
)
```

Example: A Basic Logger

Listing 5-4 shows an example program that provides a basic logging implementation using log.Logger type. The log messages are categorized as *Trace*, *Information*, *Warning* and *Error*, and four log.Logger objects are used for each log category.

Listing 5-4. A Basic Logging Implementation with Categorized Logging for Trace, Information, Warning, and Error Messages

```
package main

import (
        "errors"
        "io"
        "io/ioutil"
        "log"
        "os"
)

// Package level variables, which are pointers to log.Logger.
 var (
        Trace    *log.Logger
        Info     *log.Logger
```

111

```go
        Warning *log.Logger
        Error   *log.Logger
)

// initLog initializes log.Logger objects
func initLog(
        traceHandle io.Writer,
        infoHandle io.Writer,
        warningHandle io.Writer,
        errorHandle io.Writer) {

        // Flags for defineing the logging properties, to log.New
        flag := log.Ldate | log.Ltime | log.Lshortfile

        // Create log.Logger objects
        Trace = log.New(traceHandle, "TRACE: ", flag)
        Info = log.New(infoHandle, "INFO: ", flag)
        Warning = log.New(warningHandle, "WARNING: ", flag)
        Error = log.New(errorHandle, "ERROR: ", flag)

}

func main() {
        initLog(ioutil.Discard, os.Stdout, os.Stdout, os.Stderr)
        Trace.Println("Main started")
        loop()
        err := errors.New("Sample Error")
        Error.Println(err.Error())
        Trace.Println("Main completed")
}
func loop() {
        Trace.Println("Loop started")
        for i := 0; i < 10; i++ {
                Info.Println("Counter value is:", i)
        }
        Warning.Println("The counter variable is not being used")
        Trace.Println("Loop completed")
}
```

Four pointers to type log.Logger are declared for categorized logging for *Trace, Information, Warning,* and *Error*. The log.Logger objects are created by calling the function initLog that receives arguments of interface io.Writer to set the destination of logging messages.

```go
// Package level variables, which are pointers to log.Logger.
var (
        Trace   *log.Logger
        Info    *log.Logger
        Warning *log.Logger
        Error   *log.Logger
)
```

```
// initLog initializes log.Logger objects
func initLog(
        traceHandle io.Writer,
        infoHandle io.Writer,
        warningHandle io.Writer,
        errorHandle io.Writer) {

        // Flags for defining the logging properties, to log.New
        flag := log.Ldate | log.Ltime | log.Lshortfile

        // Create log.Logger objects
        Trace = log.New(traceHandle, "TRACE: ", flag)
        Info = log.New(infoHandle, "INFO: ", flag)
        Warning = log.New(warningHandle, "WARNING: ", flag)
        Error = log.New(errorHandle, "ERROR: ", flag)

}
```

The function log.New creates a new log.Logger. In the function New, the first parameter sets the destination of the log data, the second parameter sets a prefix that appears at the beginning of each generated log line, and the third parameter defines the logging properties. The given logging properties provide date, time, and a short file name in the log data. The log data can be written to any destination that supports the interface io.Writer. The function initLog is invoked from the function main.

```
initLog(ioutil.Discard, os.Stdout, os.Stdout, os.Stderr)
```

The ioutil.Discard is given to the destination for *Trace*, which is a null device so that all log write calls for this destination will succeed without doing anything. The os.Stdout is given to the destination for both *Information* and *Warning* so that all log write calls for this destination will appear in the console window. The os.Stderr is given to the destination for *Error* so that all log write calls for this destination will appear in the console window as standard errors. In this example program, Logger objects for *Trace*, *Information*, *Warning*, and *Error* are used for logging messages. Because the destination of *Trace* is configured as ioutil.Discard, the log data will not appear in the console window.

You should see the output similar to the following:

```
INFO: 2016/06/11 18:47:28 main.go:48: Counter value is: 0
INFO: 2016/06/11 18:47:28 main.go:48: Counter value is: 1
INFO: 2016/06/11 18:47:28 main.go:48: Counter value is: 2
INFO: 2016/06/11 18:47:28 main.go:48: Counter value is: 3
INFO: 2016/06/11 18:47:28 main.go:48: Counter value is: 4
INFO: 2016/06/11 18:47:28 main.go:48: Counter value is: 5
INFO: 2016/06/11 18:47:28 main.go:48: Counter value is: 6
INFO: 2016/06/11 18:47:28 main.go:48: Counter value is: 7
INFO: 2016/06/11 18:47:28 main.go:48: Counter value is: 8
INFO: 2016/06/11 18:47:28 main.go:48: Counter value is: 9
WARNING: 2016/06/11 18:47:28 main.go:50: The counter variable is not being used
ERROR: 2016/06/11 18:47:28 main.go:42: Sample Error
```

Example: A Configurable Logger

In the preceding example, the log data is written into the Stdout and Stderr interfaces. When you develop real-world applications, however, you might use *persistent storage* as the destination for log data. You might also require a configurable option for specifying the log level to *Trace*, *Information*, *Warning*, or *Error*. This enables you to change the log level at any time. For example, you might set the log level to *Trace*, but you might not need the *Trace* level log when you move your application into production.

Listing 5-5 shows an example program that provides a logging infrastructure that lets you configure the log level to *Trace*, *Information*, *Warning*, or *Error*, and then writes log data into a text file. The option for log level can be configured using a command-line flag.

Listing 5-5. A Logging Infrastructure with an Option to Set the Log Level and Write Log Data into a Text File, in logger.go

```go
package main

import (
        "io"
        "io/ioutil"
        "log"
        "os"
)

const (
        // UNSPECIFIED logs nothing
        UNSPECIFIED Level = iota // 0 :
        // TRACE logs everything
        TRACE // 1
        // INFO logs Info, Warnings and Errors
        INFO // 2
        // WARNING logs Warning and Errors
        WARNING // 3
        // ERROR just logs Errors
        ERROR // 4
)

// Level holds the log level.
type Level int

// Package level variables, which are pointers to log.Logger.
var (
        Trace   *log.Logger
        Info    *log.Logger
        Warning *log.Logger
        Error   *log.Logger
)

// initLog initializes log.Logger objects
func initLog(
        traceHandle io.Writer,
        infoHandle io.Writer,
        warningHandle io.Writer,
```

```go
        errorHandle io.Writer,
        isFlag bool) {

        // Flags for defining the logging properties, to log.New
        flag := 0
        if isFlag {
                flag = log.Ldate | log.Ltime | log.Lshortfile
        }

        // Create log.Logger objects.
        Trace = log.New(traceHandle, "TRACE: ", flag)
        Info = log.New(infoHandle, "INFO: ", flag)
        Warning = log.New(warningHandle, "WARNING: ", flag)
        Error = log.New(errorHandle, "ERROR: ", flag)

}


// SetLogLevel sets the logging level preference
func SetLogLevel(level Level) {

        // Creates os.*File, which has implemented io.Writer interface
        f, err := os.OpenFile("logs.txt", os.O_RDWR|os.O_CREATE|os.O_APPEND, 0666)
        if err != nil {
                log.Fatalf("Error opening log file: %s", err.Error())
        }

        // Calls function initLog by specifying log level preference.
        switch level {
        case TRACE:
                initLog(f, f, f, f, true)
                return

        case INFO:
                initLog(ioutil.Discard, f, f, f, true)
                return

        case WARNING:
                initLog(ioutil.Discard, ioutil.Discard, f, f, true)
                return
        case ERROR:
                initLog(ioutil.Discard, ioutil.Discard, ioutil.Discard, f, true)
                return

        default:
                initLog(ioutil.Discard, ioutil.Discard, ioutil.Discard, ioutil.Discard,
                false)
                f.Close()
                return

        }
}
```

The `logger.go` source provides two functions: `initLog` and `SetLogLevel`. The function `SetLogLevel` creates a file object by calling the function `OpenFile` of the standard library package `os`, then calling the function `initLog` to initialize `Logger` objects by providing the log level preference. It opens the named file with the specified flag. The function `initLog` creates the `Logger` objects based on the log preferences provided by the function.

Constant variables are declared for specifying the log level preference at various levels. The identifier `iota` is used to construct a set of related constants; here it is used for organizing the available log levels in the application, which produces an autoincremented `integer` constant. It resets the value to 0 whenever the `const` appears in the source and increments after each value within a constant declaration.

```
const (
        // UNSPECIFIED logs nothing
        UNSPECIFIED Level = iota // 0 :
        // TRACE logs everything
        TRACE // 1
        // INFO logs Info, Warnings and Errors
        INFO // 2
        // WARNING logs Warning and Errors
        WARNING // 3
        // ERROR just logs Errors
        ERROR // 4
)

// Level holds the log level.
type Level int
```

In many programming languages, *enumerations* or simply *enums*, are the idiomatic way for declaring constants with similar behavior. Unlike some programming languages, Go does not support a keyword for declaring enumerations. The idiomatic way for declaring enumerations in Go is to declare constants with `iota`. Here a type named `Level` with type `int` is used for specifying the type for constants. The value of the constant `UNSPECIFIED` resets to 0, then it autoincrements for each constant declaration, 1 for TRACE, 2 for INFO, and so on.

Listing 5-6 shows a Go source file that uses the logging infrastructure implemented in `logger.go` (see Listing 5-5).

Listing 5-6. Logging Demo in `main.go`, Using `logger.go`

```
package main

import (
        "errors"
        "flag"
)

func main() {
        // Parse log level from command line
        logLevel := flag.Int("loglevel", 0, "an integer value (0-4)")
        flag.Parse()
        // Calling the SetLogLevel with the command-line argument
        SetLogLevel(Level(*logLevel))
        Trace.Println("Main started")
        loop()
```

```
        err := errors.New("Sample Error")
        Error.Println(err.Error())
        Trace.Println("Main completed")
}
// A simple function for the logging demo
func loop() {
        Trace.Println("Loop started")
        for i := 0; i < 10; i++ {
                Info.Println("Counter value is:", i)
        }
        Warning.Println("The counter variable is not being used")
        Trace.Println("Loop completed")
}
```

In the function main, the value for log level preference is accepted from command-line flag and the function SetLogLevel of logger.go is called to create the Logger objects by specifying the log level preference.

```
logLevel := flag.Int("loglevel", 0, "an integer value (0-4)")
flag.Parse()
// Calling the SetLogLevel with the command-line argument
SetLogLevel(Level(*logLevel))
```

In this example, logging is performed using Logger objects for *Trace, Information, Warning,* and *Error.* Let's run the program by providing log level preference to *Trace* (value 1).

```
$ go build
$ ./log -loglevel=1
```

This writes log data into the text file named logs.txt. The log level to *Trace* writes log data for Trace, Information, Warning, and Error. You should see log data similar to the following in logs.txt.

```
TRACE: 2016/06/13 22:04:28 main.go:14: Main started
TRACE: 2016/06/13 22:04:28 main.go:23: Loop started
INFO: 2016/06/13 22:04:28 main.go:25: Counter value is: 0
INFO: 2016/06/13 22:04:28 main.go:25: Counter value is: 1
INFO: 2016/06/13 22:04:28 main.go:25: Counter value is: 2
INFO: 2016/06/13 22:04:28 main.go:25: Counter value is: 3
INFO: 2016/06/13 22:04:28 main.go:25: Counter value is: 4
INFO: 2016/06/13 22:04:28 main.go:25: Counter value is: 5
INFO: 2016/06/13 22:04:28 main.go:25: Counter value is: 6
INFO: 2016/06/13 22:04:28 main.go:25: Counter value is: 7
INFO: 2016/06/13 22:04:28 main.go:25: Counter value is: 8
INFO: 2016/06/13 22:04:28 main.go:25: Counter value is: 9
WARNING: 2016/06/13 22:04:28 main.go:27: The counter variable is not being used
TRACE: 2016/06/13 22:04:28 main.go:28: Loop completed
ERROR: 2016/06/13 22:04:28 main.go:17: Sample Error
TRACE: 2016/06/13 22:04:28 main.go:18: Main completed
```

Let's run the program by specifying the log level to *Information* (value of loglevel to 2).

```
$ ./log -loglevel=2
```

117

You should see log data similar to the following appended into `logs.txt`.

```
INFO: 2016/06/13 22:13:25 main.go:25: Counter value is: 0
INFO: 2016/06/13 22:13:25 main.go:25: Counter value is: 1
INFO: 2016/06/13 22:13:25 main.go:25: Counter value is: 2
INFO: 2016/06/13 22:13:25 main.go:25: Counter value is: 3
INFO: 2016/06/13 22:13:25 main.go:25: Counter value is: 4
INFO: 2016/06/13 22:13:25 main.go:25: Counter value is: 5
INFO: 2016/06/13 22:13:25 main.go:25: Counter value is: 6
INFO: 2016/06/13 22:13:25 main.go:25: Counter value is: 7
INFO: 2016/06/13 22:13:25 main.go:25: Counter value is: 8
INFO: 2016/06/13 22:13:25 main.go:25: Counter value is: 9
WARNING: 2016/06/13 22:13:25 main.go:27: The counter variable is not being used
ERROR: 2016/06/13 22:13:25 main.go:17: Sample Error
```

Because we specified the log level to *Information*, log data for *Information*, *Warning*, and *Error* are appended into the output file `logs.txt`, but log data for *Trace* is written into a null device.

5-4. Archiving Files in Tar and Zip Formats

Problem

You would like to write and read files in tar and zip formats.

Solution

The standard library package `archive` that comes with two sub packages - package `archive/tar` and package `archive/zip,` is used to write and read archive files in tar and zip formats.

How It Works

The standard library package `archive` provides support for archiving files in two file formats. To support archiving capability in both tar and zip formats, it provides two separate packages: `archive/tar` and `archive/zip`. The `archive/tar` and `archive/zip` packages provide support for reading and writing in tar and zip formats, respectively.

io.Writer and io.Reader Interfaces

Let's take a look into the `io.Writer` and `io.Reader` interfaces before diving into writing and reading archive files. The standard library package `io` provides basic interfaces for performing I/O operations. The `Writer` interface of package `io` provides an abstraction for write operations. The `Writer` interface declares a method called `Write` that accepts a value of `byte slice` as an argument.

Here is the declation of interface `io.Writer`:

```
type Writer interface {
        Write(p []byte) (n int, err error)
}
```

Here is the Go documentation for the Write method:

Write writes len(p) bytes from p to the underlying data stream. It returns the number of bytes written from p (0 <= n <= len(p)) and any error encountered that caused the write to stop early. Write must return a non-nil error if it returns n < len(p). Write must not modify the slice data, even temporarily.

The Reader interface of package io provides an abstraction for read operations. The Reader interface declares a method called Read that accepts a value of byte slice as an argument.

Here is the declaration of io.Reader interface:

```
type Reader interface {
        Read(p []byte) (n int, err error)
}
```

Here is the Go documentation about the Read method:

Read reads up to len(p) bytes into p. It returns the number of bytes read (0 <= n <= len(p)) and any error encountered. Even if Read returns n < len(p), it may use all of p as scratch space during the call. If some data is available but not len(p) bytes, Read conventionally returns what is available instead of waiting for more. When Read encounters an error or end-of-file condition after successfully reading n > 0 bytes, it returns the number of bytes read. It may return the (non-nil) error from the same call or return the error (and n == 0) from a subsequent call. An instance of this general case is that a Reader returning a non-zero number of bytes at the end of the input stream may return either err == EOF or err == nil. The next Read should return 0, EOF.

You will leverage both io.Writer and io.Reader interfaces when you work with writing and reading archive files.

Writing and Reading Tar Files

The package archive/tar is used to write and read tar files. Tar (Tape ARchive) files are archive files used in Unix-based systems. A tar archive has the file suffix .tar. The tar Unix shell command creates a single archive file from a number of specified files or extracts the files from an archive file. To work with the package archive/tar, you must add it to the list of imports:

```
import (
        "archive/tar"
)
```

The struct type tar.Writer is used to write files to the tar file. The Writer object is created by calling the function tar.NewWriter that accepts a value of type io.Writer, to which you can pass the tar archive file as an object of type os.File to be written to the provided tar file. The struct type os.File has implemented the io.Writer interface so that it can be used as the argument to call function tar.NewWriter.

The struct type tar.Reader is used to read files from the tar file. The Reader object is created by calling the function tar.NewReader that accepts a value of type io.Reader as an argument to which you can pass the tar archive file as an object of type os.File to read the contents of the tar file. The struct type os.File has implemented the interface io.Reader so that it can be used as the argument to call the function tar.NewReader.

Listing 5-7 shows an example program that demonstrates how to archive files by writing two files into a tar file and later reading the tar file by iterating through tar file and reading the contents of each file.

Listing 5-7. Writing and Reading a Tar File

```go
package main

import (
        "archive/tar"
        "fmt"
        "io"
        "log"
        "os"
)

// addToArchive writes a given file into a .tar file
// Returns nill if the operation is succeeded
func addToArchive(filename string, tw *tar.Writer) error {
        // Open the file to archive into tar file.
        file, err := os.Open(filename)
        if err != nil {
                return err
        }
        defer file.Close()
        // Get the FileInfo struct that describes the file.
        fileinfo, err := file.Stat()
        // Create a pointer to tar.Header struct
        hdr := &tar.Header{
                ModTime: fileinfo.ModTime(),             // modified time
                Name:    filename,                       // name of header
                Size:    fileinfo.Size(),                // length in bytes
                Mode:    int64(fileinfo.Mode().Perm()),  // permission and mode bits
        }
        // WriteHeader writes tar.Header and prepares to accept the file's contents.
        if err := tw.WriteHeader(hdr); err != nil {
                return err
        }
        // Write the file contents to the tar file.
        copied, err := io.Copy(tw, file)
        if err != nil {
                return err
        }
        // Check the size of copied file with the source file.
        if copied < fileinfo.Size() {
                return fmt.Errorf("Size of the copied file doesn't match with source file
                %s: %s", filename, err)
        }
        return nil
}

// archiveFiles archives a group of given files into a tar file.
func archiveFiles(files []string, archive string) error {
        // Flags for open the tar file.
        flags := os.O_WRONLY | os.O_CREATE | os.O_TRUNC
        // Open the tar file
```

```go
	file, err := os.OpenFile(archive, flags, 0644)
	if err != nil {
		return err
	}
	defer file.Close()
	// Creates a new Writer writing to given file object.
	// Writer provides sequential writing of a tar archive in POSIX.1 format.
	tw := tar.NewWriter(file)
	defer tw.Close()
	// Iterate through the files to write each file into the tar file.
	for _, filename := range files {
		// Write the file into tar file.
		if err := addToArchive(filename, tw); err != nil {
			return err
		}
	}
	return nil
}

// readArchive reads the file contents from tar file.
func readArchive(archive string) error {
	// Open the tar archive file.
	file, err := os.Open(archive)
	if err != nil {
		return err
	}
	defer file.Close()
	// Create the tar.Reader to read the tar archive.
	// A Reader provides sequential access to the contents of a tar archive.
	tr := tar.NewReader(file)
	// Iterate through the files in the tar archive.
	for {
		hdr, err := tr.Next()
		if err == io.EOF {
			// End of tar archive
			break
		}
		if err != nil {
			return err
		}
		size := hdr.Size
		contents := make([]byte, size)
		read, err := io.ReadFull(tr, contents)
		// Check the size of file contents
		if int64(read) != size {
			return fmt.Errorf("Size of the opened file doesn't match with the
			file %s", hdr.Name)
		}
		fmt.Printf("Contents of the file %s:\n", hdr.Name)
		// Writing the file contents into Stdout.
		fmt.Fprintf(os.Stdout, "\n%s", contents)
```

```
        }
        return nil
}

func main() {
        // Name of the tar file
        archive := "source.tar"
        // Files to be archived in tar format
        files := []string{"main.go", "readme.txt"}
        // Archive files into tar format
        err := archiveFiles(files, archive)
        if err != nil {
                log.Fatalf("Error while writing to tar file:%s", err)
        }
        // Archiving is successful.
        fmt.Println("The tar file source.tar has been created")
        // Read the file contents of tar file
        err = readArchive(archive)
        if err != nil {
                log.Fatalf("Error while reading the tar file:%s", err)
        }
}
```

In the function main, a variable archive is declared to provide the file name for the tar file. A variable files is declared to provide the file names as string slice to write the provided files to the tar file. A function archiveFiles is called to archive the file and another function readArchive is called to read the contents of the tar file, which is written using the function archiveFiles.

```
func main() {
        // Name of the tar file
        archive := "source.tar"
        // Files to be archived in tar format
        files := []string{"main.go", "readme.txt"}
        // Archive files into tar format
        err := archiveFiles(files, archive)
        if err != nil {
                log.Fatalf("Error while writing to tar file:%s", err)
        }
        // Archiving is successful.
        fmt.Println("The tar file source.tar has been created")
        // Read the file contents of tar file
        err = readArchive(archive)
        if err != nil {
                log.Fatalf("Error while reading the tar file:%s", err)
        }
}
```

Inside the function archiveFiles, an os.File object is created by opening the tar file and then creating a new tar.Writer by passing a File object to the function tar.NewWriter. The Writer is used to write files to the tar file.

```
// Open the tar file
file, err := os.OpenFile(archive, flags, 0644)
if err != nil {
        return err
}
defer file.Close()
// Create a new Writer writing to given file object.
// Writer provides sequential writing of a tar archive in POSIX.1 format.
tw := tar.NewWriter(file)
```

To write a collection of files to the tar file, you iterate through the variable files, which holds the file names as a value of string slice, and calls the function addToArchive that writes the provided file to the tar file.

```
for _, filename := range files {
        // Write the file into tar file.
        if err := addToArchive(filename, tw); err != nil {
                return err
        }
}
```

The function addToArchive writes the provided file to the tar file using tar.Writer. To write a new file to the tar file, the function WriteHeader of the tar.Writer object is called by providing the value of tar.Header. It then calls io.Copy to write the file's data to the tar file. A value of tar.Header contains metadata of a file that is being written to the tar file.

```
file, err := os.Open(filename)
if err != nil {
        return err
}
defer file.Close()
// Get the FileInfo struct that describes the file.
fileinfo, err := file.Stat()
// Create a pointer to tar.Header struct
hdr := &tar.Header{
        ModTime: fileinfo.ModTime(),            // modified time
        Name:    filename,                      // name of header
        Size:    fileinfo.Size(),               // length in bytes
        Mode:    int64(fileinfo.Mode().Perm()), // permission and mode bits
}
// WriteHeader writes tar.Header and prepares to accept the file's contents.
if err := tw.WriteHeader(hdr); err != nil {
        return err
}
// Write the file contents to the tar file.
copied, err := io.Copy(tw, file)
```

The function readArchive is used to read the file contents of the tar file. A pointer to tar.Reader is used to read the tar file and it is created by calling the function tar.NewReader and passing a value of os.File.

```
// Open the tar archive file.
file, err := os.Open(archive)
if err != nil {
        return err
}
defer file.Close()
// Create the tar.Reader to read the tar archive.
// A Reader provides sequential access to the contents of a tar archive.
tr := tar.NewReader(file)
```

You iterate through the files in the tar file using tar.Reader and read the contents that write into os.Stdout. The function Next of tar.Reader advances to the next entry in the file and returns an error value of io.EOF at the end of the file. When the call to function Next returns io.EOF, you can exit from the read operation because it indicates that you went through all the file contents and reached the end of the file.

```
// Iterate through the files in the tar archive.
for {
        hdr, err := tr.Next()
        if err == io.EOF {
                // End of tar archive
                fmt.Println("end")
                break
        }
        if err != nil {
                return err
        }
        size := hdr.Size
        contents := make([]byte, size)
        read, err := io.ReadFull(tr, contents)
        // Check the size of file contents
        if int64(read) != size {
                return fmt.Errorf("Size of the opened file doesn't match with the file %s",
                hdr.Name)
        }
        // hdr.Name returns the file name.
        fmt.Printf("Contents of the file %s:\n", hdr.Name)
        // Writing the file contents into Stdout.
        fmt.Fprintf(os.Stdout, "\n%s", contents)
}
```

In this example, you are trying to archive the source file main.go and readme.txt into the source.tar file. When you run the program you should see the archive file source.tar in the application directory as the output for the write operation and the contents of file main.go and readme.txt as the output for the read operation.

Writing and Reading Zip Files

The archive/zip package is used to write and read zip files. To work with package archive/zip, you must add it to the list of imports:

```
import (
        "archive/zip"
)
```

124

Package archive/zip provides similar kind of functionality to package archive/tar and the process for writing and reading zip files with package zip is similar to the process for tar files. The struct type zip.Writer is used to write files to the zip file. A new zip.Writer is created by calling the function zip.NewWriter that accepts a value of type io.Writer.

The struct type zip.ReadCloser can be used to read files from the zip file. The Reader object can be created by calling the function zip.OpenReader, which will open the zip file given by name and return a zip.ReadCloser. The package zip also provides a type Reader; a new Reader is created by calling the function zip.NewReader.

Listing 5-8 shows an example program that demonstrates how to archive files by writing two files into a zip file and later reading the zip file by iterating through the files contained in the zip file and reading the contents of each file.

Listing 5-8. Writing and Reading a Zip File

```
package main

import (
        "archive/zip"
        "fmt"
        "io"
        "log"
        "os"
)

// addToArchive writes a given file into a zip file.
func addToArchive(filename string, zw *zip.Writer) error {
        // Open the given file to archive into a zip file.
        file, err := os.Open(filename)
        if err != nil {
                return err
        }
        defer file.Close()
        // Create adds a file to the zip file using the given name/
        // Create returns a io.Writer to which the file contents should be written.
        wr, err := zw.Create(filename)
        if err != nil {
                return err
        }
        // Write the file contents to the zip file.
        if _, err := io.Copy(wr, file); err != nil {
                return err
        }
        return nil
}

// archiveFiles archives a group of given files into a zip file.
func archiveFiles(files []string, archive string) error {
        flags := os.O_WRONLY | os.O_CREATE | os.O_TRUNC
        // Open the tar file
        file, err := os.OpenFile(archive, flags, 0644)
        if err != nil {
                return err
        }
```

125

```go
        defer file.Close()
        // Create zip.Writer that implements a zip file writer.
        zw := zip.NewWriter(file)
        defer zw.Close()
        // Iterate through the files to write each file into the zip file.
        for _, filename := range files {
                // Write the file into tar file.
                if err := addToArchive(filename, zw); err != nil {
                        return err
                }
        }
        return nil
}

// readArchive reads the file contents from tar file.
func readArchive(archive string) error {
        // Open the zip file specified by name and return a ReadCloser.
        rc, err := zip.OpenReader(archive)
        if err != nil {
                return err
        }
        defer rc.Close()
        // Iterate through the files in the zip file to read the file contents.
        for _, file := range rc.File {
                frc, err := file.Open()
                if err != nil {
                        return err
                }
                defer frc.Close()
                fmt.Fprintf(os.Stdout, "Contents of the file %s:\n", file.Name)
                // Write the contents into Stdout
                copied, err := io.Copy(os.Stdout, frc)
                if err != nil {
                        return err
                }
                // Check the size of the file.
                if uint64(copied) != file.UncompressedSize64 {
                        return fmt.Errorf("Length of the file contents doesn't match with
                        the file %s", file.Name)
                }
                fmt.Println()
        }
        return nil
}

func main() {
        // Name of the zip file
        archive := "source.zip"
        // Files to be archived in zip format.
        files := []string{"main.go", "readme.txt"}
        // Archive files into zip format.
```

```
        err := archiveFiles(files, archive)
        if err != nil {
                log.Fatalf("Error while writing to zip file:%s\n", err)
        }
        // Read the file contents of tar file.
        err = readArchive(archive)
        if err != nil {
                log.Fatalf("Error while reading the zip file:%s\n", err)

        }
}
```

This example is similar to Listing 8-7 with just a few differences in the implementation for writing and reading files for tar and zip formats. When you run the program you should see the archive file source.zip in the application directory as the output for the write operation and the contents of files main.go and readme.txt as the output for the read operation.

CHAPTER 6

Data Persistence

When you build real-world applications, you might need to persist your application data into persistent storage. You can define the data model of your application using various Go types, especially structs. In most use cases, you might need to persist your application data into databases. This chapter shows you how to persist application data into databases such as MongoDB, RethinkDB, InfluxDB, and PostgreSQL. MongoDB is a popular NoSQL database that is widely used for many modern applications. RethinkDB is another NoSQL database that comes with real-time capabilities that allow you to build real-time web applications. Time series databases are becoming the next big thing in data management technologies, and hence this chapter includes recipes for working with InfluxDB, a popular time series database written in Go. This chapter also provides recipes for working with traditional SQL databases.

6-1. Persisting Data with MongoDB

Problem

You would like to work with MongoDB as the database for your Go applications.

Solution

The third-party package mgo provides a full-featured MongoDB driver for Go, which allows you to work with MongoDB from your Go applications. The mgo driver has been widely used for production Go applications.

How It Works

MongoDB is a popular NoSQL database that is widely used as the database for a variety of modern applications, including web and mobile applications. MongoDB is an open source document database that provides high performance, high availability, and automatic scaling. MongoDB stores data as documents in a binary representation called Binary JSON (BSON). In short, MongoDB is the data store for BSON documents. A collection of BSON documents is analogous to a database table in a relational database, and a single document in a collection is analogous to a row of a table in a relational database, if you want to compare MongoDB with a relational database management system (RDBMS). Because MongoDB stores data as documents, you can't compare a collection with a table. For example, you can have embedded documents within a document to implement a parent–child relationship, whereas you might keep the data in two separate tables by specifying a foreign key in a relational database. Even NoSQL databases don't support constraints in its data model. Like most of the NoSQL databases, MongoDB is a schemaless database, which means that the database can have varying sets of fields in each document inside the collections and can also have different types for each field. To get more details on MongoDB, along with instructions for download and install, check out the MongoDB web site at https://www.mongodb.org/.

© Shiju Varghese 2016
S. Varghese, *Go Recipes*, DOI 10.1007/978-1-4842-1188-5_6

■ **Note**   A NoSQL (often interpreted as not only SQL) database provides a mechanism for storage and retrieval of data, which provides an approach to a design data model other than the tabular relations used in relational databases. A NoSQL database is designed to cope with modern application development challenges such as dealing with large volumes of data with easier scalability and better performance. When compared to relational databases, a NoSQL database can provide high performance, better scalability, and cheaper storage. NoSQL databases are available in different types: document databases, graph stores, key/value stores, and wide-column stores.

The third-party package mgo, pronounced "mango," provides support for working with MongoDB database, and its subpackage bson does the implementation for BSON specification to work with BSON documents. The values of Go types such as slice, map, and struct can be persisted into MongoDB. When a write operation is performed onto MongoDB, the package mgo automatically serializes the values of Go types into BSON documents. In most use cases, you can define your data model by using structs and perform the CRUD operations against it.

Installing mgo

To install the package mgo, run the following command:

```
go get gopkg.in/mgo.v2
```

This will fetch package mgo and its subpackage bson. To work with the mgo package, you must add gopkg.in/mgo.v2 to the list of imports.

```
import "gopkg.in/mgo.v2"
```

If you want to use the bson package, you must add gopkg.in/mgo.v2/bson to the list of imports:

```
import (
        "gopkg.in/mgo.v2"
        "gopkg.in/mgo.v2/bson"
)
```

Connecting to MongoDB

To perform CRUD operations with MongoDB, you first obtain a MongoDB *session* using the function Dial as shown here:

```
session, err := mgo.Dial("localhost")
```

The function Dial establishes a connection to the cluster of MongoDB servers identified by the url parameter and returns a pointer to mgo.Session, which is used to perform CRUD operations against the MongoDB database. The function Dial supports connection with a cluster of servers as shown here:

```
session, err := mgo.Dial("server1.mongolab.com,server2.mongolab.com")
```

You can also use the function `DialWithInfo` to establish connection to one or a cluster of servers, which returns `mgo.Session`. This function allows you to pass customized information to the server using type `mgo. DialInfo` as shown here:

```
mongoDialInfo := &mgo.DialInfo{
        Addrs:    []string{"localhost"},
        Timeout:  60 * time.Second,
        Database: "bookmarkdb",
        Username: "shijuvar",
        Password: "password123",
    }

 session, err := mgo.DialWithInfo(mongoDialInfo)
```

All session methods are concurrency-safe so that you can call them from multiple goroutines. The read operations are performed based on the consistency mode specified via `mgo.Session`. The method `SetMode` of a session is used to change the consistency mode for the session object. There are three types of available consistency modes: Eventual, Monotonic, and Strong. If you haven't explicitly specified the consistency mode the default mode is Strong. In the Strong consistency mode, reads and writes will always be made to the primary server using a unique connection so that they are fully consistent, ordered, and observing the most up-to-date data.

Working with Collections

MongoDB stores data as documents, which are organized into collections. The CRUD operations are performed against a collection, which is mapped to the type `mgo.Collection` in the package mgo. The method `C` of type `mgo.Database` is used to create an `mgo.Collection` object. The `mgo.Database` type represents the named database of MongoDB, which is created by calling the method `DB` of type `mgo.Session`.

The following statement creates a pointer to `mgo.Collection` that represents the MongoDB collection named "bookmarks" in the "bookmarkdb" database.

```
collection := session.DB("bookmarkdb").C("bookmarks")
```

Performing CRUD Operations

Once you obtain a `Session`, you can perform CRUD operations against a `Collection` value. Let's write an example program to demonstrate persistence and read operations against a `Collection` value. First, we write the example program in two source files: bookmark_store.go and main.go. Listing 6-1 shows the source of bookmark_store.go file that contains a struct named Bookmark for defining the data model, and a struct type BookmarkStore that provides persistence logic for performing CRUD operations.

Listing 6-1. Data Model and Persistence Logic in bookmark_store.go

```
package main

import (
        "time"

        "gopkg.in/mgo.v2"
```

```
        "gopkg.in/mgo.v2/bson"
)

// Bookmark type represents the metadata of a bookmark.
type Bookmark struct {
        ID                        bson.ObjectId `bson:"_id,omitempty"`
        Name, Description, Location string
        Priority                  int // Priority (1 -5)
        CreatedOn          time.Time
        Tags                      []string
}

// BookmarkStore provides CRUD operations against the collection "bookmarks".
type BookmarkStore struct {
        C *mgo.Collection
}

// Create inserts the value of struct Bookmark into collection.
func (store BookmarkStore) Create(b *Bookmark) error {
        // Assign a new bson.ObjectId
        b.ID = bson.NewObjectId()
        err := store.C.Insert(b)
        return err
}

//Update modifies an existing value of a collection.
func (store BookmarkStore) Update(b Bookmark) error {
        // partial update on MogoDB
        err := store.C.Update(bson.M{"_id": b.ID},
                bson.M{"$set": bson.M{
                        "name":        b.Name,
                        "description": b.Description,
                        "location":    b.Location,
                        "priority":    b.Priority,
                        "tags":        b.Tags,
                }})
        return err
}

// Delete removes an existing value from the collection.
func (store BookmarkStore) Delete(id string) error {
        err := store.C.Remove(bson.M{"_id": bson.ObjectIdHex(id)})
        return err
}

// GetAll returns all documents from the collection.
func (store BookmarkStore) GetAll() []Bookmark {
        var b []Bookmark
        iter := store.C.Find(nil).Sort("priority", "-createdon").Iter()
        result := Bookmark{}
        for iter.Next(&result) {
```

```
                    b = append(b, result)
        }
        return b
}


// GetByID returns single document from the collection.
func (store BookmarkStore) GetByID(id string) (Bookmark, error) {
        var b Bookmark
        err := store.C.FindId(bson.ObjectIdHex(id)).One(&b)
        return b, err
}


// GetByTag returns all documents from the collection filtering by tags.
func (store BookmarkStore) GetByTag(tags []string) []Bookmark {
        var b []Bookmark
        iter := store.C.Find(bson.M{"tags": bson.M{"$in": tags}}).Sort("priority",
"-createdon").Iter()
        result := Bookmark{}
        for iter.Next(&result) {
                b = append(b, result)
        }
        return b
}
```

A struct named Bookmark is declared as the data model for the example program.

```
type Bookmark struct {
        ID                        bson.ObjectId `bson:"_id,omitempty"`
        Name, Description, Location string
        Priority                  int // Priority (1 -5)
        CreatedOn                 time.Time
        Tags                      []string
}
```

The type of field ID is specified as bson.ObjectId which is a 12-byte value, and mapped this field with _id in BSON representation. When you insert a document you need to provide a unique value of ObjectId to the field _id that acts as a primary key. If a document does not contain the field _id in its root level (top-level field) during an insert operation, the mgo driver adds the field _id by providing a unique value of ObjectId.

A struct named BookmarkStore is declared for providing persistence logic that uses the struct Bookmark; for insert and update operations it accepts a value of it, and for read operations it returns values of the same type. The struct BookmarkStore has a field C with type mgo.Collection. All CRUD operations are performed by accessing the field C. From the source file main.go (see Listing 6-2), the Collection object is provided to BookmarkStore value and performs CRUD operations by accessing the methods of BookmarkStore.

```
type BookmarkStore struct {
        C *mgo.Collection
}
```

Create a Document in a Collection

The method Create of BookmarkStore is used to insert values into the MongoDB collection named "bookmarks". It accepts a pointer to Bookmark and inserts the value of Bookmark into the MongoDB collection using the Insert method of Collection. When an insert operation is performed, the package mgo automatically encodes the values of Go types into BSON specification.

```go
func (store BookmarkStore) Create(b *Bookmark) error {
        // Assign a new bson.ObjectId
        b.ID = bson.NewObjectId()
        err := store.C.Insert(b)
        return err
}
```

A unique value of ObjectId is generated by calling the function bson.NewObjectId, and assigning this to the field ID that tags to the field _id in BSON documents. The function Insert of type Collection is used to insert the documents into a collection.

Update a Document in a Collection

The function Update of type Collection is used to update an existing document. The method Update finds a single document from the collection matching with the provided selector document and modifies the document with the values provided. The keyword "$set" is used to perform a partial update on the document.

```go
func (store BookmarkStore) Update(b Bookmark) error {
        // partial update on MogoDB
        err := store.C.Update(bson.M{"_id": b.ID},
                bson.M{"$set": bson.M{
                        "name":        b.Name,
                        "description": b.Description,
                        "location":    b.Location,
                        "priority":    b.Priority,
                        "tags":        b.Tags,
                }})
        return err
}
```

The type bson.M is used for providing values to the method Update of Collection. This type is a convenient alias for the type map with signature of map[string]interface{}, which is useful for dealing with BSON in a native way. Whenever you want to deal with BSON documents in a native way, you can provide the value of bson.M, which is useful for Update, Read, and Delete operations of Collection object.

Delete a Document from a Collection

The Remove function of Collection is used to remove documents from the collection. Here the document is removed for the given id.

```go
func (store BookmarkStore) Delete(id string) error {
        err := store.C.Remove(bson.M{"_id": bson.ObjectIdHex(id)})
        return err
}
```

Read Documents from a Collection

The method GetAll of BookmarkStore returns all documents from the collection. The method Find of Collection is used to query documents from the collection. The method Find returns a pointer to mgo. Query that can later be used to retrieve documents using functions such as One, For, Iter, or Tail.

```go
func (store BookmarkStore) GetAll() []Bookmark {
        var b []Bookmark
        iter := store.C.Find(nil).Sort("priority", "-createdon").Iter()
        result := Bookmark{}
        for iter.Next(&result) {
                b = append(b, result)
        }
        return b
}
```

A nil value is provided as the selector document to the method Find to get all documents from the collection. The resulting mgo.Query value represents the result set that performed against a given selector document. Using the function Sort, the resulting Query value can be used for sorting the document based on the values of fields. Here the sort operation is performed for the field priority in ascending order and createdon in descending order. To sort in descending order, just place "-" as the prefix for field names, as shown here for the field createdon.

```go
iter := store.C.Find(nil).Sort("priority", "-createdon").Iter()
```

The method Iter of Query returns an iterator that is capable of iterating over all the generated results, and the function Next retrieves the next document from the result set.

The method GetByID of BookmarkStore returns a single document for the given id (_id in BSON document). Here the id is provided as string so that it is being converted to bson.ObjectId using the function bson.ObjectIdHex.

```go
func (store BookmarkStore) GetByID(id string) (Bookmark, error) {
        var b Bookmark
        err := store.C.FindId(bson.ObjectIdHex(id)).One(&b)
        return b, err
}
```

In this example, the documents in the Collection are also queried for the given tags as a slice of string, which returns the documents matching with the given tags.

```go
func (store BookmarkStore) GetByTag(tags []string) []Bookmark {
        var b []Bookmark
        iter := store.C.Find(bson.M{"tags": bson.M{"$in": tags}}).Sort("priority",
        "-createdon").Iter()
        result := Bookmark{}
        for iter.Next(&result) {
                b = append(b, result)
        }
        return b
}
```

The query operator $in allows you to filter documents with an expression that matches any value in a list of values. Here the $in operator is used for filtering the documents on the field tag. Here the query returns all documents if any of the given tags matches with the field tags.

Let's reuse the functions of bookmark_store.go to perform CRUD operations against the MongoDB database. Listing 6-2 shows the source file main.go that creates an instance of type BookmarkStore by providing an mgo.Collection value and calling its methods.

Listing 6-2. Perform CRUD Operations on a MongoDB Collection by Using the Type BookmarkStore, in main.go

```go
package main

import (
        "fmt"
        "log"
        "time"

        "gopkg.in/mgo.v2"
)

var store BookmarkStore
var id string

// init will invoke before the function main.
func init() {
        session, err := mgo.DialWithInfo(&mgo.DialInfo{
                Addrs:   []string{"127.0.0.1"},
                Timeout: 60 * time.Second,
        })
        if err != nil {
                log.Fatalf("[MongoDB Session]: %s\n", err)
        }
        collection := session.DB("bookmarkdb").C("bookmarks")

        store = BookmarkStore{
                C: collection,
        }
}

// Create and update documents.
func createUpdate() {
        bookmark := Bookmark{
                Name:        "mgo",
                Description: "Go driver for MongoDB",
                Location:    "https://github.com/go-mgo/mgo",
                Priority:    2,
                CreatedOn:   time.Now(),
                Tags:        []string{"go", "nosql", "mongodb"},
        }
        // Insert a new document.
        if err := store.Create(&bookmark); err != nil {
                log.Fatalf("[Create]: %s\n", err)
        }
```

```go
        id = bookmark.ID.Hex()
        fmt.Printf("New bookmark has been inserted with ID: %s\n", id)
        // Update an existing document.
        bookmark.Priority = 1
        if err := store.Update(bookmark); err != nil {
                log.Fatalf("[Update]: %s\n", err)
        }
        fmt.Println("The value after update:")
             // Retrieve the updated document
        getByID(id)

        bookmark = Bookmark{
                Name:        "gorethink",
                Description: "Go driver for RethinkDB",
                Location:    "https://github.com/dancannon/gorethink",
                Priority:    3,
                CreatedOn:   time.Now(),
                Tags:        []string{"go", "nosql", "rethinkdb"},
        }
        // Insert a new document.
        if err := store.Create(&bookmark); err != nil {
                log.Fatalf("[Create]: %s\n", err)
        }
        id = bookmark.ID.Hex()
        fmt.Printf("New bookmark has been inserted with ID: %s\n", id)

}

// Get a document by given id.
func getByID(id string) {
        bookmark, err := store.GetByID(id)
        if err != nil {
                log.Fatalf("[GetByID]: %s\n", err)
        }
        fmt.Printf("Name:%s, Description:%s, Priority:%d\n",
                bookmark.Name, bookmark.Description, bookmark.Priority)
}

// Get all documents from the collection.
func getAll() {
        // Layout for formatting dates.
        layout := "2006-01-02 15:04:05"
        // Retrieve all documents.
        bookmarks := store.GetAll()
        fmt.Println("Read all documents")
        for _, v := range bookmarks {
                fmt.Printf("Name:%s, Description:%s, Priority:%d, CreatedOn:%s\n",
                        v.Name, v.Description, v.Priority, v.CreatedOn.Format(layout))
        }
}
```

```go
// Get documents by tags.
func getByTags() {
        layout := "2006-01-02 15:04:05"
        fmt.Println("Query with Tags - 'go, nosql'")
        bookmarks := store.GetByTag([]string{"go", "nosql"})
        for _, v := range bookmarks {
                fmt.Printf("Name:%s, Description:%s, Priority:%d, CreatedOn:%s\n",
                        v.Name, v.Description, v.Priority, v.CreatedOn.Format(layout))
        }
        fmt.Println("Query with Tags - 'mongodb'")
        bookmarks = store.GetByTag([]string{"mongodb"})
        for _, v := range bookmarks {
                fmt.Printf("Name:%s, Description:%s, Priority:%d, CreatedOn:%s\n",
                        v.Name, v.Description, v.Priority, v.CreatedOn.Format(layout))
        }
}

// Delete an existing document from the collection.
func delete() {
        if err := store.Delete(id); err != nil {
                log.Fatalf("[Delete]: %s\n", err)
        }
        bookmarks := store.GetAll()
        fmt.Printf("Number of documents in the collection after delete:%d\n",
        len(bookmarks))
}

// main - entry point of the program.
func main() {
        createUpdate()
        getAll()
        getByTags()
        delete()
}
```

In the function init, which is executed before invoking the function main, an mgo.Session value is obtained using the function DialWithInfo, and then an mgo.Collection value is created to provide type BookmarkStore. The value of BookmarkStore is used for performing CRUD operations against the collection named "bookmarks" in the database "bookmarkdb".

```go
var store BookmarkStore
var id string

func init() {
        session, err := mgo.DialWithInfo(&mgo.DialInfo{
                Addrs:   []string{"127.0.0.1"},
                Timeout: 60 * time.Second,
        })
        if err != nil {
                log.Fatalf("[MongoDB Session]: %s\n", err)
        }
```

```
        collection := session.DB("bookmarkdb").C("bookmarks")
        store = BookmarkStore{
                C: collection,
        }
}
```

The create and update operations are implemented in the function createUpdate, in which two documents are inserted into the collection and an existing document is updated.

```
func createUpdate() {
        bookmark := Bookmark{
                Name:        "mgo",
                Description: "Go driver for MongoDB",
                Location:    "https://github.com/go-mgo/mgo",
                Priority:    2,
                CreatedOn:   time.Now(),
                Tags:        []string{"go", "nosql", "mongodb"},
        }
        // Insert a new document.
        if err := store.Create(&bookmark); err != nil {
                log.Fatalf("[Create]: %s\n", err)
        }
        id = bookmark.ID.Hex()
        fmt.Printf("New bookmark has been inserted with ID: %s\n", id)
        // Update an existing document.
        bookmark.Priority = 1
        if err := store.Update(bookmark); err != nil {
                log.Fatalf("[Update]: %s\n", err)
        }
        fmt.Println("The value after update:")
        // Retrieve the updated document.
        getByID(id)

        bookmark = Bookmark{
                Name:        "gorethink",
                Description: "Go driver for RethinkDB",
                Location:    "https://github.com/dancannon/gorethink",
                Priority:    3,
                CreatedOn:   time.Now(),
                Tags:        []string{"go", "nosql", "rethinkdb"},
        }
        // Insert a new document.
        if err := store.Create(&bookmark); err != nil {
                log.Fatalf("[Create]: %s\n", err)
        }
        id = bookmark.ID.Hex()
        fmt.Printf("New bookmark has been inserted with ID: %s\n", id)

}
```

The function getByID is used for retrieving an existing document by a given id. This function is being called from function createUpdate to get the values after made an update operation.

```
func getByID(id string) {
        bookmark, err := store.GetByID(id)
        if err != nil {
                log.Fatalf("[GetByID]: %s\n", err)
        }
        fmt.Printf("Name:%s, Description:%s, Priority:%d\n", bookmark.Name, bookmark.
        Description, bookmark.Priority)
}
```

The function getAll retrieves all documents from the collection sorting by priority in ascending order and createdon in descending order, respectively.

```
func getAll() {
        // Layout for formatting dates.
        layout := "2006-01-02 15:04:05"
        // Retrieve all documents.
        bookmarks := store.GetAll()
        fmt.Println("Read all documents")
        for _, v := range bookmarks {
                fmt.Printf("Name:%s, Description:%s, Priority:%d, CreatedOn:%s\n",
                        v.Name, v.Description, v.Priority, v.CreatedOn.Format(layout))
        }
}
```

The function getByTags retrieves documents by filtering with tags. The MongoDB query operator $in is used for filtering the documents. The function GetByTag of BookmarkStore is executed two times. The first time, it is executed by providing tags, go and nosql, so you will get all documents that have any of the tags provided; here you will get two documents. The second time, it is executed by providing tags mongodb so you will get a single document as the result because only one document has the given tag.

```
func getByTags() {
        layout := "2006-01-02 15:04:05"
        fmt.Println("Query with Tags - 'go, nosql'")
        bookmarks := store.GetByTag([]string{"go", "nosql"})
        for _, v := range bookmarks {
                fmt.Printf("Name:%s, Description:%s, Priority:%d, CreatedOn:%s\n",
                        v.Name, v.Description, v.Priority, v.CreatedOn.Format(layout))
        }
        fmt.Println("Query with Tags - 'mongodb'")
        bookmarks = store.GetByTag([]string{"mongodb"})
        for _, v := range bookmarks {
                fmt.Printf("Name:%s, Description:%s, Priority:%d, CreatedOn:%s\n",
                        v.Name, v.Description, v.Priority, v.CreatedOn.Format(layout))
        }
}
```

The function delete is used for deleting an existing document by given id.

```go
func delete() {
        if err := store.Delete(id); err != nil {
                log.Fatalf("[Delete]: %s\n", err)
        }
        bookmarks, err := store.GetAll()
        if err != nil {
                log.Fatalf("[GetAll]: %s\n", err)
        }
        fmt.Printf("Number of documents in the table after delete:%d\n", len(bookmarks))
}
```

From the function main, functions are called for demonstrating the CRUD operations.

```go
func main() {
        createUpdate()
        getAll()
        getByTags()
        delete()
}
```

Let's run the example program. You should see output similar to the following:

```
New bookmark has been inserted with ID: 57809514f7e02124b042281d
The value after update:
Name:mgo, Description:Go driver for MongoDB, Priority:1
New bookmark has been inserted with ID: 57809514f7e02124b042281e
Read all documents
Name:mgo, Description:Go driver for MongoDB, Priority:1, CreatedOn:2016-07-09 11:39:24
Name:gorethink, Description:Go driver for RethinkDB, Priority:3, CreatedOn:2016-07-09
11:39:24
Query with Tags - 'go, nosql'
Name:mgo, Description:Go driver for MongoDB, Priority:1, CreatedOn:2016-07-09 11:39:24
Name:gorethink, Description:Go driver for RethinkDB, Priority:3, CreatedOn:2016-07-09
11:39:24
Query with Tags - 'mongodb'
Name:mgo, Description:Go driver for MongoDB, Priority:1, CreatedOn:2016-07-09 11:39:24
Number of documents in the collection after delete:1
```

6-2. Persisting Data with RethinkDB

Problem

You would like to work with RethinkDB as the database for your Go applications. You also would like to use the real-time capabilities of RethinkDB.

Solution

The third-party package gorethink provides a full-featured RethinkDB driver for Go, which allows you to work with RethinkDB from your Go applications. This package also allows you to subscribe and change feeds of data in real time with RethinkDB.

How It Works

RethinkDB is a NoSQL, scalable JSON database that provides a lot of capabilities similar to MongoDB. RethinkDB stores JSON documents that are organized into tables. A Table in RethinkDB is a collection of JSON documents. In addition to the familiar capabilities of a NoSQL database, RethinkDB provides real-time capabilities to its database engine that makes building real-time web applications dramatically easier. A real-time web application can push real-time updates to the client applications instead of client applications checking the server for new updates periodically. This enables a greater level of productivity when you write real-time applications. Using a Go implementation of the WebSocket protocol, you can make your web application a real-time application. By combining this with the real-time capabilities of the RethinkDB database, you can make great real-time web applications. When your real-time web application uses RethinkDB, you can subscribe to real-time change feeds; when there is any change in the database you can push those change feeds to your client applications. For more details on RethinkDB, including installation instructions, check out the website at https://www.rethinkdb.com/.

■ **Note**   The Go packages golang.org/x/net/websocket and github.com/gorilla/websocket implement a client and server for the WebSocket protocol as specified in RFC 6455 (https://tools.ietf.org/html/rfc6455).

Installing gorethink

To install the package gorethink, run the following command:

```
go get github.com/dancannon/gorethink
```

To work with the package gorethink, you must add github.com/dancannon/gorethink to the list of imports.

```
import " github.com/dancannon/gorethink"
```

Connecting to RethinkDB

To perform CRUD operations with RethinkDB, you first obtain a RethinkDB session using the function Connect as shown here:

```
session, err := gorethink.Connect(r.ConnectOpts{
            Address:  "localhost:28015",
                      Database: "bookmarkdb",
 })
```

To configure the connection pool, properties of type ConnectOpts such as MaxIdle, MaxOpen, and Timeout can be specified when calling the function Connect as shown here:

```
session, err := gorethink.Connect(gorethink.ConnectOpts{
            Address:  "localhost:28015",
                      Database: "bookmarkdb",
            MaxIdle:  10,
            MaxOpen:  10,
 })
```

You can change the `MaxIdle` and `MaxOpen` properties by calling methods of `Session` as shown here:

```
session.SetMaxIdleConns(57)
session.SetMaxOpenConns(5)
```

To connect to a cluster of RethinkDB servers that has multiple nodes you can use the following syntax. When connecting to a cluster with multiple nodes, queries are distributed among these nodes.

```
session, err := gorethink.Connect(gorethink.ConnectOpts{
    Addresses: []string{"localhost:28015", "localhost:28016"},
    Database: " bookmarkdb",
    AuthKey:   "14daak1cad13dj",
    DiscoverHosts: true,
})
```

The `AuthKey` is used for securing the RethinkDB cluster.

Performing CRUD Operations

Once you obtain a `Session` object, you can perform CRUD operations against a `Table` that represents a collection of JSON documents.

Let's write an example program to demonstrate persistence and read operations with RethinkDB. Let's write the example program in two source files: bookmark_store.go and main.go. Listing 6-3 shows the source of bookmark_store.go file that contains a struct named Bookmark for defining the data model, and a struct type BookmarkStore that provides persistence logic for performing CRUD operations against the table named "bookmarks".

Listing 6-3. Data Model and Persistence Logic in bookmark_store.go

```
package main

import (
        "time"

        r "github.com/dancannon/gorethink"
)

// Bookmark type represents the metadata of a bookmark.
type Bookmark struct {
        ID                          string `gorethink:"id,omitempty" json:"id"`
        Name, Description, Location string
        Priority                    int // Priority (1 -5)
        CreatedOn                   time.Time
        Tags                        []string
}

// BookmarkStore provides CRUD operations against the Table "bookmarks".
type BookmarkStore struct {
        Session *r.Session
}
```

```go
// Create inserts the value of struct Bookmark into Table.
func (store BookmarkStore) Create(b *Bookmark) error {

        resp, err := r.Table("bookmarks").Insert(b).RunWrite(store.Session)
        if err == nil {
                b.ID = resp.GeneratedKeys[0]
        }

        return err
}

// Update modifies an existing value of a Table.
func (store BookmarkStore) Update(b *Bookmark) error {

        var data = map[string]interface{}{
                "name":        b.Name,
                "description": b.Description,
                "location":    b.Location,
                "priority":    b.Priority,
                "tags":        b.Tags,
        }
        // partial update on RethinkDB
        _, err := r.Table("bookmarks").Get(b.ID).Update(data).RunWrite(store.Session)
        return err
}

// Delete removes an existing value from the Table.
func (store BookmarkStore) Delete(id string) error {
        _, err := r.Table("bookmarks").Get(id).Delete().RunWrite(store.Session)
        return err
}

// GetAll returns all documents from the Table.
func (store BookmarkStore) GetAll() ([]Bookmark, error) {
        bookmarks := []Bookmark{}

        res, err := r.Table("bookmarks").OrderBy("priority", r.Desc("date")).Run(store.
Session)
        err = res.All(&bookmarks)
        return bookmarks, err
}

// GetByID returns single document from the Table.
func (store BookmarkStore) GetByID(id string) (Bookmark, error) {
        var b Bookmark
        res, err := r.Table("bookmarks").Get(id).Run(store.Session)
        res.One(&b)
        return b, err
}
```

A struct named Bookmark is declared as the data model for the example program.

```go
type Bookmark struct {
        ID                              string `gorethink:"id,omitempty" json:"id"`
        Name, Description, Location string
        Priority                        int // Priority (1 -5)
        CreatedOn               time.Time
        Tags                            []string
}
```

The struct field ID is tagged with id of RethinkDB Table, and id in the JSON representation of the document. RethinkDB will autogenerate a UUID for the field id.

A struct named BookmarkStore is declared for providing persistence logic that uses the data model struct Bookmark. The struct BookmarkStore has a field Session with type gorethink.Session. All CRUD operations are performed by accessing the methods of BookmarkStore that use the field Session.

```go
type BookmarkStore struct {
        Session *r.Session
}
```

Create a Document in a Table

The method Create of BookmarkStore is used to insert values into the table named bookmarks. It accepts a pointer to Bookmark and inserts the value of Bookmark into the table. When insert and update operations are performed, the gorethink package encodes the struct values into a map before being sent to the server.

```go
func (store BookmarkStore) Create(b *Bookmark) error {

        resp, err := r.Table("bookmarks").Insert(b).RunWrite(store.Session)
        if err == nil {
                b.ID = resp.GeneratedKeys[0]
        }
        return err
}
```

The type gorethink.Term represents both write and read queries. In the package gorethink, methods are chainable so that you can easily construct queries. In the preceding method, function Table and method Insert return a gorethink.Term value. The function RunWrite runs a query and then returns a value of type WriteResponse. By accessing the GeneratedKeys field of WriteResponse value, you can get the id value. The function RunWrite is used for executing write queries such as Insert, Update, Delete, DBCreate, TableCreate, and so on.

Update a Document in a Table

To update an existing document, a value of map with the signature map[string]interface{} is provided as the value to be updated in the table.

```go
func (store BookmarkStore) Update(b *Bookmark) error {

        var data = map[string]interface{}{
                "name":           b.Name,
                "description": b.Description,
```

```
                "location":    b.Location,
                "priority":    b.Priority,
                "tags":        b.Tags,
        }

        // partial update on RethinkDB
        _, err := r.Table("bookmarks").Get(b.ID).Update(data).RunWrite(store.Session)
        return err
}
```

Delete a Document from a Table

The method Delete of type Term is used to run a delete query to delete an existing document from the table.

```
func (store BookmarkStore) Delete(id string) error {
        _, err := r.Table("bookmarks").Get(id).Delete().RunWrite(store.Session)
        return err
}
```

Read a Document from a Table

The function Run is used to run a read query. The function Run returns a gorethink.Cursor value that is the result of a query. By using the methods, such as One, All, Next, and NextResponse, you can retrieve the documents into your Go types. The method GetAll of type BookmarkStore returns all documents from the bookmarks table, which is sorting by priority in ascending order and createdon in descending order. By default, the sort is executing by ascending order, so if you want to sort by descending order, you can use the function Desc.

```
func (store BookmarkStore) GetAll() ([]Bookmark, error) {
        bookmarks := []Bookmark{}
        res, err := r.Table("bookmarks").OrderBy("priority", r.Desc("createdon")).Run(store.
Session)
        err = res.All(&bookmarks)
        return bookmarks, err
}
```

The method GetByID of type BookmarkStore returns a single document for the given id.

```
func (store BookmarkStore) GetByID(id string) (Bookmark, error) {
        var b Bookmark
        res, err := r.Table("bookmarks").Get(id).Run(store.Session)
        res.One(&b)
        return b, err
}
```

Let's reuse the functions of bookmark_store.go to perform CRUD operations against the RethinkDB Table. Listing 6-4 shows the source in the main.go file that creates an instance of type BookmarkStore by providing a gorethink.Session value, and calling its methods for performing CRUD operations. This main.go also provides the implementation of real-time capabilities of RethinkDB by subscribing to the change feeds for a table.

Listing 6-4. Perform CRUD Operations on a RethinkDB Table Using the Type BookmarkStore, in main.go

```go
package main

import (
        "fmt"
        "log"
        "time"

        r "github.com/dancannon/gorethink"
)

var store BookmarkStore
var id string

// initDB creates new database and
func initDB(session *r.Session) {
        var err error
        // Create Database
        _, err = r.DBCreate("bookmarkdb").RunWrite(session)
        if err != nil {
                log.Fatalf("[initDB]: %s\n", err)
        }
        // Create Table
        _, err = r.DB("bookmarkdb").TableCreate("bookmarks").RunWrite(session)
        if err != nil {
                log.Fatalf("[initDB]: %s\n", err)
        }
}

// changeFeeds subscribes real-time changes on table bookmarks.
func changeFeeds(session *r.Session) {
        bookmarks, _ := r.Table("bookmarks").Changes().Field("new_val").Run(session)
                if err != nil {
                log.Fatalf("[changeFeeds]: %s\n", err)
        }

        // Launch a goroutine to print real-time updates.
        go func() {
                var bookmark Bookmark
                for bookmarks.Next(&bookmark) {
                        if bookmark.ID == "" { // for delete, new_val will be null.
                                fmt.Println("Real-time update: Document has been deleted")
                        } else {
                                fmt.Printf("Real-time update: Name:%s, Description:%s,
                                Priority:%d\n",
                                        bookmark.Name, bookmark.Description, bookmark.
                                        Priority)
                        }
                }
        }()
}
```

```go
// init will invoke before the function main
func init() {
        session, err := r.Connect(r.ConnectOpts{
                Address:  "localhost:28015",
                Database: "bookmarkdb",
                MaxIdle:  10,
                MaxOpen:  10,
        })

        if err != nil {
                log.Fatalf("[RethinkDB Session]: %s\n", err)
        }

        // Create Database and Table.
        initDB(session)
        store = BookmarkStore{
                Session: session,
        }
        // Subscribe real-time changes
        changeFeeds(session)
}

// Create and update documents.
func createUpdate() {
        bookmark := Bookmark{
                Name:        "mgo",
                Description: "Go driver for MongoDB",
                Location:    "https://github.com/go-mgo/mgo",
                Priority:    1,
                CreatedOn:   time.Now(),
                Tags:        []string{"go", "nosql", "mongodb"},
        }
        // Insert a new document.
        if err := store.Create(&bookmark); err != nil {
                log.Fatalf("[Create]: %s\n", err)
        }
        id = bookmark.ID
        fmt.Printf("New bookmark has been inserted with ID: %s\n", id)
        // Update an existing document.
        bookmark.Priority = 2
        if err := store.Update(bookmark); err != nil {
                log.Fatalf("[Update]: %s\n", err)
        }
        fmt.Println("The value after update:")
        // Retrieve the updated document.
        getByID(id)
        bookmark = Bookmark{
                Name:        "gorethink",
                Description: "Go driver for RethinkDB",
                Location:    "https://github.com/dancannon/gorethink",
                Priority:    1,
```

```go
                CreatedOn:    time.Now(),
                Tags:         []string{"go", "nosql", "rethinkdb"},
        }
        // Insert a new document.
        if err := store.Create(&bookmark); err != nil {
                log.Fatalf("[Create]: %s\n", err)
        }
        id = bookmark.ID
        fmt.Printf("New bookmark has been inserted with ID: %s\n", id)

}

// Get a document by given id.
func getByID(id string) {
        bookmark, err := store.GetByID(id)
        if err != nil {
                log.Fatalf("[GetByID]: %s\n", err)
        }
        fmt.Printf("Name:%s, Description:%s, Priority:%d\n", bookmark.Name, bookmark.
Description, bookmark.Priority)
}

// Get all documents from bookmarks table.
func getAll() {
        // Layout for formatting dates.
        layout := "2006-01-02 15:04:05"
        // Retrieve all documents.
        bookmarks, err := store.GetAll()
        if err != nil {
                log.Fatalf("[GetAll]: %s\n", err)
        }
        fmt.Println("Read all documents")
        for _, v := range bookmarks {
                fmt.Printf("Name:%s, Description:%s, Priority:%d, CreatedOn:%s\n", v.Name,
v.Description, v.Priority, v.CreatedOn.Format(layout))
        }

}

// Delete an existing document from bookmarks table.
func delete() {
        if err := store.Delete(id); err != nil {
                log.Fatalf("[Delete]: %s\n", err)
        }
        bookmarks, err := store.GetAll()
        if err != nil {
                log.Fatalf("[GetAll]: %s\n", err)
        }
        fmt.Printf("Number of documents in the table after delete:%d\n", len(bookmarks))
}
```

```
// main - entry point of the program
func main() {
        createUpdate()
        getAll()
        delete()
}
```

In the init function, a Session value is obtained by connecting to the RethinkDB server using the function Connect. Unlike MongoDB, in RethinkDB, you have to create databases and tables manually. From Go code itself, a database named bookmarkdb and a table named bookmarks are created by calling the function initDB. If you execute the function initDB more than once, you will get an exception. The function changeFeeds, which is used to demonstrate the real-time capabilities of RethinkDB, is also called from the init. We will look into the function changeFeeds later in this section. The function init will be invoked before the function main.

```
func init() {
        session, err := r.Connect(r.ConnectOpts{
                Address:  "localhost:28015",
                Database: "bookmarkdb",
                MaxIdle:  10,
                MaxOpen:  10,
        })

        if err != nil {
                log.Fatalf("[RethinkDB Session]: %s\n", err)
        }

        // Create Database and Table.
        initDB(session)
        store = BookmarkStore{
                Session: session,
        }
        // Subscribe real-time changes
        changeFeeds(session)
}
```

The create and update operations are implemented in the function createUpdate, in which two documents are inserted into bookmarks table and an existing document is updated.

```
func createUpdate() {
        bookmark := Bookmark{
                Name:        "mgo",
                Description: "Go driver for MongoDB",
                Location:    "https://github.com/go-mgo/mgo",
                Priority:    1,
                CreatedOn:   time.Now(),
                Tags:        []string{"go", "nosql", "mongodb"},
        }
        // Insert a new document.
        if err := store.Create(&bookmark); err != nil {
                log.Fatalf("[Create]: %s\n", err)
        }
```

```
    id = bookmark.ID
    fmt.Printf("New bookmark has been inserted with ID: %s\n", id)
    // Update an existing document.
    bookmark.Priority = 2
    if err := store.Update(bookmark); err != nil {
            log.Fatalf("[Update]: %s\n", err)
    }
    fmt.Println("The value after update:")
    // Retrieve the updated document.
    getByID(id)
    bookmark = Bookmark{
            Name:        "gorethink",
            Description: "Go driver for RethinkDB",
            Location:    "https://github.com/dancannon/gorethink",
            Priority:    1,
            CreatedOn:   time.Now(),
            Tags:        []string{"go", "nosql", "rethinkdb"},
    }
    // Insert a new document.
    if err := store.Create(&bookmark); err != nil {
            log.Fatalf("[Create]: %s\n", err)
    }
    id = bookmark.ID
    fmt.Printf("New bookmark has been inserted with ID: %s\n", id)
}
```

The function getByID is used for retrieving an existing document by a given id. This function is being called from function createUpdate to get the values after an update operation.

```
func getByID(id string) {
    bookmark, err := store.GetByID(id)
    if err != nil {
            log.Fatalf("[GetByID]: %s\n", err)
    }
    fmt.Printf("Name:%s, Description:%s, Priority:%d\n", bookmark.Name, bookmark.
    Description, bookmark.Priority)
}
```

The function getAll retrieves all documents from the table sorted by priority in ascending order and createdon in descending order, respectively.

```
func getAll() {
    // Layout for formatting dates.
    layout := "2006-01-02 15:04:05"
    // Retrieve all documents.
    bookmarks, err := store.GetAll()
    if err != nil {
            log.Fatalf("[GetAll]: %s\n", err)
    }
    fmt.Println("Read all documents")
    for _, v := range bookmarks {
```

```
        fmt.Printf("Name:%s, Description:%s, Priority:%d, CreatedOn:%s\n", v.Name,
        v.Description, v.Priority, v.CreatedOn.Format(layout))
    }

}
```

The function delete is used to delete an existing document by a given id.

```
func delete() {
    if err := store.Delete(id); err != nil {
            log.Fatalf("[Delete]: %s\n", err)
    }
    bookmarks, err := store.GetAll()
    if err != nil {
            log.Fatalf("[GetAll]: %s\n", err)
    }
    fmt.Printf("Number of documents in the table after delete:%d\n", len(bookmarks))
}
```

From the function main, functions are called for demonstrating the CRUD operations.

```
func main() {
    createUpdate()
    getAll()
    delete()
}
```

Changefeeds in RethinkDB

RethinkDB's real-time functionality is implemented using Changefeeds, which allows the clients of a RethinkDB database to receive changes to a table in real time. Using the gorethink driver, you can subscribe to the feed for changed data by calling the function Changes on a Table value. In Listing 6-4, the function changeFeeds in main.go does an implementation of RethinkDB's Changefeeds to subscribe to data on the table bookmarks whenever any update is performed on it so that the application can receive those feeds whenever any insert, update, or delete operation is executed on the table bookmarks.

```
func changeFeeds(session *r.Session) {
    bookmarks, _ := r.Table("bookmarks").Changes().Field("new_val").Run(session)
            if err != nil {
            log.Fatalf("[changeFeeds]: %s\n", err)
    }
    // Launch a goroutine to print real-time updates.
    go func() {
            var bookmark Bookmark
            for bookmarks.Next(&bookmark) {
                    if bookmark.ID == "" {  // for delete, new_val will be null.
                            fmt.Println("Real-time update: Document has been deleted")
                    } else {
                            fmt.Printf("Real-time update: Name:%s, Description:%s,
                            Priority:%d\n",
```

```
                                    bookmark.Name, bookmark.Description, bookmark.
                                    Priority)
                    }
                }
        }()
}
```

The function Changes is called for subscribing to RethinkDB's Changefeeds for the field "new_val". The Changefeeds functionality can provide two values when any update is performed on the table: old_val and new_val. The old_val is the old version of the document and the new_val is a new version of the document. On an insert, old_val will be null; on a delete, new_val will be null. On an update, both old_val and new_val are present. In the function changeFeeds, it is subscribed for new_val. The output of Changefeeds can be subscribed in the handler function to perform actions on the values provided by Changefeeds. Here the handler function is implemented in a goroutine so that it will be executed asynchronously in the background without blocking any execution. By combining with goroutines and channels, you can create efficient real-time applications with Go and RethinkDB. Here the Changefeeds for the field new_val result is printed in the console window. The new_val will be null for delete so that you don't access any values for the Changefeeds for delete operations. The Changefeeds functionality will provide feeds when any insert, update, or delete operation is performed on the table bookmarks. The new_val values for the Changefeeds are accessible from the Cursor value provided by the function Changes by executing with Run. By calling the function Next of Cursor value, you can retrieve the values provided by Changefeeds.

Let's run the program written in Listing 6-4. You should see output similar to the following:

```
Real-time update: Name:mgo, Description:Go driver for MongoDB, Priority:1
New bookmark has been inserted with ID: f487b133-6f19-4b3b-8dfa-4d652b2f1c1b
Real-time update: Name:mgo, Description:Go driver for MongoDB, Priority:2
The value after update:
Name:mgo, Description:Go driver for MongoDB, Priority:2
Real-time update: Name:gorethink, Description:Go driver for RethinkDB, Priority:1
New bookmark has been inserted with ID: ee6a19c8-efa5-4672-ae62-37d8b0ea060f
Read all documents
Name:gorethink, Description:Go driver for RethinkDB, Priority:1, CreatedOn:2016-07-08
20:03:50
Name:mgo, Description:Go driver for MongoDB, Priority:2, CreatedOn:2016-07-08 20:03:49
Real-time update: Document has been deleted
Number of documents in the table after delete:1
```

The output shows that Changefeeds functionality provides real-time updates on table bookmarks.

6-3. Working on Time Series Data with InfluxDB

Problem

You would like to work with time series data to be used for building time series graphs and real-time data analysis.

Solution

InfluxDB is a time series database written in Go. InfluxDB provides a native Go client library (github.com/influxdata/influxdb/client/v2) to work with InfluxDB from Go applications.

How It Works

Time series data processing and real-time data analysis are the next big thing in big data and data management technologies. InfluxDB, part of the InfluxData platform, is a time series database that allows you to efficiently store time series data. InfluxDB includes a native Go client library that provides convenience functions to read and write time series data. It uses the HTTP protocol to communicate with your InfluxDB cluster.

Time Series Database

Time series data is a sequence of data points, typically consisting of successive measurements made over a time interval. When you build graphs based on time series data, one of your axes would always be time (years, days, hours, minutes). Time series data processing is an important data management approach for building prediction models and forecasting. A time series database (TSDB) is a database in which you manage and store time series data. InfluxDB, provided by the InfluxData platform, is one of the most popular TSDBs available on the market.

Key Concepts InfluxDB

Data management in InfluxDB is different than traditional data management systems. Here is a summary of the key concepts in InfluxDB:

- *Database*: The high-level entity in InfluxDB. You can have multiple databases in one InfluxDB instance.

- *Measurement*: You persist time series data into measurements. A measurement is analogous to a relational table. When you build graphs based on the time series data, a measurement is a name of the graph.

- *Point*: A measurement contains points much like a relational table contains records. A point contains mandatory fields(s) and a timestamp. A timestamp specifies the time of the point and fields are used for storing the data for that timestamp. A point can have tags, which are metadata of time series data.

- *Timestamp*: Each point in a measurement contains a timestamp because InfluxDB is a TSDB. If you don't provide a timestamp when you create a new point, InfluxDB automatically creates a new timestamp for that point. A timestamp in a point specifies the time it was created. When you build graphs, one axis would be time and another would be the value of fields.

- *Fieldset*: The collection of fields is known as a fieldset.

- *Tags*: Tags in a point are metadata, which are indexed. Keep in mind that measurements are indexed on tags and not on fields.

- *Tagset*: The collection of all the tags is known as a tagset.

- *Series*: A combination of a measurement and tags is known as a series.

Line Protocol

The line protocol is a text-based format for writing points to measurements in InfluxDB. It consists of a measurement, tags, fields, and a timestamp. When you write points to InfluxDB using the HTTP API of InfluxDB, the body of HTTP POST would be a line protocol that represents the time series data to be inserted to InfluxDB. Each line in the line protocol defines a single point. Multiple lines must be separated by the newline character \n. The format of the line protocol consists of three parts:

```
[key] [fields] [timestamp]
```

154

Each section in the line protocol is separated by spaces. It must provide a measurement name and at least one field. Tags are optional, but in real-world scenarios, you should include tags. Tag keys and tag values are strings. Field keys are strings, and, by default, field values are floats. If a point does not contain a timestamp, it will be written using the server's local nanosecond timestamp. Timestamps are assumed to be in nanoseconds unless a precision value is provided. Here is the line protocol that represents a single point:

```
cpu,host=server01,region=uswest cpu_usage=46.26 1434055562000000000
```

Here cpu is the name of measurement, host and region are the keys of tags, and cpu_usage is the name of the field and its value is 46.26. The value 1434055562000000000 is the timestamp. When you write records into InfluxDB using the Go client library, you don't need to make data in line protocol format, as it is done by the client library.

Install InfluxDB

It is recommended that you install InfluxDB using one of the prebuilt packages available from https://www.influxdata.com/downloads/#influxdb. You can also install InfluxDB from source that is available at https://github.com/influxdata/influxdb.

In macOS, you can install InfluxDB using brew:

```
brew install influxdb
```

Creating a Database in InfluxDB

Let's create a database and user account in InfluxDB using its command-line interface, influx. The influx tool provides an interactive shell for the database to write data, query data interactively, and view query output in different formats. To launch the InfluxDB command-line interface, run the command influx:

```
$ influx
```

The next command creates a user account named opsadmin:

```
> create user opsadmin with password 'pass123'
```

This command grants privileges to the newly created user opsadmin:

```
> grant all privileges to opsadmin
```

The final command creates a database named metricsdb:

```
> create database metricsdb
```

Working on InfluxDB with Go Client

The v2 version of the Go client library for InfluxDB is available from github.com/influxdata/influxdb/client/v2. The Go client library is maintained by the InfluxDB team. To install the v2 version of the package, run the following command:

```
go get github.com/influxdata/influxdb/client/v2
```

To work with the package, you must add github.com/influxdata/influxdb/client/v2 to the list of imports.

```
import "github.com/influxdata/influxdb/client/v2"
```

Connecting to InfluxDB

By default, InfluxDB listens on port 8086. The following code block connects to InfluxDB with user account opsadmin.

```
c, err := client.NewHTTPClient(client.HTTPConfig{
            Addr:     "http://localhost:8086",
            Username: "opsadmin",
            Password: "pass123",
    })
```

The function NewHTTPClient returns a new InfluxDB Client from the given configuration. Struct type HTTPConfig is used to provide configuration for creating the InfluxDB Client. Here is the definition of struct HTTPConfig:

```
// HTTPConfig is the config data needed to create an HTTP Client
type HTTPConfig struct {
        // Addr should be of the form "http://host:port"
        // or "http://[ipv6-host%zone]:port".
        Addr string

        // Username is the influxdb username, optional
        Username string

        // Password is the influxdb password, optional
        Password string

        // UserAgent is the http User Agent, defaults to "InfluxDBClient"
        UserAgent string

        // Timeout for influxdb writes, defaults to no timeout
        Timeout time.Duration

        // InsecureSkipVerify gets passed to the http client, if true, it will
        // skip https certificate verification. Defaults to false
        InsecureSkipVerify bool

        // TLSConfig allows the user to set their own TLS config for the HTTP
        // Client. If set, this option overrides InsecureSkipVerify.
        TLSConfig *tls.Config
}
```

Once you have created an InfluxDB Client, you can use it for both write and query operations.

Writing Points to InfluxDB

When you write points to measurement for persisting data into InfluxDB, you should do so in batches. To write points in batches, you first create a new BatchPoints value as shown here:

```
bp, err := client.NewBatchPoints(client.BatchPointsConfig{
            Database:  "metricsdb",
            Precision: "s",
     })
```

A BatchPoints value is created by providing a configuration. The property Precision specifies the precision for timestamp created for each point. By default, all timestamps in Unix are in nanoseconds. If you want to provide timestamps in any unit other than nanoseconds, you must provide the appropriate precision. Use n, u, ms, s, m, and h for nanoseconds, microseconds, milliseconds, seconds, minutes, and hours, respectively.

The following code block creates a new point by providing values for tags, fields, and timestamp to the measurement named cpu.

```
// tagset - "host" and "region"
tags := map[string]string{
 "host":   "host1"
 "region": "us-west"
}

// field - "cpu_usage"
fields := map[string]interface{}{
 "cpu_usage": 46.22
}

// New point to measurement named "cpu"
pt, err := client.NewPoint("cpu ", tags, fields, time.Now())

 if err != nil {
       log.Fatalln("Error: ", err)
}

bp.AddPoint(pt)
```

Because you write points in batches, you add n number of points to BatchPoints using the function AddPoint. Once all points are added to BatchPoints, call the function Write of the InfluxDB Client instance to complete the write operation.

```
// Write the batch
c.Write(bp) // c is the instance of InfluxDB Client instance
```

Reading Points from InfluxDB

InfluxDB provides the ability to query data using familiar SQL constructs. This code block determines the count value of points in measurement cpu.

```
command:= fmt.Sprintf("SELECT count(%s) FROM %s", "cpu_usage", "cpu")
q := client.Query{
                Command:  command,
                Database: DB,
        }
        // Query the Database
        if response, err := c.Query(q)  // // c is the instance of InfluxDB Client instance
        if err != nil {
                log.Fatalln("Error: ", err)
        }
        count :=response.Results[0].Series[0].Values[0][1]
```

Example: Writing and Reading on InfluxDB

Listing 6-5 shows an example program that writes points to InfluxDB in batches and reads points from the database.

Listing 6-5. Writing and Reading of Points to a Measurement "cpu" in InfluxDB

```go
package main

import (
        "encoding/json"
        "fmt"
        "log"
        "math/rand"
        "time"

        client "github.com/influxdata/influxdb/client/v2"
)

const (
        // DB provides the database name of the InfluxDB
        DB       = "metricsdb"
        username = "opsadmin"
        password = "pass123"
)

func main() {
        // Create client
        c := influxDBClient()
        // Write operations
        // Create metrics data for measurement "cpu"
        createMetrics(c)
        // Read operations
        // Read with limit of 10
        readWithLimit(c, 10)
        // Read mean value of "cpu_usage" for a region
        meanCPUUsage(c, "us-west")
        // Read count of records for a region
```

```go
        countRegion(c, "us-west")

}

// influxDBClient returns InfluxDB Client
func influxDBClient() client.Client {
        c, err := client.NewHTTPClient(client.HTTPConfig{
                Addr:     "http://localhost:8086",
                Username: username,
                Password: password,
        })
        if err != nil {
                log.Fatalln("Error: ", err)
        }
        return c
}

// createMetrics write batch points to create the metrics data
func createMetrics(clnt client.Client) {
        batchCount := 100
        rand.Seed(42)

        // Create BatchPoints by giving config for InfluxDB
        bp, _ := client.NewBatchPoints(client.BatchPointsConfig{
                Database:  DB,
                Precision: "s",
        })
        // Batch update to adds Points
        for i := 0; i < batchCount; i++ {
                regions := []string{"us-west", "us-central", "us-north", "us-east"}
                // tagset - "host" and "region"
                tags := map[string]string{
                        "host":   fmt.Sprintf("192.168.%d.%d", rand.Intn(100), rand.
                        Intn(100)),
                        "region": regions[rand.Intn(len(regions))],
                }

                value := rand.Float64() * 100.0
                // field - "cpu_usage"
                fields := map[string]interface{}{
                        "cpu_usage": value,
                }

                pt, err := client.NewPoint("cpu", tags, fields, time.Now())

                if err != nil {
                        log.Fatalln("Error: ", err)
                }
                // Add a Point
                bp.AddPoint(pt)

        }
```

```go
        // Writes the batch update to add points to measurement "cpu"
        err := clnt.Write(bp)
        if err != nil {
                log.Fatalln("Error: ", err)
        }
}

// queryDB query the database
func queryDB(clnt client.Client, command string) (res []client.Result, err error) {
        // Create the query
        q := client.Query{
                Command:  command,
                Database: DB,
        }
        // Query the Database
        if response, err := clnt.Query(q); err == nil {
                if response.Error() != nil {
                        return res, response.Error()
                }
                res = response.Results
        } else {
                return res, err
        }
        return res, nil
}

// readWithLimit reads records with a given limit
func readWithLimit(clnt client.Client, limit int) {
        q := fmt.Sprintf("SELECT * FROM %s LIMIT %d", "cpu", limit)
        res, err := queryDB(clnt, q)
        if err != nil {
                log.Fatalln("Error: ", err)
        }

        for i, row := range res[0].Series[0].Values {
                t, err := time.Parse(time.RFC3339, row[0].(string))
                if err != nil {
                        log.Fatalln("Error: ", err)
                }
                val, err := row[1].(json.Number).Float64()
                fmt.Printf("[%2d] %s: %f\n", i, t.Format(time.Stamp), val)
        }
}

// meanCPUUsage reads the mean value of cpu_usage
func meanCPUUsage(clnt client.Client, region string) {
        q := fmt.Sprintf("select mean(%s) from %s where region = '%s'", "cpu_usage", "cpu",
        region)
        res, err := queryDB(clnt, q)
        if err != nil {
                log.Fatalln("Error: ", err)
        }
```

```
        value, err := res[0].Series[0].Values[0][1].(json.Number).Float64()
        if err != nil {
                log.Fatalln("Error: ", err)
        }

        fmt.Printf("Mean value of cpu_usage for region '%s':%f\n", region, value)
}

// countRegion reads the count of records for a given region
func countRegion(clnt client.Client, region string) {
        q := fmt.Sprintf("SELECT count(%s) FROM %s where region = '%s'", "cpu_usage", "cpu",
region)
        res, err := queryDB(clnt, q)
        if err != nil {
                log.Fatalln("Error: ", err)
        }
        count := res[0].Series[0].Values[0][1]
        fmt.Printf("Found a total of %v records for region '%s'\n", count, region)
}
```

The function influxDBClient returns a Client object, which is being used for write and read operations with InfluxDB. The function createMetrics is used to write points in batches. For the sake of the example, 100 points are inserted into a measurement named cpu. Two tags are included in the tagset: host and region. The measurement cpu has one field named cpu_usage.

To perform read operations, the function queryDB is used as a helper function that returns a slice of client.Result after executing the given query command. In this example, three query operations are executed using the helper function queryDB. The function readWithLimit reads the data from measurement cpu with a limit of 10. The function meanCPUUsage reads the mean value of cpu_usage from measurement cpu for region "us-west". Finally, function countRegion reads the count of points from measurement cpu for region us-west.

When the read operations are performed, you should see output similar to the following:

```
[ 0] Sep 17 10:49:42: 11.901734
[ 1] Sep 17 10:49:42: 15.471216
[ 2] Sep 17 10:49:42: 32.904423
[ 3] Sep 17 10:49:42: 15.973031
[ 4] Sep 17 10:49:42: 88.648864
[ 5] Sep 17 10:49:42: 92.049809
[ 6] Sep 17 10:49:42: 83.304049
[ 7] Sep 17 10:49:42: 18.495674
[ 8] Sep 17 10:49:42: 23.389015
[ 9] Sep 17 10:49:42: 46.009337
Mean value of cpu_usage for region 'us-west':46.268998
Found a total of 27 records for region 'us-west'
```

You can perform query operations from the influx command-line interface tool. Let's run the tool and execute a query:

```
$ influx
> select * from cpu limit 10
```

The preceding command provides data similar to the following:

```
name: cpu
---------
time                    cpu_usage           host            region
1474109382000000000     11.901733613473244  192.168.1.21    us-west
1474109382000000000     15.47121626535387   192.168.99.62   us-east
1474109382000000000     32.9044231821345    192.168.98.18   us-north
1474109382000000000     15.97303140480521   192.168.97.1    us-central
1474109382000000000     88.64886440612389   192.168.96.13   us-north
1474109382000000000     92.04980918501607   192.168.95.74   us-central
1474109382000000000     83.30404929547693   192.168.91.22   us-west
1474109382000000000     18.495673741297637  192.168.90.58   us-west
1474109382000000000     23.38901519689525   192.168.9.91    us-west
1474109382000000000     46.00933676790605   192.168.9.30    us-central
```

6-4. Working with SQL Databases

Problem

You would like to work with relational databases such as PostgreSQL, MySQL, and so on, from your Go applications.

Solution

The standard library package `database/sql` provides a generic interface for working with SQL databases. To work with any specific SQL databases, you must use a database-specific driver along with package `database/sql`. A list of third-party SQL drivers that work with package `database/sql` can be found at `http://golang.org/s/sqldrivers`.

How It Works

Package `database/sql` provides a generic interface for working with various SQL databases. Although `database/sql` provides a generic interface for SQL databases, it does not include any specific database drivers. Hence you must use a third-party package that provides an implementation for package `database/sql`. For example, if you want to work with a PostgreSQL database, you must use a database driver for PostgreSQL for `database/sql`.

Working with PostgreSQL

Third-party package pq (`github.com/lib/pq`) is a PostgreSQL driver for `database/sql`, which is written in Go. To install package pq, run the following command:

```
go get github.com/lib/pq
```

To working with package pq, you only need to import the driver and can use the full APIs provided by package `database/sql`. The `init` function in the following code block opens a PostgreSQL database:

```
import (
        "database/sql"
```

```
        _ "github.com/lib/pq"
)

var db *sql.DB

func init() {
        var err error
        db, err = sql.Open("postgres", "postgres://user:pass@localhost/dbname")
        if err != nil {
                log.Fatal(err)
        }
}
```

When you work with SQL databases you typically use the API of package database/sql, but you might not need to directly access the functions of packages for the specific database driver. Here you use package pq only for invoking its init function for registering your driver ("postgres") with database/sql. Because the package pq is importing just for invoking its init function, a *blank identifier* (_) is used as the package alias to avoid compilation error.

The function Open of package database/sql opens a database specified by its database driver name and a driver-specific data source name, usually consisting of at least a database name and connection information. Here the database driver name is "postgres". The function Open returns *sql.DB, which represents a pool of connections that the package sql provides for your database.

Working with MySQL

Third-party package mysql (github.com/go-sql-driver/mysql) is a MySQL driver for database/sql. To install package mysql, run the following command:

```
go get github.com/go-sql-driver/mysql
```

To work with package mysql, you only need to import the driver and can use the full APIs provided by package database/sql. The init function in the following code block opens a MySQL database:

```
import (
        "database/sql"

        _ " github.com/go-sql-driver/mysql"
)

var db *sql.DB

func init() {
        var err error
        db, err = sql.Open("mysql", "user:password@/dbname")
        if err != nil {
                log.Fatal(err)
        }
}
```

The function Open of package database/sql opens a database with driver name "mysql" and given data source name.

Example with PostgreSQL Database

Let's write an example program to demonstrate how to work with the PostgreSQL database using packages database/sql and pq. The following SQL statement is used for creating the table structure for the example program:

```
create table products (
  id                serial primary key,
  title          varchar(255) NOT NUL,
  description    varchar(255) NOT NUL,
  price             decimal(5,2) NOT NULL
);
```

Listing 6-6 shows an example program that demonstrates insert and read operations with PostgreSQL database on a database named productstore.

Listing 6-6. Insert and Read Operation with a Database productstore in PostgreSQL

```
package main

import (
        "database/sql"
        "fmt"
        "log"

        _ "github.com/lib/pq"
)

// Product struct provides the data model for productstore
type Product struct {
        ID          int
        Title       string
        Description string
        Price       float32
}

var db *sql.DB

func init() {
        var err error
        db, err = sql.Open("postgres", "postgres://user:pass@localhost/productstore")
        if err != nil {
                log.Fatal(err)
        }
}
func main() {
        product := Product{
                Title:       "Amazon Echo",
                Description: "Amazon Echo - Black",
                Price:       179.99,
        }
        // Insert a product
```

```go
        createProduct(product)
        // Read all product records
        getProducts()
}

// createProduct inserts product values into product table
func createProduct(prd Product) {
        result, err := db.Exec("INSERT INTO products(title, description, price) VALUES($1,
        $2, $3)", prd.Title, prd.Description, prd.Price)
        if err != nil {
                log.Fatal(err)
        }

        lastInsertID, err := result.LastInsertId()
        rowsAffected, err := result.RowsAffected()
        fmt.Printf("Product with id=%d created successfully (%d row affected)\n",
        lastInsertID, rowsAffected)
}

// getProducts reads all records from the product table
func getProducts() {
        rows, err := db.Query("SELECT * FROM products")
        if err != nil {
                if err == sql.ErrNoRows {
                        fmt.Println("No Records Found")
                        return
                }
                log.Fatal(err)
        }
        defer rows.Close()

        var products []*Product
        for rows.Next() {
                prd := &Product{}
                err := rows.Scan(&prd.Title, &prd.Description, &prd.Price)
                if err != nil {
                        log.Fatal(err)
                }
                products = append(products, prd)
        }
        if err = rows.Err(); err != nil {
                log.Fatal(err)
        }

        for _, pr := range products {
                fmt.Printf("%s, %s, $%.2f\n", pr.Title, pr.Description, pr.Price)
        }
}
```

A *sql.DB object is created in the function init by providing database driver name as "postgres" and the name of the data source to work with PostgreSQL database.

```
var db *sql.DB

func init() {
        var err error
        db, err = sql.Open("postgres", "postgres://user:pass@localhost/productstore")
        if err != nil {
                log.Fatal(err)
        }
}
```

The *sql.DB object is used for performing insert and read operations. To insert records into a database table, the function Exec of the sql.DB object is used to execute a query without returning any rows. The values for inserting records are passed using placeholder parameters using $N notation. The syntax for the placeholder parameter is different in different databases. For example, MySQL and SQL Server are using the character ? as a placeholder. The function Exec returns a sql.Result value that has two methods: LastInsertId and RowsAffected. LastInsertId returns the integer value generated by the database, which can be used for getting the value of and auto increment column when inserting a new row. RowsAffected returns the number of rows affected by an update, insert, or delete operation.

```
func createProduct(prd Product) {
        result, err := db.Exec("INSERT INTO products(title, description, price) VALUES($1,
$2, $3)", prd.Title, prd.Description, prd.Price)
        if err != nil {
                log.Fatal(err)
        }

        lastInsertID, err := result.LastInsertId()
        rowsAffected, err := result.RowsAffected()
        fmt.Printf("Product with id=%d created successfully (%d row affected)\n",
lastInsertID, rowsAffected)
}
```

To perform the SQL statement SELECT for querying data, the function Query of the sql.DB object is used, which returns a value of struct type Rows.

```
rows, err := db.Query("SELECT * FROM products")
```

By calling the method Next of Rows object, you can read the values of the next row using the Scan method.

```
var products []*Product
        for rows.Next() {
                prd := &Product{}
                err := rows.Scan(&prd.Title, &prd.Description, &prd.Price)
                if err != nil {
                        log.Fatal(err)
                }
                products = append(products, prd)
        }
        if err = rows.Err(); err != nil {
                log.Fatal(err)
        }
}
```

When you execute a query for getting a single row, you can use the function QueryRow to execute a query and return one row. Here is an example code block that uses QueryRow to get one row:

```
    id := 1
    var product string
  err := db.QueryRow("SELECT title FROM products WHERE id=$1", id).Scan(&product)
switch {
    case err == sql.ErrNoRows:
            log.Printf("No product with that ID.")
    case err != nil:
            log.Fatal(err)
    default:
            fmt.Printf("Product is %s\n", product)
    }
```

When you run the program in Listing 6-6, you should see output similar to the following:

```
Product with id=1 created successfully (1 row affected)
Amazon Echo, Amazon Echo - Black, $179.99
```

Using the standard library package database/sql and a third-party package for a specific database driver like github.com/lib/pq for PostgreSQL database, you can work with variety of SQL databases. The advantages of using package database/sql is that you can use the same interface to work with different databases.

CHAPTER 7

■ ■ ■

Building HTTP Servers

Go is a general-purpose programming language that can be used for building variety of applications. When it comes to web programming, Go is a great technology stack for building back-end APIs. Go might not be an ideal choice for building conventional web applications where the web application performs UI rendering using server-side templates. When you build RESTful APIs for powering back-end systems for a variety of systems including web front-end, mobile applications, and many modern application scenarios, Go is the finest stack. Some of the existing technology stacks are good for building lightweight RESTful APIs, but these systems eventually fail when the HTTP requests have CPU-intensive tasks and the APIs are communicating with other back-end systems in a distributed environment. Go is an ideal technology stack for building massively scalable back-end systems and RESTful APIs. In this chapter, you learn how to build HTTP servers for building your back-end APIs.

The standard library package net/http, which comes with lot of extensibility, provides the foundational layer for writing web applications in Go. If you would like to use server-side templates for your Go web applications, you can leverage the standard library package html/template to render the user interface. In Go, by simply using standard library packages, you can build full-featured web applications and RESTful APIs, so you don't need a web framework for most of the web programming scenarios, especially building RESTful services. In most of the use cases, use standard library packages; whenever you need extra functionality, use third-party libraries that extend the standard library packages.

In a nutshell, web programming is based on a request–response paradigm, where clients send an HTTP request to the web server, the request is processed on the web server, and it sends an HTTP response back to the clients. To process HTTP requests and send HTTP responses in this way, package net/http provides two major components:

- **ServeMux** is an HTTP request multiplexer (HTTP request router) that compares uniform resource identifiers (URIs) of incoming HTTP requests against a list of predefined URI patterns and then executes the associated handler configured for the URI pattern. The struct type http.ServeMux provides an implementation for working as an HTTP request multiplexer.

- **Handler** is responsible for writing headers and bodies into the HTTP responses. In package net/http, Handler is an interface, so it provides greater level of extensibility when you write HTTP applications. Because the Handler implementation is just looking for a concrete type of Handler interface, you can provide your own implementations for serving HTTP requests.

Package net/http is designed for extensibility and composability, so it gives you a great deal of flexibility to write your web applications by extending the functionality provided by net/http. The Go community has delivered a lot of third-party packages to extend the package net/http, which can be used for your Go web applications.

© Shiju Varghese 2016
S. Varghese, *Go Recipes*, DOI 10.1007/978-1-4842-1188-5_7

7-1. Creating Custom HTTP Handlers

Problem

How do you create custom handlers for serving HTTP requests for an HTTP server?

Solution

HTTP handlers are created by providing an implementation of the http.Handler interface.

How It Works

In Go, any object can be an implementation of HTTP handler if you could provide an implementation of the http.Handler interface. Here is the definition of interface Handler in the package http:

```
type Handler interface {
        ServeHTTP(ResponseWriter, *Request)
}
```

The interface http.Handler has a method ServeHTTP, which has two parameters: an interface type http.ResponseWriter and a pointer to struct type http.Request. The method ServeHTTP should be used for writing headers and data to the ResponseWriter.

Let's create a custom handler by providing the method ServeHTTP to a struct type:

```
type textHandler struct {
        responseText string
}

func (th *textHandler) ServeHTTP(w http.ResponseWriter, r *http.Request) {
        fmt.Fprintf(w, th.responseText)
}
```

A struct type textHandler is declared, which has a field responseText that will be used for writing data to the ResponseWriter. The method ServeHTTP is attached to the textHandler so that it is an implementation of interface http.Handler. The struct type textHandler is ready for serving HTTP requests by configuring it as the handler with a ServeMux. Listing 7-1 shows an example HTTP server that uses two custom handlers for serving HTTP requests.

Listing 7-1. HTTP Server with Custom Handlers

```
package main

import (
        "fmt"
        "log"
        "net/http"
)

type textHandler struct {
        responseText string
}
```

```go
func (th *textHandler) ServeHTTP(w http.ResponseWriter, r *http.Request) {
        fmt.Fprintf(w, th.responseText)
}

type indexHandler struct {
}

func (ih *indexHandler) ServeHTTP(w http.ResponseWriter, r *http.Request) {
        w.Header().Set(
                "Content-Type",
                "text/html",
        )
        html :=
                `<doctype html>
<html>
<head>
        <title>Hello Gopher</title>
</head>
<body>
        <b>Hello Gopher!</b>
<p>
  <a href="/welcome">Welcome</a> |  <a href="/message">Message</a>
</p>
</body>
</html>`
        fmt.Fprintf(w, html)

}

func main() {
        mux := http.NewServeMux()
        mux.Handle("/", &indexHandler{})

        thWelcome := &textHandler{"Welcome to Go Web Programming"}
        mux.Handle("/welcome", thWelcome)

        thMessage := &textHandler{"net/http package is used to build web apps"}
        mux.Handle("/message", thMessage)

        log.Println("Listening...")
        http.ListenAndServe(":8080", mux)
}
```

The HTTP server uses two handler implementations: textHandler and indexHandler; both are struct types that have implemented the http.Handler interface by providing an implementation of the method ServeHTTP. The method ServeHTTP of textHandler writes the text string that is accessed through its property to the ResponseWriter using the function fmt.Fprintf.

```go
func (th *textHandler) ServeHTTP(w http.ResponseWriter, r *http.Request) {
        fmt.Fprintf(w, th.responseText)
}
```

For the indexHandler, method ServeHTTP declares an HTML string and writes this to the ResponseWriter.

```go
func (ih *indexHandler) ServeHTTP(w http.ResponseWriter, r *http.Request) {
        w.Header().Set(
                "Content-Type",
                "text/html",
        )
        html :=
                `<doctype html>
        <html>
        <head>
                <title>Hello Gopher</title>
        </head>
        <body>
                <b>Hello Gophe!</b>
        <p>
          <a href="/welcome">Welcome</a> |   <a href="/message">Message</a>
        </p>
        </body>
</html>`
        fmt.Fprintf(w, html)

}
```

Inside the function main, an object of ServeMux is created and then configures the HTTP request multiplexer by providing a uniform resource locator (URL) pattern and its corresponding handler values.

```go
func main() {
        mux := http.NewServeMux()
        mux.Handle("/", &indexHandler{})

        thWelcome := &textHandler{"Welcome to Go Web Programming"}
        mux.Handle("/welcome", thWelcome)

        thMessage := &textHandler{"net/http package is used to build web apps"}
        mux.Handle("/message", thMessage)

        log.Println("Listening...")
        http.ListenAndServe(":8080", mux)
}
```

The function Handle of ServeMux allows you to register a URL pattern with an associated handler. Here the URL "/" is mapped with an indexHandler value as the handler, and URLs "/welcome" and "/message" are mapped for textHandler values as the handlers for serving HTTP requests. Because you have implemented an HTTP request multiplexer with a ServeMux value that has used two custom handlers for serving HTTP requests, you can now start your HTTP server. The function ListenAndServe starts an HTTP server with a given address and handler.

```go
http.ListenAndServe(":8080", mux)
```

The first parameter of the function ListenAndServe is an address for an HTTP server to listen at a given Transmission Control Protocol (TCP) network address, and the second parameter is an implementation of the http.Handler interface. Here you have given a ServeMux value as the handler. The struct type ServeMux has also implemented the method ServeHTTP so that it can be given as a handler for calling the function ListenAndServe. Typically you provide a ServeMux value as the second argument to call the function ListenAndServe. We cover this in greater detail later in this chapter.

The function http.ListenAndServe creates an instance of struct type http.Server by using the given arguments, calls its (http.Server value) ListenAndServe method that listens on the TCP network address, and then calls the method Serve (of http.Server value) with a handler to handle requests on incoming connections. The http.Server defines parameters for running an HTTP server.

Let's run the program to start an HTTP server that will listen at port number 8080. Figure 7-1 shows the response from the HTTP server for the request to "/".

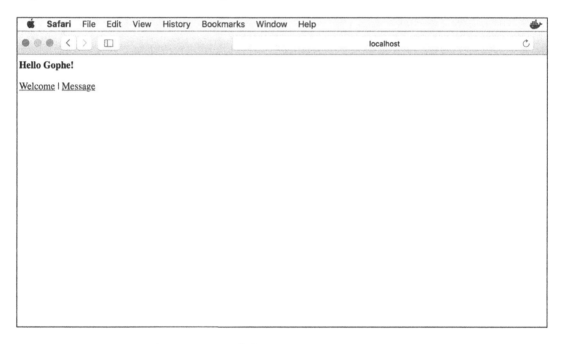

Figure 7-1. *Server response for the request to "/"*

Figure 7-2 shows the response from the HTTP server for the request to "/welcome".

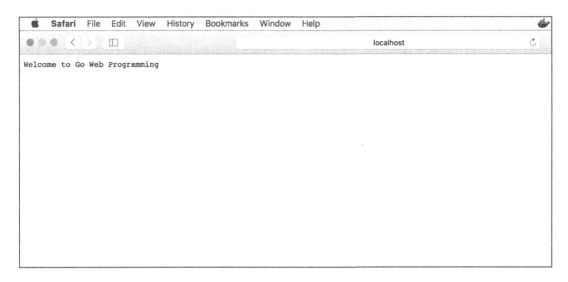

Figure 7-2. *Server response for the request to* "/welcome"

Figure 7-3 shows the response from the HTTP server for the request to "/message".

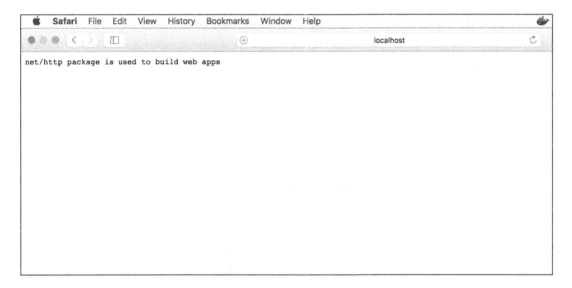

Figure 7-3. *Server response for the request to* "/message"

7-2. Using an Adapter to Use Normal Functions as Handlers

Problem

It would be a tedious job to create custom handlers for serving HTTP requests. How do you use an adapter to use normal functions as HTTP handlers so that you don't need to create custom handler types?

Solution

By using the func type http.HandlerFunc, you can use normal functions as HTTP handlers. HandlerFunc has an implementation of interface http.Handler so that it can be used as HTTP handlers. You can provide normal functions with the appropriate signature, as an argument to the HandlerFunc to use it as HTTP handlers. Here func type HandlerFunc works as an adapter to your normal functions to be used as HTTP handlers.

How It Works

HandlerFunc is an adapter that allows you to use normal functions as HTTP handlers. Here is the declaration of type HandlerFunc in the package http:

```
type HandlerFunc func(ResponseWriter, *Request)
```

If fn is a function with the appropriate signature (func(ResponseWriter, *Request)), HandlerFunc(fn) is a handler that calls fn. Listing 7-2 shows an example HTTP server that uses HandlerFunc to use normal functions as HTTP handlers.

Listing 7-2. HTTP Server That Uses Normal Functions as HTTP Handlers

```go
package main

import (
        "fmt"
        "log"
        "net/http"
)

func index(w http.ResponseWriter, r *http.Request) {
        w.Header().Set(
                "Content-Type",
                "text/html",
        )
        html :=
                `<doctype html>
        <html>
        <head>
                <title>Hello Gopher</title>
        </head>
        <body>
                <b>Hello Gopher!</b>
        <p>
            <a href="/welcome">Welcome</a> |  <a href="/message">Message</a>
        </p>
        </body>
</html>`
        fmt.Fprintf(w, html)
}

func welcome(w http.ResponseWriter, r *http.Request) {
```

175

```
        fmt.Fprintf(w, "Welcome to Go Web Programming")
}
func message(w http.ResponseWriter, r *http.Request) {
        fmt.Fprintf(w, "net/http package is used to build web apps")
}

func main() {
        mux := http.NewServeMux()
        mux.Handle("/", http.HandlerFunc(index))
        mux.Handle("/welcome", http.HandlerFunc(welcome))
        mux.Handle("/message", http.HandlerFunc(message))

        log.Println("Listening...")
        http.ListenAndServe(":8080", mux)
}
```

Here functions are declared with the signature func(ResponseWriter, *Request) to use them as HTTP handlers by providing these functions to HandlerFunc.

```
mux := http.NewServeMux()
mux.Handle("/", http.HandlerFunc(index))
mux.Handle("/welcome", http.HandlerFunc(welcome))
mux.Handle("/message", http.HandlerFunc(message))
```

Comparing this approach with the program written in Listing 7-1, where you created a struct type and provided a method ServeHTTP to implement the interface http.Handler, this approach is easier because you can simply use normal functions as HTTP handlers.

7-3. Using Normal Functions as HTTP Handlers Using ServeMux.HandleFunc

Problem

How do you use normal functions as HTTP handlers without explicitly calling the http.HandlerFunc type?

Solution

The ServeMux provides a method HandleFunc that allows you to register a normal function as a handler for the given URI pattern without explicitly calling the func type http.HandlerFunc.

How It Works

The method HandleFunc of ServeMux is a helper function that internally calls the method Handle of ServeMux in which the given handler function is used to call the http.HandlerFunc to provide an implementation of http.Handler. Here is the source of function HandleFunc in package http:

```
func (mux *ServeMux) HandleFunc(pattern string, handler func(ResponseWriter, *Request)) {
        mux.Handle(pattern, HandlerFunc(handler))
}
```

Listing 7-3 shows an example HTTP server that uses `HandleFunc` of `ServeMux` to use normal functions as HTTP handlers without explicitly using `HandlerFunc`.

Listing 7-3. HTTP Server That Uses `HandleFunc` of `ServeMux`

```go
package main

import (
        "fmt"
        "log"
        "net/http"
)

func index(w http.ResponseWriter, r *http.Request) {
        w.Header().Set(
                "Content-Type",
                "text/html",
        )
        html :=
                `<doctype html>
<html>
<head>
        <title>Hello Gopher</title>
</head>
<body>
        <b>Hello Gopher!</b>
        <p>
            <a href="/welcome">Welcome</a> |  <a href="/message">Message</a>
        </p>
        </body>
</html>`
        fmt.Fprintf(w, html)
}

func welcome(w http.ResponseWriter, r *http.Request) {
        fmt.Fprintf(w, "Welcome to Go Web Programming")
}
func message(w http.ResponseWriter, r *http.Request) {
        fmt.Fprintf(w, "net/http package is used to build web apps")
}

func main() {
        mux := http.NewServeMux()
        mux.HandleFunc("/", index)
        mux.HandleFunc("/welcome", welcome)
        mux.HandleFunc("/message", message)
        log.Println("Listening...")
        http.ListenAndServe(":8080", mux)
}
```

The `HandleFunc` is just a helper function that calls the function `Handle` of `ServeMux` by providing `http.HandlerFunc` as a handler.

7-4. Using Default ServeMux Value

Problem

How do you use the default ServeMux value provided by the package http, as the ServeMux, and how do you register handler functions when you use the default ServeMux value?

Solution

The package http provides a default ServeMux value named DefaultServeMux, which can be used as the HTTP request multiplexer so that you don't need to create a ServeMux from your code. When you use DefaultServeMux as the ServeMux value, you can configure HTTP routes using the function http.HandleFunc, which registers the handler function for the given pattern into the DefaultServeMux.

How It Works

By default, package http provides an instance of ServeMux named DefaultServeMux. When you call the function http.ListenAndServe for running your HTTP server you can provide a nil value as the argument for the second parameter (an implementation of http.Handler).

```
http.ListenAndServe(":8080", nil)
```

If you provide a nil value, package http will take DefaultServeMux as the ServeMux value. When you work with DefaultServeMux as the ServeMux value, you can use the function http.HandleFunc to register a handler function for the given URL pattern. Inside the function http.HandleFunc, it calls the function HandleFunc of DefaultServeMux. The HandleFunc of ServeMux then calls the function Handle of ServeMux by providing the http.HandlerFunc call using the given handler function.

Listing 7-4 shows an example HTTP server that uses DefaultServeMux as the ServeMux value, and using http.HandleFunc to register a handler function.

Listing 7-4. HTTP Server That Uses DefaultServeMux and http.HandleFunc

```
package main

import (
        "fmt"
        "log"
        "net/http"
)

func index(w http.ResponseWriter, r *http.Request) {
        w.Header().Set(
                "Content-Type",
                "text/html",
        )
        html :=
                `<doctype html>
        <html>
        <head>
                <title>Hello Gopher</title>
```

```
        </head>
        <body>
                <b>Hello Gopher!</b>
        <p>
            <a href="/welcome">Welcome</a> |  <a href="/message">Message</a>
        </p>
        </body>
</html>`
        fmt.Fprintf(w, html)
}

func welcome(w http.ResponseWriter, r *http.Request) {
        fmt.Fprintf(w, "Welcome to Go Web Programming")
}
func message(w http.ResponseWriter, r *http.Request) {
        fmt.Fprintf(w, "net/http package is used to build web apps")
}

func main() {
        http.HandleFunc("/", index)
        http.HandleFunc("/welcome", welcome)
        http.HandleFunc("/message", message)
        log.Println("Listening...")
        http.ListenAndServe(":8080", nil)
}
```

The function http.HandleFunc is used to register a handler function to the DefaultServeMux.

7-5. Customizing http.Server

Problem

How do you customize the values of http.Server to be used for running an HTTP server?

Solution

To customize http.Server and use it to run the HTTP server, create an instance of http.Server with the desired value and then call its method ListenAndServe.

How It Works

In the previous recipes, you have used the function http.ListenAndServe for running an HTTP server. When you call the function http.ListenAndServe, it internally creates an instance of http.Server by providing a string value of address and an http.Handler value and runs the server using the http.Server value. Because the instance of http.Server is created from inside the function http.ListenAndServe, you could not customize the values of http.Server. The http.Server defines parameters for running an HTTP server. If you want to customize the http.Server value, you can explicitly create an instance of http.Server from your program and then call its method ListenAndServe.

Listing 7-5 shows an example HTTP server that customizes http.Server and calls its method ListenAndServe to run the HTTP server.

Listing 7-5. HTTP Server That Uses the Method ListenAndServe of http.Server

```
package main

import (
        "fmt"
        "log"
        "net/http"
        "time"
)

func index(w http.ResponseWriter, r *http.Request) {
        fmt.Fprintf(w, "Welcome to Go Web Programming")
}

func main() {

        http.HandleFunc("/", index)

        server := &http.Server{
                Addr:         ":8080",
                ReadTimeout:  60 * time.Second,
                WriteTimeout: 60 * time.Second,
        }

        log.Println("Listening...")
        server.ListenAndServe()
}
```

This example customizes the fields ReadTimeout and WriteTimeout of http.Server to be used for running the HTTP server.

7-6. Writing HTTP Middleware

Problem

How do you write an HTTP middleware function to wrap HTTP handlers with a pluggable piece of code to provide shared behavior to HTTP applications?

Solution

To write HTTP middleware functions, write functions with the signature func(http.Handler) http.Handler, thus HTTP middleware functions can accept a handler as a parameter value and can provide a pluggable piece of code inside the middleware function. Because it returns http.Handler, the middleware function can be used as a Handler to register with the HTTP request multiplexer.

How It Works

HTTP middlewares are pluggable and self-contained piece of code that wrap HTTP handlers of web applications. These are like typical HTTP handlers, but they wrap another HTTP handler, typically normal application handlers to provide shared behaviors to web applications. It works as an another layer in the HTTP request-handling cycle to inject some pluggable code for executing shared behaviors such as authentication and authorization, logging, caching, and so on.

Here is the basic pattern for writing HTTP middleware:

```
func middlewareHandler(next http.Handler) http.Handler {
  return http.HandlerFunc(func(w http.ResponseWriter, r *http.Request) {
    // Middleware logic goes here before executing application handler
    next.ServeHTTP(w, r)
   // Middleware logic goes here after executing application handler
  })
}
```

Here the middleware function accepts an http.Handler value and returns an http.Handler value. Because the middleware function returns http.Handler, it can register as a Handler with http.ServeMux by wrapping the application handler as an argument to the middleware function. To invoke the logic of a given handler from middleware, call its method ServeHTTP.

```
next.ServeHTTP(w, r)
```

Middleware logic can be executed before and after executing application handlers. To write middleware logic before executing the given Handler (handler getting as a parameter value), write it before calling the ServeHTTP and write the logic after calling the ServeHTTP to execute the middleware logic after executing the Handler of parameter value.

Listing 7-6 shows an example HTTP server that wraps application handlers with a middleware function named loggingHandler.

Listing 7-6. HTTP Middleware That Wraps Application Handlers

```
package main

import (
        "fmt"
        "log"
        "net/http"
        "time"
)

// loggingHandler is an HTTP Middleware that logs HTTP requests.
func loggingHandler(next http.Handler) http.Handler {
        return http.HandlerFunc(func(w http.ResponseWriter, r *http.Request) {
                // Middleware logic before executing given Handler
                start := time.Now()
                log.Printf("Started %s %s", r.Method, r.URL.Path)
                next.ServeHTTP(w, r)
                // Middleware logic after executing given Handler
                log.Printf("Completed %s in %v", r.URL.Path, time.Since(start))
        })
}
```

```go
func index(w http.ResponseWriter, r *http.Request) {
        w.Header().Set(
                "Content-Type",
                "text/html",
        )
        html :=
                `<doctype html>
        <html>
        <head>
                <title>Hello Gopher</title>
        </head>
        <body>
                <b>Hello Gopher!</b>
        <p>
            <a href="/welcome">Welcome</a> |  <a href="/message">Message</a>
        </p>
        </body>
</html>`
        fmt.Fprintf(w, html)
}

func welcome(w http.ResponseWriter, r *http.Request) {
        fmt.Fprintf(w, "Welcome to Go Web Programming")
}
func message(w http.ResponseWriter, r *http.Request) {
        fmt.Fprintf(w, "net/http package is used to build web apps")
}

func main() {
        http.Handle("/", loggingHandler(http.HandlerFunc(index)))
        http.Handle("/welcome", loggingHandler(http.HandlerFunc(welcome)))
        http.Handle("/message", loggingHandler(http.HandlerFunc(message)))
        log.Println("Listening...")
        http.ListenAndServe(":8080", nil)
}
```

An HTTP middleware named loggingHandler is used for logging all HTTP requests and their response times. The function loggingHandler accepts an http.Handler value so you can pass an application handler as an argument to the middleware function, and can register the middleware handler to ServeMux because it returns http.Handler.

```go
http.Handle("/", loggingHandler(http.HandlerFunc(index)))
http.Handle("/welcome", loggingHandler(http.HandlerFunc(welcome)))
http.Handle("/message", loggingHandler(http.HandlerFunc(message)))
```

Because the type of the parameter of middleware function is `http.Handler`, application handler functions are converted into `http.Handler` by using `http.HandlerFunc` to call the middleware. You can have chain of middleware functions to wrap your application handlers because you write middleware functions with `signature func(http.Hanlder) http.Handler`.

Let's run the application and navigate to the all configured URL patterns. You should see the log messages provided by HTTP middleware, similar to the following:

```
2016/08/05 15:34:29 Started GET /
2016/08/05 15:34:29 Completed / in 5.0039ms
2016/08/05 15:34:34 Started GET /welcome
2016/08/05 15:34:34 Completed /welcome in 9.0082ms
2016/08/05 15:34:40 Started GET /message
2016/08/05 15:34:40 Completed /message in 6.0077ms
```

7-7. Writing RESTful API with Go and MongoDB

Problem

You would like to write RESTful APIs in Go with MongoDB as the persistence store.

Solution

The standard library package `http` provides all essential components for building RESTful APIs. Package `http` is designed for extensibility so that you can extend the functionality of the package with third-party packages and your own custom packages when you write HTTP applications. The package `mgo` is the most popular package for working with MongoDB, which is used for the data persistence for the REST API example.

How It Works

Let's build a REST API example to demonstrate how to build a RESTful API with Go and MongoDB. Although package `http` is sufficient for building web applications, we would like to use third-party package Gorilla mux (github.com/gorilla/mux) as the HTTP request multiplexer instead of `http.ServeMux`. Package `mux` provides rich functionality for specifying the HTTP routes, which is useful for specifying the RESTful endpoints. For example, `http.ServeMux` doesn't support specifying HTTP verbs for the URL patterns, which is essential for defining RESTful endpoints, but package `mux` provides lot of flexibility for defining routes of the application, including specifying the HTTP verbs for the URL pattern. The third-party package `mgo` is used for performing persistence on the MongoDB database, a popular NoSQL database.

Directory Structure of the Application

We organize the REST API application into multiple packages. Figure 7-4 shows the high-level directory structure used for the REST API application.

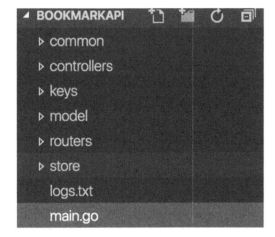

Figure 7-4. *Directory structure of the REST API application*

Figure 7-5 shows the directory structure and associated files of the completed version of the REST API application.

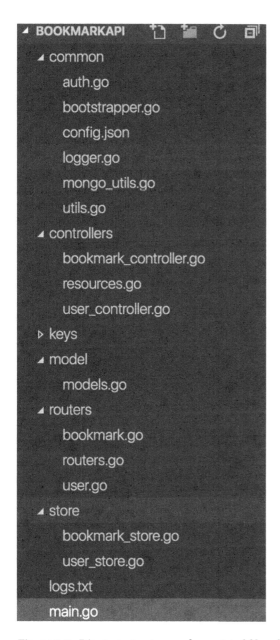

Figure 7-5. Directory structure and associated files of the completed application

Except the directory keys, all other directories represent Go packages. The keys directory contains cryptographic keys for signing JSON web tokens (JWT) and its verification. This is used for the authentication of APIs with JWT.

The REST API application has been divided into the following packages:

- **Common:** Package `common` provides utility functions and provides initialization logic for the application.

- **Controllers:** Package `controllers` provides HTTP handler functions for the application.

- **Store:** Package `store` provides persistence logic with MongoDB database.

- **model:** Package `model` describes the data model of the application.

- **routers:** Package `routers` implements HTTP request routers for the REST API.

The example code in the book primarily focuses on an entity named Bookmark and discusses basic parts for building a REST API. The completed version of the REST API application, which includes authentication with JWT, logging, and so, is available from the code repository of the book at `https://github.com/shijuvar/go-recipes`.

Data Model

Package `model` provides the data model for the REST API application. Listing 7-7 shows the data model of the REST API example.

Listing 7-7. Data Model in `models.go`

```
package model

import (
        "time"

        "gopkg.in/mgo.v2/bson"
)

// Bookmark type represents the metadata of a bookmark.

type Bookmark struct {
                ID          bson.ObjectId `bson:"_id,omitempty"`
                Name        string        `json:"name"`
                Description string        `json:"description"`
                Location    string        `json:"location"`
                Priority    int           `json:"priority"` // Priority (1 -5)
                CreatedBy   string        `json:"createdby"`
                CreatedOn   time.Time     `json:"createdon,omitempty"`
                Tags        []string      `json:"tags,omitempty"`
        }
```

The type Bookmark represents the metadata of bookmarks in the application. This model is designed to be working with MongoDB so that type of field ID is specified as `bson.ObjectId`. The example application allows the users to add, edit, delete, and view metadata of bookmarks that can be organized with a priority and with tags.

Resource Model

The previous step defined the data model for the application to be worked with, a NoSQL database, MongoDB. As you have done the data modeling against a database, let's define the resource model for our REST APIs. Resource modeling defines a REST API that provides endpoints of an API to its client applications. This can leverage URIs, API operations using various HTTP methods, and so on. According to Roy Fielding's dissertation on REST, "The key abstraction of information in REST is a resource. Any information that can be named can be a resource: a document or image, a temporal service (e.g., "today's weather in Los Angeles"), a collection of other resources, a non-virtual object (e.g., a person), and so on. In other words, any concept that might be the target of an author's hypertext reference must fit within the definition of a resource. A resource is a conceptual mapping to a set of entities, not the entity that corresponds to the mapping at any particular point in time."

Here you define a resource named "/bookmarks", which represents the collection of a bookmark entity. By using an HTTP Post on the resource "/bookmarks", you can create a new resource. The URI "/bookmarks/{id}" can be used to represent a single bookmark entity. By using an HTTP Get on the "/bookmarks/{id}", you can retrieve data for a single bookmark. Table 7-1 shows the resource model that is designed against the bookmark entity.

Table 7-1. *Resource Model for the Bookmark Entity*

URI	HTTP Verb	Functionality
/bookmarks	Post	Creates a new bookmark
/bookmarks/{id}	Put	Updates an existing bookmark for a given ID
/bookmarks	Get	Gets all bookmarks
/bookmarks/{id}	Get	Gets a single bookmark for a given ID
/bookmarks/users/{id}	Get	Gets all bookmarks associated with a single user
/bookmarks/{id}	Delete	Deletes an existing bookmark for a given ID

Configuring REST API Resources into the HTTP Multiplexer

Let's map the resources of REST API into the HTTP request multiplexer. Package mux is used as the HTTP request multiplexer for this application. The following command installs package mux:

```
go get github.com/gorilla/mux
```

To use package mux, you must add github.com/gorilla/mux to the list of imports.

```
import " github.com/gorilla/mux "
```

Listing 7-8 shows the function SetBookmarkRoutes that registers resource endpoints and the corresponding application handlers for the Bookmark entity, into a HTTP request multiplexer. Here you would like to organize the multiplexer configuration for each entity in individual functions so that you can easily maintain the HTTP routes of the applications. If you want to add a multiplexer configuration for the User entity, you organize this in another function. These functions are finally called from the function InitRoutes of routers.go. Application handlers are organized into the package controllers.

Listing 7-8. Configuration for the HTTP Request Multiplexer in routers/bookmark.go

```
package routers

import (
        "github.com/gorilla/mux"

        "github.com/shijuvar/go-recipes/ch07/bookmarkapi/controllers"
)

// SetBookmarkRoutes registers routes for bookmark entity.
func SetBookmarkRoutes(router *mux.Router) *mux.Router {
        router.HandleFunc("/bookmarks", controllers.CreateBookmark).Methods("POST")
        router.HandleFunc("/bookmarks/{id}", controllers.UpdateBookmark).Methods("PUT")
        router.HandleFunc("/bookmarks", controllers.GetBookmarks).Methods("GET")
        router.HandleFunc("/bookmarks/{id}", controllers.GetBookmarkByID).Methods("GET")
        router.HandleFunc("/bookmarks/users/{id}", controllers.GetBookmarksByUser).
        Methods("GET")
        router.HandleFunc("/bookmarks/{id}", controllers.DeleteBookmark).Methods("DELETE")
        return router
}
```

The type mux.Router is used to register HTTP routes and their corresponding handler functions. It implements the interface http.Handler so it is compatible with the type ServeMux of package http. The function HandleFunc registers a new route with a matcher for the URL path. This function is working similar to the function HandleFunc of http.ServeMux. The function SetBookmarkRoutes is invoked from the function InitRoutes of routers.go as shown in Listing 7-9.

Listing 7-9. Initializing Routes in routers/routers.go

```
package routers

import (
        "github.com/gorilla/mux"
)

// InitRoutes registers all routes for the application.
func InitRoutes() *mux.Router {
        router := mux.NewRouter().StrictSlash(false)
        // Routes for the Bookmark entity
        router = SetBookmarkRoutes(router)
        // Call other router configurations
        return router
}
```

A new mux.router instance is created by calling the function mux.NewRouter. The function InitRoutes is called from main.go of package main to configure routes of the application to be used with the HTTP server.

Managing mgo.Session

CChapter 6 discussed how to work with MongoDB database using package mgo. When package mgo is used for working with MongoDB, you first obtain an mgo.Session value by calling mgo.Dial or mgo.DialWithInfo. The mgo.Session instance is used to perform CRUD operations against the MongoDB collections. It is not a recommended practice to use a global mgo.Session value for all CRUD operations in your application, however. A good practice for using the mgo.Session value is to use a copied value of mgo.Session from the global mgo.Session value for a data persistence session. When you write web applications, a good practice is to use a copied value of the global mgo.Session value for each HTTP request life cycle. Type mgo.Session provides the function Copy, which can be used for creating a copy of an mgo.Session value. You can also use the function Clone that provides a cloned version of the mgo.Session value to make a copy of mgo.Session to perform CRUD operations for a data persistence session. Both copied and cloned sessions will reuse the same pool of connections from the global mgo.Session, which is obtained using Dial or DialWithInfo. Function Clone works just like Copy, but also reuses the same socket as the original session. The REST API example uses the function Copy for making a copied mgo.Session value that is used across the single HTTP request life cycle.

Listing 7-10 shows the source of mongo_utils.go in package common, which provides helper functions for working with MongoDB, including a struct type named DataStore that provides a copy of the global mgo.Session to be used for each HTTP request life cycle.

Listing 7-10. Helper Functions for mgo.Session in common/mongo_utils.go

```go
package common

import (
        "log"
        "time"

        "gopkg.in/mgo.v2"
)

var session *mgo.Session

// GetSession returns a MongoDB Session
func getSession() *mgo.Session {
        if session == nil {
                var err error
                session, err = mgo.DialWithInfo(&mgo.DialInfo{
                        Addrs:    []string{AppConfig.MongoDBHost},
                        Username: AppConfig.DBUser,
                        Password: AppConfig.DBPwd,
                        Timeout:  60 * time.Second,
                })
                if err != nil {
                        log.Fatalf("[GetSession]: %s\n", err)
                }
        }
        return session
}
func createDBSession() {
        var err error
        session, err = mgo.DialWithInfo(&mgo.DialInfo{
```

```
                Addrs:    []string{AppConfig.MongoDBHost},
                Username: AppConfig.DBUser,
                Password: AppConfig.DBPwd,
                Timeout:  60 * time.Second,
        })
        if err != nil {
                log.Fatalf("[createDbSession]: %s\n", err)
        }
}


// DataStore for MongoDB
type DataStore struct {
        MongoSession *mgo.Session
}


// Close closes an mgo.Session value.
// Used to add defer statements for closing the copied session.
func (ds *DataStore) Close() {
        ds.MongoSession.Close()
}


// Collection returns mgo.collection for the given name
func (ds *DataStore) Collection(name string) *mgo.Collection {
        return ds.MongoSession.DB(AppConfig.Database).C(name)
}


// NewDataStore creates a new DataStore object to be used for each HTTP request.
func NewDataStore() *DataStore {
        session := getSession().Copy()
        dataStore := &DataStore{
                MongoSession: session,
        }
        return dataStore
}
```

The function createDBSession creates a global mgo.Session value and this function will be called at once before running the HTTP server. The function getSession returns the global mgo.Session value. Instances of struct type DataStore are created from applications handlers to work with MongoDB database by creating a copy of mgo.Session. The function NewDataStore creates a new instance of DataStore by providing a copy of the global mgo.Session value.

```
func NewDataStore() *DataStore {
        session := getSession().Copy()
        dataStore := &DataStore{
                MongoSession: session,
        }
        return dataStore
}
```

Models for JSON Resources

The example REST API application is a JSON-based REST API where the JSON format is used for sending and receiving data in HTTP requests and responses. To meet JSON API specifications (http://jsonapi. org/), let's define data models to be used for HTTP requests and HTTP responses. Here you define models for JSON representation in which the element name "data" is defined as the root for all JSON representations in the body of HTTP requests and HTTP responses. Listing 7-11 shows the data models for JSON representation.

Listing 7-11. Data Models for JSON Resources in `controllers/resources.go`

```
package controllers

import (
        "github.com/shijuvar/go-recipes/ch07/bookmarkapi/model"
)
//Models for JSON resources
type (
        // BookmarkResource for Post and Put - /bookmarks
        // For Get - /bookmarks/id
        BookmarkResource struct {
                Data model.Bookmark `json:"data"`
        }
        // BookmarksResource for Get - /bookmarks
        BookmarksResource struct {
                Data []model.Bookmark `json:"data"`
        }
)
```

   This type is used from application handler to receive data from the body of `http.Request` and to write data to the `http.ResponseWriter`.

HTTP Handlers for Bookmarks Resource

Here are the routes configured for the Bookmarks resource:

```
router.HandleFunc("/bookmarks", controllers.CreateBookmark).Methods("POST")
router.HandleFunc("/bookmarks/{id}", controllers.UpdateBookmark).Methods("PUT")
router.HandleFunc("/bookmarks", controllers.GetBookmarks).Methods("GET")
router.HandleFunc("/bookmarks/{id}", controllers.GetBookmarkByID).Methods("GET")
router.HandleFunc("/bookmarks/users/{id}", controllers.GetBookmarksByUser).Methods("GET")
router.HandleFunc("/bookmarks/{id}", controllers.DeleteBookmark).Methods("DELETE")
```

   The HTTP handler functions for the Bookmarks resource are written in `bookmark_controller.go`, which is organized into the package `controllers`. Listing 7-12 shows the handler functions for serving HTTP requests to the Bookmarks resources.

Listing 7-12. HTTP Handler Functions for Bookmarks Resource in controllers/bookmark_controller.go

```go
package controllers

import (
        "encoding/json"
        "net/http"

        "github.com/gorilla/mux"
        "gopkg.in/mgo.v2"
        "gopkg.in/mgo.v2/bson"

        "github.com/shijuvar/go-recipes/ch07/bookmarkapi/common"
        "github.com/shijuvar/go-recipes/ch07/bookmarkapi/store"
)

// CreateBookmark insert a new Bookmark.
// Handler for HTTP Post - "/bookmarks
func CreateBookmark(w http.ResponseWriter, r *http.Request) {
        var dataResource BookmarkResource
        // Decode the incoming Bookmark json
        err := json.NewDecoder(r.Body).Decode(&dataResource)
        if err != nil {
                common.DisplayAppError(
                        w,
                        err,
                        "Invalid Bookmark data",
                        500,
                )
                return
        }
        bookmark := &dataResource.Data
        // Creates a new DataStore value to work with MongoDB store.
        dataStore := common.NewDataStore()
        // Add to the mgo.Session.Close()
        defer dataStore.Close()
        // Get the mgo.Collection for "bookmarks"
        col := dataStore.Collection("bookmarks")
        // Creates an instance of BookmarkStore
        bookmarkStore := store.BookmarkStore{C: col}
        // Insert a bookmark document
        err = bookmarkStore.Create(bookmark)
        if err != nil {
                common.DisplayAppError(
                        w,
                        err,
                        "Invalid Bookmark data",
                        500,
                )
                return
        }
```

```go
        j, err := json.Marshal(BookmarkResource{Data: *bookmark})
        // If error has occurred,
        // Send JSON response using helper function common.DisplayAppError
        if err != nil {
                common.DisplayAppError(
                        w,
                        err,
                        "An unexpected error has occurred",
                        500,
                )
                return
        }
        w.Header().Set("Content-Type", "application/json")
        w.WriteHeader(http.StatusCreated)
        // Write the JSON data to the ResponseWriter
        w.Write(j)

}


// GetBookmarks returns all Bookmark documents
// Handler for HTTP Get - "/Bookmarks"
func GetBookmarks(w http.ResponseWriter, r *http.Request) {
        dataStore := common.NewDataStore()
        defer dataStore.Close()
        col := dataStore.Collection("bookmarks")
        bookmarkStore := store.BookmarkStore{C: col}
        bookmarks := bookmarkStore.GetAll()
        j, err := json.Marshal(BookmarksResource{Data: bookmarks})
        if err != nil {
                common.DisplayAppError(
                        w,
                        err,
                        "An unexpected error has occurred",
                        500,
                )
                return
        }
        w.WriteHeader(http.StatusOK)
        w.Header().Set("Content-Type", "application/json")
        w.Write(j)
}

// GetBookmarkByID returns a single bookmark document by id
// Handler for HTTP Get - "/Bookmarks/{id}"
func GetBookmarkByID(w http.ResponseWriter, r *http.Request) {
        // Get id from the incoming url
        vars := mux.Vars(r)
        id := vars["id"]

        dataStore := common.NewDataStore()
        defer dataStore.Close()
```

```go
        col := dataStore.Collection("bookmarks")
        bookmarkStore := store.BookmarkStore{C: col}

        bookmark, err := bookmarkStore.GetByID(id)
        if err != nil {
                if err == mgo.ErrNotFound {
                        w.WriteHeader(http.StatusNoContent)

                } else {
                        common.DisplayAppError(
                                w,
                                err,
                                "An unexpected error has occurred",
                                500,
                        )

                }
                return
        }
        j, err := json.Marshal(bookmark)
        if err != nil {
                common.DisplayAppError(
                        w,
                        err,
                        "An unexpected error has occurred",
                        500,
                )
                return
        }
        w.Header().Set("Content-Type", "application/json")
        w.WriteHeader(http.StatusOK)
        w.Write(j)
}

// GetBookmarksByUser returns all Bookmarks created by a User
// Handler for HTTP Get - "/Bookmarks/users/{id}"
func GetBookmarksByUser(w http.ResponseWriter, r *http.Request) {
        // Get id from the incoming url
        vars := mux.Vars(r)
        user := vars["id"]
        dataStore := common.NewDataStore()
        defer dataStore.Close()
        col := dataStore.Collection("bookmarks")
        bookmarkStore := store.BookmarkStore{C: col}
        bookmarks := bookmarkStore.GetByUser(user)
        j, err := json.Marshal(BookmarksResource{Data: bookmarks})
        if err != nil {
                common.DisplayAppError(
                        w,
                        err,
                        "An unexpected error has occurred",
```

```
                        500,
                )
                return
        }
        w.WriteHeader(http.StatusOK)
        w.Header().Set("Content-Type", "application/json")
        w.Write(j)
}

// UpdateBookmark update an existing Bookmark document
// Handler for HTTP Put - "/Bookmarks/{id}"
func UpdateBookmark(w http.ResponseWriter, r *http.Request) {
        // Get id from the incoming url
        vars := mux.Vars(r)
        id := bson.ObjectIdHex(vars["id"])
        var dataResource BookmarkResource
        // Decode the incoming Bookmark json
        err := json.NewDecoder(r.Body).Decode(&dataResource)
        if err != nil {
                common.DisplayAppError(
                        w,
                        err,
                        "Invalid Bookmark data",
                        500,
                )
                return
        }
        bookmark := dataResource.Data
        bookmark.ID = id
        dataStore := common.NewDataStore()
        defer dataStore.Close()
        col := dataStore.Collection("bookmarks")
        bookmarkStore := store.BookmarkStore{C: col}
        // Update an existing Bookmark document
        if err := bookmarkStore.Update(bookmark); err != nil {
                common.DisplayAppError(
                        w,
                        err,
                        "An unexpected error has occurred",
                        500,
                )
                return
        }
        w.WriteHeader(http.StatusNoContent)

}

// DeleteBookmark deletes an existing Bookmark document
// Handler for HTTP Delete - "/Bookmarks/{id}"
func DeleteBookmark(w http.ResponseWriter, r *http.Request) {
        vars := mux.Vars(r)
```

```
        id := vars["id"]
        dataStore := common.NewDataStore()
        defer dataStore.Close()
        col := dataStore.Collection("bookmarks")
        bookmarkStore := store.BookmarkStore{C: col}
        // Delete an existing Bookmark document
        err := bookmarkStore.Delete(id)
        if err != nil {
                common.DisplayAppError(
                        w,
                        err,
                        "An unexpected error has occurred",
                        500,
                )
                return
        }
        w.WriteHeader(http.StatusNoContent)
}
```

HTTP handler functions for the HTTP Post and HTTP Put decode the JSON data from the request body and parse it into the models created for the JSON resources. Here it is parsed into the struct type BookmarkResource. Here is the declaration of BookmarkResource written in resources.go of package controllers.

```
BookmarkResource struct {
        Data model.Bookmark `json:"data"`
}
```

By accessing the property Data of BookmarkResource, the incoming data is mapped to the domain model model.Bookmark and performs the data persistence logic using the value of it.

```
var dataResource BookmarkResource
// Decode the incoming Bookmark json
err := json.NewDecoder(r.Body).Decode(&dataResource)
bookmark := &dataResource.Data
```

Struct type common.DataStore is used for maintaining a copied version of global mgo.Session value, to be used throughout the single HTTP request life cycle. The method Collection of DataStore returns an mgo.Collection value. The mgo.Collection value is used for creating an instance of store.BookmarkStore. The struct type BookmarkStore of package store, provides persistence logic against the data model Bookmark that is working against the MongoDB collection named "bookmarks".

```
dataStore := common.NewDataStore()
// Add to the mgo.Session.Close()
defer dataStore.Close()
// Get the mgo.Collection for "bookmarks"
col := dataStore.Collection("bookmarks")
// Creates an instance of BookmarkStore
bookmarkStore := store.BookmarkStore{C: col}
```

Methods of BookmarkStore are used to perform CRUD operations into the MongoDB database. The function Create of BookmarkStore is used to insert a new document into the MongoDB collection.

```
// Insert a bookmark document
err=bookmarkStore.Create(bookmark)
```

If the returned error value is nil after executing the persistence logic of BookmarkStore, an appropriate HTTP response is sent to the HTTP clients. Here is the HTTP response sent from the handler function for the HTTP Post to "/bookmarks":

```
j, err := json.Marshal(BookmarkResource{Data: *bookmark})


w.Header().Set("Content-Type", "application/json")
w.WriteHeader(http.StatusCreated)
// Write the JSON data to the ResponseWriter
w.Write(j)
```

Here, a struct type BookmarkResource is created using the value of model.Bookmark and encode it into JSON using json.Marshal. If any error value is received from handler functions, a helper function common. DisplayAppError is used for sending HTTP error messages in JSON format.

```
// Insert a bookmark document
err = bookmarkStore.Create(bookmark)
if err != nil {
        common.DisplayAppError(
                w,
                err,
                "Invalid Bookmark data",
                500,
        )
        return
}
```

Here is the implementation of helper function DisplayAppError:

```
// DisplayAppError provides app specific error in JSON
func DisplayAppError(w http.ResponseWriter, handlerError error, message string, code int) {
        errObj := appError{
                Error:      handlerError.Error(),
                Message:    message,
                HTTPStatus: code,
        }
        w.Header().Set("Content-Type", "application/json; charset=utf-8")
        w.WriteHeader(code)
        if j, err := json.Marshal(errorResource{Data: errObj}); err == nil {
                w.Write(j)
        }
}
```

Handler functions for HTTP Put, Get, and Delete retrieve values from the route variables from the URL of HTTP request. The package mux provides a function Vars that returns route variables for the current request as a key/value pair of collection with type map[string]string. The following code block retrieves the value of route variable "id".

```
vars := mux.Vars(r)
id := vars["id"]
```

Data Persistence with MongoDB

HTTP handler functions of bookmark_controller.go use struct type BookmarkStore for data persistence logic to perform CRUD operations against a MongoDB collection named "bookmarks". Listing 7-13 shows the data persistence logic provided by BookmarkStore.

Listing 7-13. Data Persistence Logic in store/bookmark_store.go

```
package store

import (
        "time"

        "gopkg.in/mgo.v2"
        "gopkg.in/mgo.v2/bson"

        "github.com/shijuvar/go-recipes/ch07/bookmarkapi/model"
)

// BookmarkStore provides CRUD operations against the collection "bookmarks".
type BookmarkStore struct {
        C *mgo.Collection
}

// Create inserts the value of struct Bookmark into collection.
func (store BookmarkStore) Create(b *model.Bookmark) error {
        // Assign a new bson.ObjectId
        b.ID = bson.NewObjectId()
        b.CreatedOn = time.Now()
        err := store.C.Insert(b)
        return err
}

// Update modifies an existing document of a collection.
func (store BookmarkStore) Update(b model.Bookmark) error {
        // partial update on MogoDB
        err := store.C.Update(bson.M{"_id": b.ID},
                bson.M{"$set": bson.M{
                        "name":        b.Name,
                        "description": b.Description,
```

```go
                        "location":   b.Location,
                        "priority":   b.Priority,
                        "tags":       b.Tags,
                }})
        return err
}

// Delete removes an existing document from the collection.
func (store BookmarkStore) Delete(id string) error {
        err := store.C.Remove(bson.M{"_id": bson.ObjectIdHex(id)})
        return err
}

// GetAll returns all documents from the collection.
func (store BookmarkStore) GetAll() []model.Bookmark {
        var b []model.Bookmark
        iter := store.C.Find(nil).Sort("priority", "-createdon").Iter()
        result := model.Bookmark{}
        for iter.Next(&result) {
                b = append(b, result)
        }
        return b
}

// GetByUser returns all documents from the collection.
func (store BookmarkStore) GetByUser(user string) []model.Bookmark {
        var b []model.Bookmark
        iter := store.C.Find(bson.M{"createdby": user}).Sort("priority", "-createdon").
Iter()
        result := model.Bookmark{}
        for iter.Next(&result) {
                b = append(b, result)
        }
        return b
}

// GetByID returns a single document from the collection.
func (store BookmarkStore) GetByID(id string) (model.Bookmark, error) {
        var b model.Bookmark
        err := store.C.FindId(bson.ObjectIdHex(id)).One(&b)
        return b, err
}
```

Running the HTTP Server

The HTTP server for the REST API is created and running from main.go. Listing 7-14 shows the source of main.go.

Listing 7-14. Running HTTP Server in main.go

```
package main

import (
        "log"
        "net/http"

        "github.com/shijuvar/go-recipes/ch07/bookmarkapi/common"
        "github.com/shijuvar/go-recipes/ch07/bookmarkapi/routers"
)

// Entry point of the program
func main() {

        // Calls startup logic
        common.StartUp()
        // Get the mux router object
        router := routers.InitRoutes()
        // Create the Server
        server := &http.Server{
                Addr:    common.AppConfig.Server,
                Handler: router,
        }
        log.Println("Listening...")
        // Running the HTTP Server
        server.ListenAndServe()
}
```

Inside the function main, some startup logics are executed using the function common.StartUp. A call to common.StartUp executes several required functions before running the HTTP server. This includes reading the application configuration file and loading the values into a struct instance, connecting to MongoDB database using the function mgo.DialWithInfo, obtaining an mgo.Session value, and so on. Package common provides the startup logic that is required before running the HTTP server. The http.Handler value is created by calling routers.InitRoutes, which returns mux.Router. The mux.Router has an implementation of interface http.Handler, thus it is used as a handler for the HTTP server.

Testing REST API Server

Let's run the HTTP server and test some of the API endpoints for the Bookmarks resource. Postman (https://www.getpostman.com/) is used to test the API endpoints. Figure 7-6 shows the HTTP Post request to "/bookmarks".

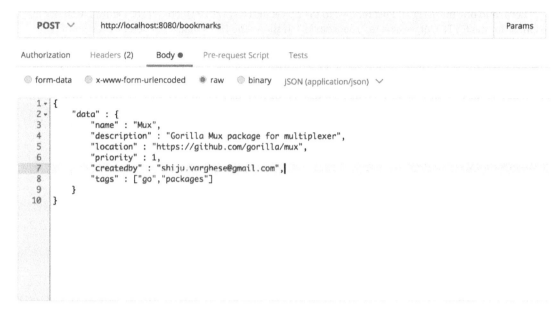

Figure 7-6. *Sending HTTP Post to "/bookmarks"*

Figure 7-7 shows the response from the API server for the HTTP Post to "/bookmarks". It shows the HTTP status code 201 and JSON for the newly created resource.

```
Body    Cookies    Headers (3)    Tests                                    Status: 201 Created

Pretty    Raw    Preview    JSON ∨    ⇉

 1 ▾ {
 2 ▾     "data": {
 3           "ID": "57a363005218e507237aa2c2",
 4           "name": "Mux",
 5           "description": "Gorilla Mux package for multiplexer",
 6           "location": "https://github.com/gorilla/mux",
 7           "priority": 1,
 8           "createdby": "shiju.varghese@gmail.com",
 9           "createdon": "2016-08-04T21:15:04.804960305+05:30",
10 ▾        "tags": [
11             "go",
12             "packages"
13           ]
14       }
15 }
```

Figure 7-7. *HTTP Response for the HTTP Post to "/bookmarks"*

Let's send one more HTTP Post request to the server and test HTTP Get requests. Figure 7-8 shows the response for the HTTP Get request to "/bookmarks". It shows the JSON data of all bookmark resources.

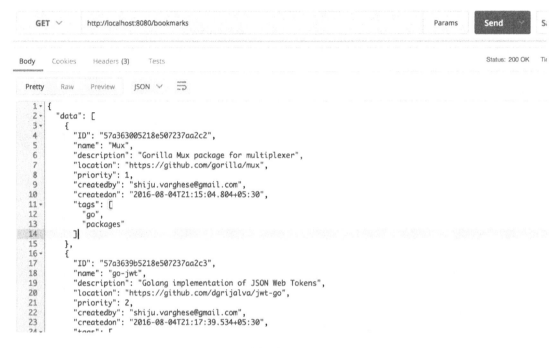

Figure 7-8. *HTTP Response for the HTTP Get to "/bookmarks"*

Figure 7-9 shows the response for the HTTP Get request to "/bookmarks/{id}". It shows the JSON data of a single bookmark resource for the given bookmark ID.

Figure 7-9. *HTTP Response for the HTTP Get request to "/bookmarks/{id}"*

Figure 7-10 shows the response for the HTTP Get request to "/bookmarks/users/{id}". It shows the JSON data of all bookmark resources associated with a user for the given user ID.

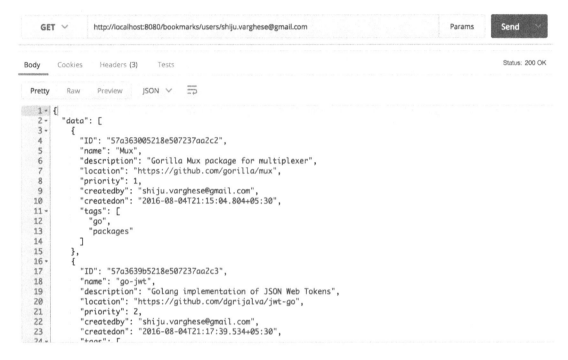

Figure 7-10. *HTTP Response for the HTTP Get request to "/bookmarks/users/{id}"*

The completed version of the REST API application is available from the code repository of this book at https://github.com/shijuvar/go-recipes.

CHAPTER 8

■ ■ ■

Testing Go Applications

Software engineering is an evolutionary process in which you develop applications as an evolutionary system and you modify and refactor the application continuously. You should be able to modify the functionality of an application and refactor its code at any time without breaking any parts of the application. When you develop applications as an evolutionary product and modify the application code, it should not break any parts of the applications. You might need to adopt some good engineering practices to ensure the quality of your applications. Automated testing is an important engineering practice that can be used to ensure the quality of software systems. In an automated testing process, you write unit tests against the smallest piece of testable software in the application, called a unit, to determine whether the functionality of each individual unit behaves exactly as you have intended. In this chapter, you learn how to write unit tests in Go.

8-1. Writing Unit Tests

Problem

How do you write unit tests to ensure your Go packages behave as you have intended?

Solution

The standard library package testing provides support for writing unit tests of Go packages. The go test command runs unit tests that are written with the package testing.

How It Works

The package testing provides all essential support for writing unit tests, which is intended to be used with the go test command for running unit tests. The go test command identifies unit test functions by looking into the following patterns in functions:

func TestXxx(*testing.T)

You write unit test functions with the prefix Test followed by an alphanumeric string that starts with an uppercase letter. To write unit test functions, you must create a test suite file with a name that ends with _test.go that contains unit test functions with the signature func TestXxx(*testing.T). You typically put the test suite file in the same package that is being tested. When you build the packages using go build or go install, it excludes the test suite files, and when you run the unit tests using go test, it includes test suite files.

© Shiju Varghese 2016
S. Varghese, *Go Recipes*, DOI 10.1007/978-1-4842-1188-5_8

For help with running go test run the following command:

```
go help test
```

For help on various flags used by the go test command run the following command:

```
go help testflag
```

Listing 8-1 shows an example package for which you will write a unit test later on.

Listing 8-1. Package calc with Two Utility Functions in calc.go

```go
package calc

import "math"

// Sum returns sum of integer values
func Sum(nums ...int) int {
        result := 0
        for _, v := range nums {
                result += v
        }
        return result
}

// Average returns average of integer values
// The output provides a float64 value in two decimal points
func Average(nums ...int) float64 {
        sum := 0
        for _, v := range nums {
                sum += v
        }
        result := float64(sum) / float64(len(nums))
        pow := math.Pow(10, float64(2))
        digit := pow * result
        round := math.Floor(digit)
        return round / pow
}
```

Listing 8-2 shows the unit tests for testing the behavior of the functions Sum and Average in package calc.

Listing 8-2. Unit Tests for Package calc in calc_test.go

```go
package calc

import "testing"

// Test case for the Sum function
func TestSum(t *testing.T) {
        input, expected := []int{7, 8, 10}, 25
```

```
        result := Sum(input...)
        if result != expected {

                t.Errorf("Result: %d, Expected: %d", result, expected)
        }

}

// Test case for the Sum function
func TestAverage(t *testing.T) {
        input, expected := []int{7, 8, 10}, 8.33
        result := Average(input...)
        if result != expected {

                t.Errorf("Result: %f, Expected: %f", result, expected)
        }
}
```

Two test cases are written for verifying the behavior of functions in package calc. The name of the unit test functions started with the Test prefix, followed by a string that starts with an uppercase letter. Inside the unit test functions, the output value of functions verify expected values and call the method Errorf to signal failure. To signal failure of a test case, you can call Error, Fail, or related methods of type testing.T. The Error and Fail methods signal the failure of a test case, but it will continue the execution of remaining unit tests. If you want to stop the execution whenever a test case fails, you can call the method FailNow or Fatal of type testing.T. The method FailNow calls the method Fail and stops the execution. Fatal is equivalent to Log followed by FailNow. In these unit test functions, the method Errorf is used to signal the failure of test cases.

```
if result != expected {

        t.Errorf("Result: %d, Expected: %d", result, expected)
}
```

Running Unit Tests

To run the unit tests, run the go test command from your package directory:

```
go test
```

You should see output similar to the following:

```
PASS
ok      github.com/shijuvar/go-recipes/ch08/calc        0.233s
```

The output of this test is not very descriptive. The verbose (-v) flag provides descriptive information when you execute unit tests.

```
go test -v
```

This results in output similar to the following:

```
=== RUN    TestSum
--- PASS: TestSum (0.00s)
=== RUN    TestAverage
--- PASS: TestAverage (0.00s)
PASS
ok        github.com/shijuvar/go-recipes/ch08/calc        0.121s
```

Note that unit tests are executing in a sequential manner. In these tests, it first executes the test function TestSum and after completing the execution, it then executes the test function TestAverage.

Test Coverage

When you run unit tests, you can measure the amount of testing performed by the test cases. The go test command provides a *coverage* (-cover) flag that helps you to get coverage of the test cases written against your code. Let's run the unit tests with the coverage flag to determine test coverage of package calc:

```
go test -v -cover
```

You should see output similar to the following:

```
=== RUN    TestSum
--- PASS: TestSum (0.00s)
=== RUN    TestAverage
--- PASS: TestAverage (0.00s)
PASS
coverage: 100.0% of statements
ok        github.com/shijuvar/go-recipes/ch08/calc        0.139s
```

This test output shows that package calc has 100% test coverage.

8-2. Skipping Long-Running Tests

Problem

You would like to have the flexibility of skipping some unit tests when running the tests. How do you skip execution of some unit tests when you run the unit tests?

Solution

The go test command allows you to pass a *short* (-short) flag that lets you skip some unit tests during execution. Inside the unit test functions, you can check whether the short flag is provided by calling the function Short of package testing, and can skip execution of tests by calling the function Skip of type testing.T if you would like to skip those tests.

How It Works

When you execute unit tests you might need to skip some of them. Sometimes, you might want to prevent some unit tests from being executed in some use cases. For example, you might want to skip some time-consuming unit tests. Another example scenario is that some unit tests might have a dependency to a configuration file or to an environment variable which is not available during the execution of those tests, so you can skip execution of those tests instead of letting them fail.

The type `testing.T` provides a method `Skip` that can be used to skip unit tests. To skip those unit tests, you can give a signal by providing a short (`-short`) flag to the go `test` command. Listing 8-3 shows three unit test functions in which one test is skipped during the execution of tests if you provide short (`-short`) flag to the go `test` command.

Listing 8-3. Unit Tests in Which One Test is Skipped in Execution

```go
package calc

import (
        "testing"
        "time"
)

// Test case for the Sum function
func TestSum(t *testing.T) {
        input, expected := []int{7, 8, 10}, 25
        result := Sum(input...)
        if result != expected {

                t.Errorf("Result: %d, Expected: %d", result, expected)
        }

}

// Test case for the Sum function
func TestAverage(t *testing.T) {
        input, expected := []int{7, 8, 10}, 8.33
        result := Average(input...)
        if result != expected {

                t.Errorf("Result: %f, Expected: %f", result, expected)
        }
}

// TestLongRun is a time-consuming test
func TestLongRun(t *testing.T) {
        // Checks whether the short flag is provided
        if testing.Short() {
                t.Skip("Skipping test in short mode")
        }
        // Long running implementation goes here
        time.Sleep(5 * time.Second)
}
```

In these unit tests, you can skip test execution of the function TestLongRun if you can provide a short flag to the go test command. The function testing.Short is used to identify whether a short flag is provided. If so, execution of the unit test is skipped by calling the function Skip. You can provide a string value when you call the function Skip.

```
// Checks whether the short flag is provided
         if testing.Short() {
       t.Skip("Skipping test in short mode")
}
```

If you are not providing the short flag, function TestLongRun will run as a normal unit test. Let's run the tests by providing the short flag:

```
go test -v -short
```

You should see output similar to the following:

```
=== RUN   TestSum
--- PASS: TestSum (0.00s)
=== RUN   TestAverage
--- PASS: TestAverage (0.00s)
=== RUN   TestLongRun
--- SKIP: TestLongRun (0.00s)
        calc_test.go:36: Skipping test in short mode
PASS
ok      github.com/shijuvar/go-recipes/ch08/calc        0.241s
```

The test output shows that the unit test function TestLongRun was skipped during the execution. Now let's run the tests without providing the short flag:

```
go test -v
```

This should result in output similar to the following:

```
=== RUN   TestSum
--- PASS: TestSum (0.00s)
=== RUN   TestAverage
--- PASS: TestAverage (0.00s)
=== RUN   TestLongRun
--- PASS: TestLongRun (5.00s)
PASS
ok      github.com/shijuvar/go-recipes/ch08/calc        5.212s
```

The test output shows that the function TestLongRun was running as normal.

8-3. Writing Benchmark Tests

Problem

How do you benchmark Go code by writing tests?

Solution

The package testing allows you to write tests for benchmark Go functions. To write benchmarks, write functions with the pattern func BenchmarkXxx(*testing.B), which are executed by the go test command when its -bench flag is provided.

How It Works

When you run tests with the go test command, you can pass the -bench flag to execute bechmark tests wherein functions with pattern func BenchmarkXxx(*testing.B) are considered benchmarks. You write benchmark functions inside the _test.go files. Listing 8-4 shows benchmark tests to benchmark functions of package calc (see Listing 8-1).

Listing 8-4. Unit Tests with Benchmarks in Package calc

```go
package calc

import "testing"

// Test case for function Sum
func TestSum(t *testing.T) {
        input, expected := []int{7, 8, 10}, 25
        result := Sum(input...)
        if result != expected {

                t.Errorf("Result: %d, Expected: %d", result, expected)
        }

}

// Test case for function Average
func TestAverage(t *testing.T) {
        input, expected := []int{7, 8, 10}, 8.33
        result := Average(input...)
        if result != expected {

                t.Errorf("Result: %f, Expected: %f", result, expected)
        }
}

// Benchmark for function Sum
func BenchmarkSum(b *testing.B) {
        for i := 0; i < b.N; i++ {
                Sum(7, 8, 10)
        }
}

// Benchmark for function Average
func BenchmarkAverage(b *testing.B) {
        for i := 0; i < b.N; i++ {
                Average(7, 8, 10)
        }
}
```

Two benchmark tests are written to benchmark the performance of the functions in package `calc`. You must run the target code for `b.N` times by using a loop construct to execute the functions to benchmark in a reliable manner. The value of the `b.N` will be adjusted during the execution of benchmark tests. The benchmark tests give you a reliable response time per loop. When you provide the -bench flag to `go test` command, you need to provide a regular expression to indicate which benchmark tests are to be included for execution. To run all benchmarks, use -bench . or -bench=.

Let's run the tests by providing -bench .

```
go test -v -bench .
```

You should see output similar to the following:

```
=== RUN    TestSum
--- PASS: TestSum (0.00s)
=== RUN    TestAverage
--- PASS: TestAverage (0.00s)
BenchmarkSum-4          100000000              23.1 ns/op
BenchmarkAverage-4       10000000             224 ns/op
PASS
ok      github.com/shijuvar/go-recipes/ch08/calc        4.985s
```

8-4. Running Unit Tests in Parallel

Problem

How do you execute unit tests in parallel?

Solution

You can run unit tests in parallel by calling the method `Parallel` of type `testing.T`. Inside the unit test functions, a call to the method `Parallel` signals that this test is to be run in parallel with other parallel tests.

How It Works

By default, unit tests are executing sequentially. If you want to run a unit test in parallel to speed up the execution, call the method `Parallel` inside the test function before writing the test logic. The method `Parallel` indicates that this unit test is to be run in parallel with other parallel tests. You can call the method `Parallel` for any unit test functions you would like to run in parallel.

Listing 8-5 provides a couple of unit tests to be run in parallel.

Listing 8-5. Unit Tests to Be Run in Parallel

```
package calc

import (
        "testing"
        "time"
)

// Test case for the function Sum to be executed in parallel
```

```
func TestSumInParallel(t *testing.T) {
        t.Parallel()
        // Delaying 1 second for the sake of demonstration
        time.Sleep(1 * time.Second)
        input, expected := []int{7, 8, 10}, 25
        result := Sum(input...)
        if result != expected {

                t.Errorf("Result: %d, Expected: %d", result, expected)
        }

}

// Test case for the function Sum to be executed in parallel
func TestAverageInParallel(t *testing.T) {
        t.Parallel()
        // Delaying 1 second for the sake of demonstration
        time.Sleep(2 * time.Second)
        input, expected := []int{7, 8, 10}, 8.33
        result := Average(input...)
        if result != expected {

                t.Errorf("Result: %f, Expected: %f", result, expected)
        }
}
```

Inside the test functions, the method Parallel is called as the first code statement to signal that this test is to be run in parallel so that execution of a parallel test will not wait for completion of the test function and run in parallel with other parallel tests.

```
t.Parallel()
```

If you write unit test functions with parallel tests and normal tests mixed, it will execute normal tests sequentially and parallel tests in parallel with other parallel tests. Run the tests with the go test command:

```
go test -v
```

You should see output similar to the following:

```
=== RUN   TestSumInParallel
=== RUN   TestAverageInParallel
--- PASS: TestSumInParallel (1.00s)
--- PASS: TestAverageInParallel (2.00s)
PASS
ok      github.com/shijuvar/go-recipes/ch08/calc        2.296s
```

The output shows that both TestSumInParallel and TestAverageInParallel are running in parallel and didn't wait for the completion of one test to run another.

8-5. Writing Tests for Verifying Example Code

Problem

How do you write tests for verifying example code?

Solution

The package `testing` provides support for writing tests to verify example code. To write example functions, declare functions with names that start with the prefix `Example`.

How It Works

Example functions verify the example code written for packages, types, and functions. The example functions will also be available in Go documentation generated by the godoc tool. When you generate Go documentation using the godoc tool, example functions will be available as example code for Go packages and various types. The example functions are declared with a name that starts with the prefix `Example`. Here are the naming conventions used to declare examples for the package, a function `F`, a type `T`, and method `M` on type `T`:

```
func Example()    // Example test for package
func ExampleF()   // Example test for function F
func ExampleT()   // Example test for type T
func ExampleT_M() // Example test for M on type T
```

Inside the example functions, you typically include a concluding line comment that begins with `Output:`. It compares the given output with the output of the function when the test functions are executed with the go test command. Listing 8-6 shows example functions in the package `calc`.

Listing 8-6. Example Functions for Package `calc`

```
package calc

import "fmt"

// Example code for function Sum
func ExampleSum() {
        fmt.Println(Sum(7, 8, 10))
        // Output: 25
}

// Example code for function Average
func ExampleAverage() {
        fmt.Println(Average(7, 8, 10))
        // Output: 8.33
}
```

The convention for writing example code for function `Sum` is `ExampleSum` and for function `Average` is `ExampleAverage`. Inside the example test functions, a concluding line comment that begins with `Output:` is provided. The output of the line comment is compared with the standard output of the function. In the example function `ExampleSum`, the output of the line comment is compared with the output of the function call to `Sum`.

Let's run the example function with the go test command:

```
go test -v
```

You should see output similar to the following:

```
=== RUN    ExampleSum
--- PASS: ExampleSum (0.00s)
=== RUN    ExampleAverage
--- PASS: ExampleAverage (0.00s)
PASS
ok      github.com/shijuvar/go-recipes/ch08/calc        0.165s
```

The example test functions will be available as example code in documentation generated by the godoc tool. Figure 8-1 shows the documentation for function Sum, which includes the example code taken from the test function ExampleSum.

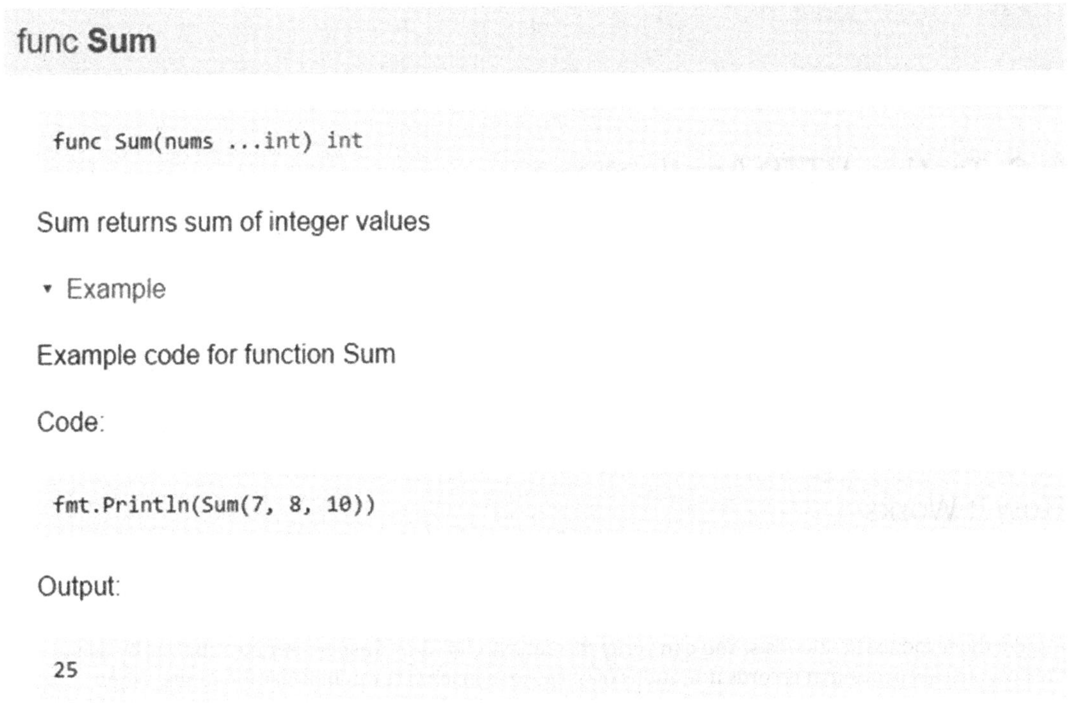

func **Sum**

```
func Sum(nums ...int) int
```

Sum returns sum of integer values

▾ Example

Example code for function Sum

Code:

```
fmt.Println(Sum(7, 8, 10))
```

Output:

```
25
```

Figure 8-1. *Documentation for function Sum generated by godoc tool*

Figure 8-2 shows the documentation for the function Average, which includes the example code taken from the test function ExampleAverage.

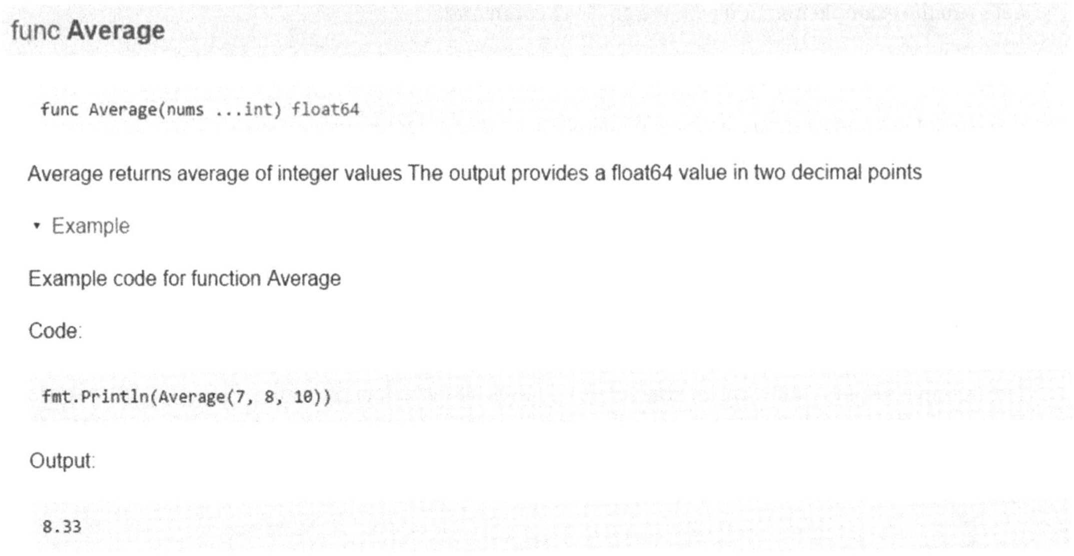

func **Average**

```
func Average(nums ...int) float64
```

Average returns average of integer values The output provides a float64 value in two decimal points

- Example

Example code for function Average

Code:

```
fmt.Println(Average(7, 8, 10))
```

Output:

```
8.33
```

Figure 8-2. *Documentation for function Average generated by godoc tool*

8-6. Testing HTTP Applications

Problem

How do you write tests for HTTP applications?

Solution

The standard library package net/http/httptest provides utilities for testing HTTP applications.

How It Works

Package httptest provides support for testing HTTP applications. To test HTTP applications, package httptest provides the ResponseRecorder and Server struct types.

ResponseRecorder is an implementation of http.ResponseWriter that records HTTP responses to inspect the response in unit tests. You can verify the behavior of http.ResponseWriter in tests by using the ResponseRecorder that records mutations of http.ResponseWriter in handler functions. When you test your HTTP applications using ResponseRecorder, you don't need to use an HTTP server. A ResponseRecorder instance is created by calling the function NewRecorder of package httptest.

```
w := httptest.NewRecorder()
```

A Server is a test HTTP server listening on a system-chosen port on the local loopback interface (127.0.0.1), for use in end-to-end HTTP tests. This allows you to test your HTTP applications using an HTTP server by sending HTTP requests to the test server from an HTTP client. The test HTTP server is created by calling the function NewServer of package httptest by providing an instance of http.Handler.

```
server := httptest.NewServer(r) // r is an instance of http.Handler
```

An HTTP API Server

Listing 8-7 shows an example HTTP API server created for writing unit tests with package httptest later on.

Listing 8-7. Example HTTP Server in main.go

```go
package main

import (
        "encoding/json"
        "net/http"

        "github.com/gorilla/mux"
)

// User model
type User struct {
        FirstName string `json:"firstname"`
        LastName  string `json:"lastname"`
        Email     string `json:"email"`
}

// getUsers serves requests for Http Get to "/users"
func getUsers(w http.ResponseWriter, r *http.Request) {
        data := []User{
                User{
                        FirstName: "Shiju",
                        LastName:  "Varghese",
                        Email:     "shiju@xyz.com",
                },

                User{
                        FirstName: "Irene",
                        LastName:  "Rose",
                        Email:     "irene@xyz.com",
                },
        }
        users, err := json.Marshal(data)
        if err != nil {
                w.WriteHeader(http.StatusInternalServerError)
                return
        }
        w.Header().Set("Content-Type", "application/json")
        w.WriteHeader(http.StatusOK)
```

```go
        w.Write(users)
}

func main() {
        r := mux.NewRouter()
        r.HandleFunc("/users", getUsers).Methods("GET")
        http.ListenAndServe(":8080", r)
}
```

Listing 8-7 creates a simple HTTP server with single endpoint: HTTP Get to "/users" that returns a collection User entity.

Testing HTTP Applications Using ResponseRecorder

Listing 8-8 shows a test with ResponseRecorder for testing the HTTP server created in Listing 8-7.

Listing 8-8. Testing HTTP API Server Using ResponseRecorder in main_test.go

```go
package main

import (
        "net/http"
        "net/http/httptest"
        "testing"

        "github.com/gorilla/mux"
)

// TestGetUsers test HTTP Get to "/users" using ResponseRecorder
func TestGetUsers(t *testing.T) {
        r := mux.NewRouter()
        r.HandleFunc("/users", getUsers).Methods("GET")
        req, err := http.NewRequest("GET", "/users", nil)
        if err != nil {
                t.Error(err)
        }
        w := httptest.NewRecorder()

        r.ServeHTTP(w, req)
        if w.Code != 200 {
                t.Errorf("HTTP Status expected: 200, got: %d", w.Code)
        }
}
```

In TestGetUsers, an HTTP multiplexer is configured for testing HTTP Get requests on "/users".

```go
r := mux.NewRouter()
r.HandleFunc("/users", getUsers).Methods("GET")
```

An HTTP request object is created using http.NewRequest to to call method ServeHTTP of handler of HTTP Get on "/users". A nil value is provided as the parameter for the HTTP request body to the function NewRequest because it is an HTTP Get request. You may provide a value for the HTTP request body for creating HTTP request object on HTTP Posts.

```
req, err := http.NewRequest("GET", "/users", nil)
if err != nil {
        t.Error(err)
}
```

A ResponseRecorder object is created using httptest.NewRecorder to record the returned HTTP responses for later inspection in tests.

```
w := httptest.NewRecorder()
```

Method ServeHTTP of the HTTP handler is called by providing ResponseRecorder and Request objects to invoke the HTTP Get request on "/users". This will invoke the handler function getUsers.

```
r.ServeHTTP(w, req)
```

The ResponseRecorder object records the returned HTTP responses (mutations on http. ResponseWriter in handler function) so that it is available for inspection. You can see that the HTTP response returns an HTTP status code of 200.

```
if w.Code != 200 {
    t.Errorf("HTTP Status expected: 200, got: %d", w.Code)
}
```

Let's run the test with the go test command:

```
go test -v
```

You should see output similar to the following:

```
=== RUN   TestGetUsers
--- PASS: TestGetUsers (0.00s)
PASS
ok      github.com/shijuvar/go-recipes/ch08/httptest    0.353s
```

Testing HTTP Application Using Server

In Listing 8-8, you wrote tests using the ResponseRecorder to inspect the values of HTTP responses. This type is sufficient for inspecting the behavior of HTTP responses. Package httptest also provides a type Server that lets you create an HTTP server for testing so that you can run your tests via HTTP pipeline by sending HTTP requests to the test HTTP server using an HTTP client. Listing 8-9 shows a test with a test Server for testing the HTTP API server created in Listing 8-7.

Listing 8-9. Testing HTTP API Server Using Server in main_test.go

```go
package main

import (
        "fmt"
        "net/http"
        "net/http/httptest"
        "testing"

        "github.com/gorilla/mux"
)

// TestGetUsersWithServer test HTTP Get to "/users" using Server
func TestGetUsersWithServer(t *testing.T) {
        r := mux.NewRouter()
        r.HandleFunc("/users", getUsers).Methods("GET")
        server := httptest.NewServer(r)
        defer server.Close()
        usersURL := fmt.Sprintf("%s/users", server.URL)
        request, err := http.NewRequest("GET", usersURL, nil)

        res, err := http.DefaultClient.Do(request)

        if err != nil {
                t.Error(err)
        }

        if res.StatusCode != 200 {
                t.Errorf("HTTP Status expected: 200, got: %d", res.StatusCode)
        }
}
```

In the test function TestGetUsersWithServer, the HTTP multiplexer is configured for testing HTTP Get requests on "/users".

```go
r := mux.NewRouter()
r.HandleFunc("/users", getUsers).Methods("GET")
```

The test HTTP server is created by calling function httptest.NewServer. The function NewServer starts and returns a new HTTP server. The method Close of Server is added to the list of deferred functions to shut down the test Server when the test is finished.

```go
server := httptest.NewServer(r)
defer server.Close()
```

An HTTP request is created using function http.NewRequest and sends an HTTP request using the method Do of HTTP client object. A nil value is provided as the parameter for the HTTP request body to the function NewRequest because it is an HTTP Get request. The HTTP client is created using http.DefaultClient, and then calls method Do to send an HTTP request to the test Server that returns an HTTP response.

```
usersURL:= fmt.Sprintf("%s/users", server.URL)
request, err := http.NewRequest("GET", usersURL, nil)
res, err := http.DefaultClient.Do(request)
```

You see that the HTTP response returns an HTTP status code of 200.

```
if res.StatusCode != 200 {
    t.Errorf("HTTP Status expected: 200, got: %d", res.StatusCode)
}
```

Let's run the test with the go test command:

```
go test -v
```

You should see output similar to the following:

```
=== RUN   TestGetUsersWithServer
--- PASS: TestGetUsersWithServer (0.01s)
PASS
ok      github.com/shijuvar/go-recipes/ch08/httptest      0.355s
```

8-7. Writing BDD-Style Tests

Problem

How do you write behavior-driven develpment (BDD)-style tests in Go?

Solution

Third-party package Ginkgo is a BDD-style testing framework for Go that allows you to write tests based BDD. Ginkgo is best paired with the Gomega matcher library.

How It Works

BDD is a software development process that evolved from test-driven development (TDD). In BDD, applications are specified and designed by describing their behavior. BDD emphasizes behavior instead of test. Ginkgo is a BDD-style testing framework that is built on top of the standard library package testing. Ginkgo is typically used with Gomega as the matcher library for test assertion.

Building a Testable HTTP API Server

Let's build a testable HTTP API server to write BDD-style tests for an application. In BDD, you typically start with writing specs (BDD-style tests) before writing production code, but for the sake of demonstration, here you start with writing application code, then you write specs. When you write tests, the most important thing is that your application code should be testable so that you can independently isolate individual components of the application and write tests to verify its behavior.

Figure 8-3 shows the directory structure of the HTTP API application. To run the example code shown later you will need to create this directory structure and ensure files are created in the correct directory. This directory structure must be in a subdirectory of GOPATH/src.

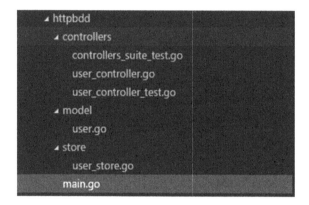

Figure 8-3. *Directory structure of the HTTP API application*

The package controllers consists of handler functions and tests. The package model defines the data model of the application. It also defines an interface for persistent store so that you can use a different implementation of the interface for your application code and also for tests. The package store provides a concrete implementation of persistent store by implementing the interface defined in the package model.

Listing 8-10 shows the source of user.go in the package model.

Listing 8-10. Data Model and Interface for Persistent Store in model/user.go

```
package model

import "errors"

// ErrorEmailExists is an error value for duplicate email id
var ErrorEmailExists = errors.New("Email Id is exists")

// User model
type User struct {
        FirstName string `json:"firstname"`
        LastName  string `json:"lastname"`
        Email     string `json:"email"`
}

// UserStore provides a contract for Data Store for User entity
type UserStore interface {
        GetUsers() []User
        AddUser(User) error
}
```

Package model declares a data model named User and provides an interface named UserStore that provides a contract for persistent store for User entity. Package store provides an implementation of interface UserStore by persisting User values into a MongoDB database.

Listing 8-11 shows the source of user_store.go in the package store.

Listing 8-11. Implementation of UserStore to Persist Data into MongoDB in store/user_store.go

```go
package store

import (
        "log"
        "time"

        "gopkg.in/mgo.v2"
        "gopkg.in/mgo.v2/bson"

        "github.com/shijuvar/go-recipes/ch08/httpbdd/model"
)

// MongoDB Session
var mgoSession *mgo.Session

// Create a MongoDB Session
func createDBSession() {
        var err error
        mgoSession, err = mgo.DialWithInfo(&mgo.DialInfo{
                Addrs:   []string{"127.0.0.1"},
                Timeout: 60 * time.Second,
        })
        if err != nil {
                log.Fatalf("[createDbSession]: %s\n", err)
        }
}

// Initializes the MongoDB Session
func init() {
        createDBSession()
}

// MongoUserStore provides persistence logic for "users" collection.
type MongoUserStore struct{}

// AddUser insert new User
func (store *MongoUserStore) AddUser(user model.User) error {
        session := mgoSession.Copy()
        defer session.Close()
        userCol := session.DB("userdb").C("users")
        // Check whether email id exists or not
        var existUser model.User
        err := userCol.Find(bson.M{"email": user.Email}).One(&existUser)
        if err != nil {
                if err == mgo.ErrNotFound { // Email is unique
                }
        }
        if (model.User{}) != existUser {
```

```
                    return model.ErrorEmailExists
            }
        err = userCol.Insert(user)
        return err
}


// GetUsers returns all documents from the collection.
func (store *MongoUserStore) GetUsers() []model.User {
        session := mgoSession.Copy()
        defer session.Close()
        userCol := session.DB("userdb").C("users")
        var users []model.User
        iter := userCol.Find(nil).Iter()
        result := model.User{}
        for iter.Next(&result) {
                users = append(users, result)
        }
        return users
}
```

Struct type MongoUserStore is a concrete implementation of interface UserStore that persists data into a MongoDB database. In the function AddUser, you check whether the email ID of a new user is unique or not. This is a behavior of our application that will be tested when you write specs for handler functions.

Listing 8-12 shows the source of user_controller.go in package controllers that provides handler functions for HTTP API applications.

Listing 8-12. Handler Functions in controllers/user_controller.go

```
package controllers

import (
        "encoding/json"
        "log"
        "net/http"

        "github.com/shijuvar/go-recipes/ch08/httpbdd/model"
)

// GetUsers serves requests for Http Get to "/users"
func GetUsers(store model.UserStore) http.Handler {
        return http.HandlerFunc(func(w http.ResponseWriter, r *http.Request) {
                data := store.GetUsers()
                users, err := json.Marshal(data)
                if err != nil {
                        w.WriteHeader(http.StatusInternalServerError)
                        return
                }
                w.Header().Set("Content-Type", "application/json")
                w.WriteHeader(http.StatusOK)
                w.Write(users)
        })

}
```

```go
// CreateUser serves requests for Http Post to "/users"
func CreateUser(store model.UserStore) http.Handler {
        return http.HandlerFunc(func(w http.ResponseWriter, r *http.Request) {
                var user model.User
                // Decode the incoming User json
                err := json.NewDecoder(r.Body).Decode(&user)
                if err != nil {
                        log.Fatalf("[Controllers.CreateUser]: %s\n", err)
                        w.WriteHeader(http.StatusInternalServerError)
                        return
                }
                // Insert User entity into User Store
                err = store.AddUser(user)
                if err != nil {
                        if err == model.ErrorEmailExists {
                                w.WriteHeader(http.StatusBadRequest)
                        } else {
                                w.WriteHeader(http.StatusInternalServerError)
                        }
                        return
                }
                w.WriteHeader(http.StatusCreated)
        })
}
```

Package controllers provides handler functions for the HTTP API. The example HTTP API has two endpoints: HTTP Get on "/users" and HTTP Post on "/users". The handler function GetUsers serves HTTP requests for HTTP Get on "/users" and handler function CreateUser serves HTTP requests for HTTP Post on "/users". The handler functions are written for better testability. They accept an implementation of interface UserStore as the persistent store, but they do not depend on any concrete implementation. Hence you can provide persistent store for your application to persist data into a real-world database and when you write tests you can provide a mock implementation of persistent store by providing an implementation of interface UserStore. Because application handlers depend on the interface UserStore you can have different implementations in application code and in tests.

Listing 8-13 shows the source of main.go that configures an HTTP multiplexer and creates an HTTP API server.

Listing 8-13. HTTP API Server in main.go

```go
package main

import (
        "net/http"

        "github.com/gorilla/mux"

        "github.com/shijuvar/go-recipes/ch08/httpbdd/controllers"
        "github.com/shijuvar/go-recipes/ch08/httpbdd/store"
)

func setUserRoutes() *mux.Router {
        r := mux.NewRouter()
```

```
        userStore := &store.MongoUserStore{}
        r.Handle("/users", controllers.CreateUser(userStore)).Methods("POST")
        r.Handle("/users", controllers.GetUsers(userStore)).Methods("GET")
        return r
}

func main() {
        http.ListenAndServe(":8080", setUserRoutes())
}
```

The application handlers are configured into an HTTP multiplexer by providing an instance of MongoUserStore as the argument to handler functions.

```
userStore := &store.MongoUserStore{}
r.Handle("/users", controllers.CreateUser(userStore)).Methods("POST")
r.Handle("/users", controllers.GetUsers(userStore)).Methods("GET")
```

Writing BDD-Style Tests for HTTP API Server

Third-party package Ginkgo and its preferred matcher library Gomega are used for specifying and verifying behavior in test cases.

Installing Ginkgo and Gomega

To install Ginkgo and Gomega, run the following commands:

```
go get github.com/onsi/ginkgo/ginkgo
go get github.com/onsi/gomega
```

When you install the package ginkgo, it will also install an executable program named ginkgo into your GOBIN location, which can be used for bootstrapping test suite files and running tests. GOBIN is the directory where the go install command installs Go binaries. The default location of GOBIN is $GOPATH/bin. If you want to change the default location, you can do so by configuring an environment variable named GOBIN.

To work with Ginkgo and Gomega, you must add these packages to the list of imports:

```
import (



    "github.com/onsi/ginkgo"
    "github.com/onsi/gomega"
)
```

Bootstrapping a Test Suite File

To write tests with Ginkgo for a package, you first create a test suite file. Let's run the following command from the controllers directory where you write the test suite file and specs.

```
ginkgo bootstrap
```

This will generate a file named `controllers_suite_test.go` that contains the code shown in Listing 8-14.

Listing 8-14. Test Suite File `controllers_suite_test.go` in `controllers_test` Package

```
package controllers_test

import (
        . "github.com/onsi/ginkgo"
        . "github.com/onsi/gomega"

        "testing"
)

func TestControllers(t *testing.T) {
        RegisterFailHandler(Fail)
        RunSpecs(t, "Controllers Suite")
}
```

The generated test suite file named `controllers_suite_test.go` will be organized into a package named `controllers_test` as you have generated the test suite file from package `controllers`. Here you organize tests and application code inside the same directory, but in different packages. Go allows you to organize packages `controllers` and `controllers_test` inside the `controllers` directory. This will isolate your tests from the application code because you organize application code and tests into different packages. If you want to change the package name to `controllers` for the test suite file and tests you can do it and Ginkgo can work with it.

In the test suite `controllers_suite_test.go`, you do the following:

- Import packages `ginkgo` and `gomega` using a dot (`.`) import. This allows you to call exported identifiers of `ginkgo` and `gomega` packages without using a qualifier.

- `RegisterFailHandler(Fail)` statement connects between Ginkgo and Gomega. Gomega is used as the matcher library for Ginkgo.

- `RunSpecs(t, "Controllers Suite")` statement tells Ginkgo to start the test suite. Ginkgo will automatically fail the `testing.T` if any of your specs fail.

Note that you don't need to write any extra code other than the code generated by `ginkgo bootstrap`. This test suite file is enough for running all specs in the same package, which you write in the next step.

Adding Specs to Suite

You just created test suite file named `controllers_suite_test.go`. To run your test suite, you need to add a test file to run the specs. You can generate a test file using the `ginkgo generate` command.

```
ginkgo generate user_controller
```

This will generate a test file named `user_controller_test.go`. Listing 8-15 shows the code generated by the `ginkgo` command-line tool.

Listing 8-15. Test File user_controller_test.go Generated by ginkgo

```
package controllers_test

import (
    . "github.com/onsi/ginkgo"
    . "github.com/onsi/gomega"
)

var _ = Describe("UserController", func() {

})
```

The specs are written inside a top-level describe container using Ginkgo's Describe function. Ginkgo uses var _ = to evaluate the Describe function at the top level without requiring an init function.

Writing Specs in Test File

The generated test file user_controller_test.go now just contains a top-level Describe container. Let's write the specs in the test file to test the HTTP API server. Let's define the basic user stories before writing specs.

1.   Let users view the list of User entities.

2.   Let users create a new User entity.

3.   The Email Id of a User entity should be unique.

Now let's write the specs in the test file based on those user stories. Listing 8-16 shows the specs written in user_controller_test.go for writing BDD-style tests against the HTTP API server.

Listing 8-16. Specs in user_controller_test.go

```
package controllers_test

import (
        "encoding/json"
        "net/http"
        "net/http/httptest"
        "strings"

        "github.com/shijuvar/go-recipes/ch08/httpbdd/controllers"
        "github.com/shijuvar/go-recipes/ch08/httpbdd/model"

        "github.com/gorilla/mux"
        . "github.com/onsi/ginkgo"
        . "github.com/onsi/gomega"
)

var _ = Describe("UserController", func() {
        var r *mux.Router
        var w *httptest.ResponseRecorder
        var store *FakeUserStore
```

```go
BeforeEach(func() {
        r = mux.NewRouter()
        store = newFakeUserStore()
})

// Specs for HTTP Get to "/users"
Describe("Get list of Users", func() {
        Context("Get all Users from data store", func() {
                It("Should get list of Users", func() {
                        r.Handle("/users", controllers.GetUsers(store)).
                        Methods("GET")
                        req, err := http.NewRequest("GET", "/users", nil)
                        Expect(err).NotTo(HaveOccurred())
                        w = httptest.NewRecorder()
                        r.ServeHTTP(w, req)
                        Expect(w.Code).To(Equal(200))
                        var users []model.User
                        json.Unmarshal(w.Body.Bytes(), &users)
                        // Verifying mocked data of 2 users
                        Expect(len(users)).To(Equal(2))
                })
        })
})

// Specs for HTTP Post to "/users"
Describe("Post a new User", func() {
        Context("Provide a valid User data", func() {
                It("Should create a new User and get HTTP Status: 201", func() {
                        r.Handle("/users", controllers.CreateUser(store)).
                        Methods("POST")
                        userJson := `{"firstname": "Alex", "lastname": "John",
                        "email": "alex@xyz.com"}`

                        req, err := http.NewRequest(
                                "POST",
                                "/users",
                                strings.NewReader(userJson),
                        )
                        Expect(err).NotTo(HaveOccurred())
                        w = httptest.NewRecorder()
                        r.ServeHTTP(w, req)
                        Expect(w.Code).To(Equal(201))
                })
        })
        Context("Provide a User data that contains duplicate email id", func() {
                It("Should get HTTP Status: 400", func() {
                        r.Handle("/users", controllers.CreateUser(store)).
                        Methods("POST")
                        userJson := `{"firstname": "Shiju", "lastname": "Varghese",
                        "email": "shiju@xyz.com"}`
```

```
                                req, err := http.NewRequest(
                                        "POST",
                                        "/users",
                                        strings.NewReader(userJson),
                                )
                                Expect(err).NotTo(HaveOccurred())
                                w = httptest.NewRecorder()
                                r.ServeHTTP(w, req)
                                Expect(w.Code).To(Equal(400))
                        })
                })
        })
})

// FakeUserStore provides a mocked implementation of interface model.UserStore
type FakeUserStore struct {
        userStore []model.User
}

// GetUsers returns all users
func (store *FakeUserStore) GetUsers() []model.User {
        return store.userStore
}

// AddUser inserts a User
func (store *FakeUserStore) AddUser(user model.User) error {
        // Check whether email exists
        for _, u := range store.userStore {
                if u.Email == user.Email {
                        return model.ErrorEmailExists
                }
        }
        store.userStore = append(store.userStore, user)
        return nil
}

// newFakeUserStore provides two dummy data for Users
func newFakeUserStore() *FakeUserStore {
        store := &FakeUserStore{}
        store.AddUser(model.User{
                FirstName: "Shiju",
                LastName:  "Varghese",
                Email:     "shiju@xyz.com",
        })

        store.AddUser(model.User{
                FirstName: "Irene",
                LastName:  "Rose",
                Email:     "irene@xyz.com",
        })
        return store
}
```

Listing 8-16 provides BDD-style tests against handler functions (see Listing 8-12) of the HTTP API server. The handler functions have a dependency to interface model.UserStore, which provides a contract for persistent store. Here is the handler function GetUsers that serves HTTP Get requests on "/users":

```
func GetUsers(store model.UserStore) http.Handler {
        return http.HandlerFunc(func(w http.ResponseWriter, r *http.Request) {
                data := store.GetUsers()
                users, err := json.Marshal(data)
                if err != nil {
                        w.WriteHeader(http.StatusInternalServerError)
                        return
                }
                w.Header().Set("Content-Type", "application/json")
                w.WriteHeader(http.StatusOK)
                w.Write(users)
        })

}
```

To test handler functions, you must provide an implementation of interface model.UserStore. The application code provides a store.MongoUserStore value as the implementation of interface model. UserStore that persists data into MongoDB database. When you write tests, you don't need to persist data into a real-world database; instead, you can provide a mock implementation for persistent store. Because handler functions are just dependent on interface model.UserStore and not any concrete implementation, you can easily provide a mock implementation to work with persistent store by providing an implementation of interface model.UserStore. Struct type FakeUserStore provides a mock implementation of interface model.UserStore.

```
type FakeUserStore struct {
        userStore []model.User
}

// GetUsers returns all users
func (store *FakeUserStore) GetUsers() []model.User {
        return store.userStore
}

// AddUser inserts a User
func (store *FakeUserStore) AddUser(user model.User) error {
        // Check whether email exists
        for _, u := range store.userStore {
                if u.Email == user.Email {
                        return model.ErrorEmailExists
                }
        }
        store.userStore = append(store.userStore, user)
        return nil
}

// newFakeUserStore provides two dummy data for Users
func newFakeUserStore() *FakeUserStore {
```

```
        store := &FakeUserStore{}
        store.AddUser(model.User{
                FirstName: "Shiju",
                LastName:  "Varghese",
                Email:     "shiju@xyz.com",
        })

        store.AddUser(model.User{
                FirstName: "Irene",
                LastName:  "Rose",
                Email:     "irene@xyz.com",
        })
        return store
}
```

Function newFakeUserStore provides an instance of FakeUserStore with two dummy User data.

When you write specs, blocks Describe, Context, and It are used to specify behaviors. A Describe block is used to describe individual behaviors of code and it is used as the container for Context and It blocks. The Context block is used to specify different contexts under an individual behavior. You can write multiple Context blocks within a Describe block. The It block is used to write individual specs inside a Describe or Context container.

The BeforeEach block runs before each It block. This block is used for writing logic before running each spec. Here it is used for creating instances of mux.Router and FakeUserStore.

```
var r *mux.Router
var w *httptest.ResponseRecorder
var store *FakeUserStore
BeforeEach(func() {
        r = mux.NewRouter()
        store = newFakeUserStore()
})
```

The values of mux.Router and FakeUserStore are used to configure an HTTP request multiplexer in It blocks.

```
r.Handle("/users", controllers.GetUsers(store)).Methods("GET")
```

Let's summarize the specs of user_controller_test.go:

- Two individual behaviors are specified in the Describe block: "Get list of Users" and "Post a new User" on "users".

- Inside the Describe block, the Context block is used to define a context under an individual behavior.

- The individual specs are written in an It block inside the Describe and Context containers.

- Inside the "Get list of Users" behavior, a context "Get all Users from data store" is specified. This context maps the functionality of HTTP Get on "/users" endpoint. Inside this context, an It block "Should get list of Users" is specified. This inspects whether the returned HTTP response has a status code of 200. The persistent store provided by FakeUserStore provides dummy data of two users so that you can check that the returned HTTP response has two users.

- Inside the "Post a new User" behavior, two contexts are defined in Context blocks: "Provide a valid User data" and "Provide a User data that contains duplicate email id". These contexts map the functionality of HTTP Post on "/users" endpoint. This should be able to create a new user if you provide valid User data. You should get an error if you provide User data with a duplicate email ID. You provide a duplicate user with an existing email ID to test behavior of the context "Provide a User data that contains duplicate email id". The provided email ID for this spec is already added into the persistent store FakeUserStore so you should get the HTTP error in response when you execute the spec. These specs are specified in the It block.

You can run the specs using either the go test command or ginkgo command. Let's run the specs using the go test command:

```
go test -v
```

You should see output similar to the following:

```
=== RUN   TestControllers
Running Suite: Controllers Suite
================================
Random Seed: 1473153169
Will run 3 of 3 specs


+++
Ran 3 of 3 Specs in 0.026 seconds
SUCCESS! -- 3 Passed | 0 Failed | 0 Pending | 0 Skipped --- PASS: TestControllers (0.03s)
PASS
ok      github.com/shijuvar/go-recipes/ch08/httpbdd/controllers 0.624s
```

You can also use the ginkgo command to run specs:

```
ginkgo test -v
```

That should result in output similar to the following:

```
Running Suite: Controllers Suite
================================
Random Seed: 1473153225
Will run 3 of 3 specs

UserController Get list of Users Get all Users from data store
  Should get list of Users
  D:/go/src/github.com/shijuvar/go-recipes/ch08/httpbdd/controllers/user_controller_test.
go:40
+
------------------------------
UserController Post a new User Provide a valid User data
  Should create a new User and get HTTP Status: 201
  D:/go/src/github.com/shijuvar/go-recipes/ch08/httpbdd/controllers/user_controller_test.
go:60
+
------------------------------
```

UserController Post a new User Provide a User data that contains duplicate email id
  Should get HTTP Status: 400
  D:/go/src/github.com/shijuvar/go-recipes/ch08/httpbdd/controllers/user_controller_test.
go:76
+
Ran 3 of 3 Specs in 0.070 seconds
SUCCESS! -- 3 Passed | 0 Failed | 0 Pending | 0 Skipped PASS

Ginkgo ran 1 suite in 4.6781235s
Test Suite Passed

Index

© Shiju Varghese 2016
S. Varghese, *Go Recipes*, DOI 10.1007/978-1-4842-1188-5

Get the eBook for only $4.99!

Why limit yourself?

Now you can take the weightless companion with you wherever you go and access your content on your PC, phone, tablet, or reader.

Since you've purchased this print book, we are happy to offer you the eBook for just $4.99.

Convenient and fully searchable, the PDF version enables you to easily find and copy code—or perform examples by quickly toggling between instructions and applications.

To learn more, go to http://www.apress.com/us/shop/companion or contact support@apress.com.

Printed in the United States
By Bookmasters